The Life of a
Q-Ship Captain

Photo: White, St. Catherines

Gordon Campbell.

The Life of a
Q-Ship Captain

**Being the
Autobiography
of**

VICE-ADMIRAL GORDON CAMPBELL
VC DSO

Periscope Publishing Limited
Penzance

First Published in Great Britain in 1932 under
the title of "Number Thirteen" by Hodder &
Stoughton Ltd.

Republished in 2002 by Periscope Publishing
Ltd.
33 Barwis Terrace
Penzance
Cornwall TR18 2AW, UK

www.periscopepublishing.com

A CIP record for this book is available from the
British Library

ISBN No 1-904381-06-5

TO

MY WIFE

Preface

My friends have persuaded me to write my reminiscences. I feel rather young to attempt such a job, as I have always thought that autobiographies were written by people whose years were so advanced as to be almost out of sight. I am told, however, that in these days reminiscences should be written before one's memory becomes atrophied.

Having decided to embark on this new adventure, I came down to the sea, set to—and here is the result.

I have not during my lifetime kept a diary regularly, so that my adventures are not always related in chronological order. It may be, too, that in one or two cases I have not been able to assign an exact date to a particular happening. Yet it is happenings that I am concerned with in this book rather than my own opinions. It is true that here and there will be found criticisms of the Admiralty, and I trust no one will for a moment harbour the thought that I have any personal feeling against any members of the Board, or, indeed, that in similar circumstances I would have acted differently from them. The state of affairs in the Navy, which culminated in the mutiny at Invergordon, however, in my opinion, has resulted in a lack of confidence in the Board of Admiralty which can only be eradicated by a Commission to enquire into the advisability of reorganising the whole system of naval government. With the best will in the world, officers serving on the active list are comparatively powerless. I realise it is commonly thought that a retired naval officer has either a bee in his bonnet or is disgruntled. As regards the former, I must leave others to judge; but I deny the latter. My affection for the Senior Service is as great now as it has ever been, and I think it is a pity that the Admiralty does not realise that retired officers of all ranks mix in the business world, gain knowledge and experience which they were unable to acquire when in the Service, and so are able to regard naval matters from a broader-minded yet still technical point of view.

As with my previous book, *My Mystery Ships*, I have had some difficulty in selecting a title. I was frequently told that the title *My Mystery Ships* suggested that I invented or owned all " mystery ships," a rather thoughtless criticism, as every Admiral talks about " my flag flying in H.M.S. ——," and every sailor says, " There's my ship lying in the harbour." I may mention, nevertheless, that the original title of my book was " Mystery

Ships," and the reason the word " My " was added was lest I should lead the public into believing that I had written a general history of " Mystery Ships," whereas the book was confined to my personal experiences.

I think there can be no misunderstanding about the title of the present book, for its meaning is explained in the opening lines.

I wish to thank Mr. Leonard P. Moore, Miss Norah Perriam, and Miss Raphael and her assistants for the help they have given me in compiling the book, and last but not least my Secretary, Miss Gwen Cumming.

GORDON CAMPBELL.

August 4th, 1932,
ST. MILDRED'S HOTEL,
WESTGATE-ON-SEA,
KENT.

Contents

Illustrations

courtesy of the Editor the fact that the book would be dedicated to her was published on the last morning she ever read, and it gave her a moment of great happiness.

Although my father left the Army at an early age to enter business, he never severed his connection with it, and later became Lieut.-Colonel and Honorary Colonel in the Volunteers.

At a large review held in Hyde Park just before the War, he had a very personal adventure. He had brought out his old uniform and very tight-fitting trousers for the occasion, and just as he reached the parade ground they split at rather an awkward place. My mother took him into one of the V.A.D. tents to have them sewn up, and all was well. But after the ceremony my mother, returning a little later than my father, found him sitting on the edge of the bed trying to struggle out of his pants which the obliging nurse had sewn through to the tail of his shirt !

Our family of sixteen was composed of eleven boys and five girls, though I never knew more than eight brothers and two sisters, the others having died at an early age. My parents being very poor in view of the number of their children, we were brought up largely on a " bread-and-butter-and-suet-pudding " sort of regime, with trousers being continually cut down for younger brothers. But we were a very happy family, and I have nothing but gratitude for the way in which I was brought up . . . even for the part accomplished by my father's swagger cane !

Like the rest of my brothers, I was educated at

Dulwich College, going to the preparatory school when I was eight and a half. It was in those days that I showed my first interest in explosives. A party of about six of us had assembled at the house of my pal, K. S. Carpmael.[1] His father had given him a shilling to entertain us with, and we decided to spend it on gunpowder. We first tried the possibilities of firing a toy brass cannon, but we found this rather dull, so we next proceeded to make some golden rain by mixing a little water with the powder. The first result was not very good, owing to there being too much water in the mixture, and just as we were making a stronger mixture, the whole lot blew up, badly burning Carpmael in particular and the rest in varying degrees. Luckily our experiments were being carried out in the coal-cellar, otherwise the results might have been worse.

During the summer holidays we were invariably sent to what was then an innovation—a public-school camp. I well remember the first that I went to—we had a great thrill one day when we were taken over Queen Victoria's yacht, and like a schoolboy, or even like some grown-ups, I was very

[1] Carpmael has had an extraordinary career. Joining the Navy as an Accountant Officer, he found himself during the Great War as a Paymaster-Lieutenant-Commander, stuck in a rather uninteresting shore office. This did not suit his energy and fighting spirit, so he transferred to the executive as a Sub-Lieutenant. He was soon promoted to Lieutenant in the Grand Fleet, and I think would have become an executive Lieutenant-Commander if the War had lasted a little longer. When peace came he was in the extraordinary position of being an executive Lieutenant and also a Paymaster-Lieutenant-Commander. Naturally he was between the devil and the deep sea. But again he grasped the situation, ate many dinners, was called to the Bar, and is now one of the legal advisers to the Admiralty.

keen on being able to say that I had lain on Queen Victoria's bed and worn her robes of the Order of the Garter.

On leaving the preparatory school at the age of thirteen, I received a most magnificent report, as in addition to being captain of the First XV and in the First XI, I was a prefect. The only master who told the Real Truth was the Greek master, and he said I was intensely idle.

I passed straight into the Upper School at Dulwich College, and, my father being very keen on Greek and Latin, I went in for the classical side, so I was not allowed to make any special preparations for the naval examination until within six months of the exam., when I was transferred to the Army Class, the Navy Class being in the Junior School, which rendered me ineligible for it.   In spite of this handicap, I was one of the few boys who passed into the *Britannia* from a public school at the age of fourteen, and my public-school training has stood me in good stead ever since. I was supposed to be fairly brainy, and my father was told I would pass in the first seven. As a matter of fact, I passed in the last seven, fifty-ninth out of a total of sixty-five! It was only my knowledge of Latin that got me through at all.

I was in Edinburgh when the news arrived, and I was the proudest boy on earth, as my great ambition had always been to go to sea. I joined the old *Britannia* at Dartmouth as a cadet or " young gentleman " in September 1900. Many stories

SELF AGE 5

have been written of life in the *Britannia*, and my experiences were much the same as those of other people, though I had one which might have cost me my life.

I was out sailing in what was known as one of the " black cutters "—there were just three of us on board. The mainsheet got jammed, and I leaned overboard to clear it ; away went the boom, and I fell overboard with my feet tangled up in the sheet, so that I was being dragged along with my head under water. It seemed hours before I was able to free myself. Eventually I was picked up by a local yacht's boat and got back on board the *Britannia* to find I had been put in the " Commander's report " for falling overboard. It was even suggested that I might have been bathing without permission !

It was during my time in the *Britannia* that I crocked my knee playing in the First XV, an event which was to have a great effect on me later on, and which, unfortunately, finished my reasonable prospects of a successful football career.

The great event of the fifteen months we spent in the *Britannia* was a week's cruise in the old *Racer*, a sailing ship with auxiliary steam power. Going aloft, making and furling sail, was a great experience for us, and it all came back vividly to my imagination the other day, when, at Dartmouth, I saw a Chilean training ship making all " plain sail," with the British cadets looking on. Steam, electricity, motors, and aeroplanes have made great strides in the development and purposes of the world, but I

2

don't know that anyone has yet found a better training-ground than a sailing ship. I am glad to think that the present Admiralty are considering the reintroduction of some similar form of training.

In January 1902 I joined my first sea-going ship, the *Prince George*, a battleship in the Channel Fleet. My father and mother came down with me to Portsmouth, and we lunched at the famous George Hotel, where Nelson is supposed to have made his last stay before Trafalgar. I hope he had as good a treacle tart as the one I had.

Our Commander in the *Prince George*, a man in whom the midshipmen were most interested, subsequently became Admiral Sir Sydney R. Fremantle, K.C.B., etc., under whom I was to serve again at a later date.

My first job was to be told off as A.D.C. to the Captain. I was frightfully thrilled, as it struck me as an appointment of great honour, till I heard it referred to as the " Skipper's Doggie "—in other words, it meant following the Captain about like a dog. I was warned that the first thing to do when the Captain gave one an order was to get out of his sight as quickly as possible, so when I received my first order from him to take a message which I didn't correctly hear, I at once dived out of sight by the nearest ladder. To my horror, I discovered that it was the Captain's own hatch and midshipmen weren't allowed to use it. My career as A.D.C. was at an end.

The next job I had was much more to my liking,

for I became a signal-midshipman. In the days before wireless all signals were made by flags or semaphore, and there was great competition in each ship to try to get the flags up first, and if any ship was particularly slack, the Flagship would hoist her " Number," which brought disgrace on the ship, as it showed the slackness to the whole Fleet. One learnt in this job to be particularly alert, and to keep one's eyes open. The job also carried a certain number of privileges, and one could use the signal-house on the after-bridge for writing. But this caused my undoing. I was tempted to smoke a cigarette there one evening, and being caught I got the inevitable justice of twelve cuts with the cane. During the night watches, the Lieutenant of the Watch would invariably visit the bridge to see that everyone was alive. One of the Lieutenants was very unpopular, and to play a joke on him, the signalmen dressed up a " dummy " one dark night, and when the Lieutenant was seen approaching, put a lighted cigarette in its mouth. Up came the Lieutenant and at once started a round of abuse at the signalman for " smoking," and got still more impatient at getting no answer to his hundred and one questions. This might have continued for a long time had not the stamping of his angry feet caused the dummy to fall down !

We had a very strict gun-room, and I seldom passed a week without being chastised. On one occasion I certainly deserved it. On being ordered by one of the senior midshipmen to go and get a

suitable book for him to read in the train, I produced
a Prayer Book. He used his best walking-stick to
administer justice. It was not so strong as my skin,
and when it broke he added another half-dozen to
the punishment.

Soon after I joined the *Prince George*, the Squadron sailed, under the late Admiral-of-the-Fleet Sir
A. K. Wilson, V.C., for foreign waters. Although
we midshipmen didn't come into any personal
contact with him, we all admired him for his leader-
ship and handling of his command, and for many
years I always hoped that, if a war came, he would be
in command of the Fleet. He was looked on as a
hard disciplinarian and certainly used to shake
everyone up, but even in these days I don't think
that either officers or men mind anything, provided
they are under a man who can lead them and whom
they can trust.

We visited various Spanish and Mediterranean
ports, returning in time for the great Coronation
Review of King Edward at Spithead. Nearly every
foreign nation was represented, and our "chummy
ship," the foreigner lying abreast of us, was the
Russian ship *Pobeida*, with whom we exchanged many
visits.

As is well remembered, the original review, which
was to consist of one hundred and forty-one vessels,
had to be postponed owing to the King's illness, and
a second one was held, consisting of one hundred
and twenty-one vessels, of which five were foreign
vessels, and sixteen torpedo-boats. It is interesting

to note that for this large Fleet there were only six Flag Officers, one of whom was Commander-in-Chief of Portsmouth, whereas the Home Fleet of the present day has the same number, although it comprises only about forty-two vessels.

By this time I had received my first naval command, that of a picket-boat, and I took great pride in her, as I have indeed in all the vessels I have commanded. I even used to spend money from my hard-earned pay of 1s. 9d. a day to buy tins of polish, etc., to ensure having the boat always spick and span.

During the review I was sent ashore in charge of a picket-boat to fetch the Commander's father, Admiral Sir Edmund Fremantle, G.C.B., a man of great fame, who had held many high positions and who lived to nearly a hundred. I was particularly instructed to be very careful to receive him with every respect, and I warned my boat's crew accordingly. I laid my boat alongside the Clarence Pier at Southsea, and refused to allow on board any of the Wardroom stewards, etc., who wanted to come. In due course an oldish-looking gentleman arrived, and said he wanted to come off to the *Prince George.* I told him I was very sorry, but I could not admit him. He insisted that he had to come off, and I said : " I cannot help it, I shall not be able to take you," and was rather snappy. After further argument, he informed me that he was Admiral Sir Edmund Fremantle—and I nearly fell flat ! I quickly brought the crew to attention, and received him with all respect possible ; luckily he never mentioned the incident to his son. The last time I saw Admiral Fremantle was when attending a meeting of the Missions to Seamen on January 16th, 1929, when he was our Chairman. He made a very inspiring speech. I think this was the last time he performed at any public function, which showed the value he placed on the work of the Missions to Seamen.

After the review we again went to the Mediterranean for combined manœuvres, and to visit various ports. Whilst in Tetuan Bay, where we had gone to do some target practice, I handled my picket-boat in a manner which got it in the line between the target and H.M.S. *Magnificent*, which was flying the Flag of Admiral Sir Assheton Curzon Howe, G.C.B. I got a very sharp signal for my misdeed, and on the completion of the firing, was ordered to repair on board the *Magnificent*. I arrived rather in fear and trembling, and was told the Admiral wanted to see me. I don't think I had ever spoken to an Admiral before. On arrival before him, he said : " What's your name ? " I told him ; he said : " Are you the son of Colonel Frederick Campbell ? " On receiving my reply, he said : " Well, I hope you will be a chip of the old block, only don't foul my range again." So all was well. He had apparently entertained my father and mother to luncheon in the *Britannia* when my elder brother Jim (Captain James D. Campbell, M.V.O., O.B.E.) was a cadet, and had been impressed with my mother's pride in her sons, and had remembered her saying she hoped her sons would be chips of the old block.

Whilst at Gibraltar in October I received an appointment as Midshipman of H.M.S. *Irresistible*, a bigger battleship belonging to the Mediterranean Fleet, and I had to join her at Malta. This of course meant missing my Christmas leave—but one gets used to such things in the Navy.

It was towards the end of November that I left the *Prince George*, as she was returning to England, and I was transferred temporarily to the old *Cleopatra*, one of the last ships to be able to pull her funnel down and her screw up, to await the arrival of the cruiser *Aboukir* on her passage to Malta.

On the day I left the *Prince George*, my last duty was to fetch the Commander, all rigged up in his cocked hat, etc., back from a court-martial. I was doing my last trip in my picket-boat, and I wanted to do it in great style. I fetched up alongside the gangway with a full speed ahead and then full astern. The Commander stepped out of the boat before it had stopped, with the result that his cocked hat fell off. This wasn't my fault, but he turned round on me, and not only informed me that I was the biggest fool he had ever seen, but also stopped my leave for two years. As I was due to leave the ship in a few minutes (which he had forgotten) I was rather tickled. After a few days in the *Cleopatra*, which were very interesting, as she was one of the last of her type in the service and it was a treat to see the hands making and furling sail, I joined the

Aboukir for passage to Malta. On arrival I found
the *Irresistible* had not yet arrived, so was again
transferred to the *Venerable* for a few days to await
the *Irresistible.* This meant I had been in five
different ships in three weeks, much to the detriment
of the school part of my education, which fact
unfortunately is not taken into consideration at
examination time.

During my time in the Mediterranean, Malta used
to be a favourite visiting-place of the Royal Family ;
and when King Edward came, great festivities took
place. On another occasion the present King and
Queen came to Malta in H.M.S. *Renown* after their
visit to India. The *Renown* looked a perfect picture,
painted in the old colours—a black side, yellow upper
works, and a salmon-coloured water-line. The
Duke of Connaught also visited Malta, and on these
occasions was generally given some display, such as
illuminated boats, and also a line of pulling boats
through which the Royalties would pass, whilst the
boats tossed their oars, or, if at night-time, fired
Very lights. I was lucky enough to be the midshipman in charge of one of these boats when King
Edward visited Malta.

Another distinguished visitor we received was the
German Emperor, who came out on the *Hohen-
zollern.* He flew the flag of Admiral-of-the-Fleet of
the British Navy, of which he was very proud. I
was present not only at Malta when he came there,
but also when he went to Corfu at the same time as
the King of Greece.

The routine in the Mediterranean was very much of the ordinary type, except that the " spit and polish " was more obvious than in the Squadron under Admiral Wilson's command. We had a very happy gun-room, but it was rather a come-down for me, as I had been a senior " snottie " or midshipman in the *Prince George,* but now once more found myself a junior. But these shocks, which at the time seem rather nasty, are all for one's good in the long run.

After Christmas we cruised in the Eastern Mediterranean, and I remember one cold morning in January, which happened to be my birthday, when we were lying at the port of Platea. By a stroke of misfortune, I was late getting up on deck when the hands fell in about 5.30. I tried to bluff the matter through, but was bowled out, with the result that I was sent to the masthead. I only had a vest on under my monkey jacket, and was nearly frozen ; I further had the chagrin of seeing all the other midshipmen going ashore on a day's leave, and it was not till late in the afternoon that the officer who had sent me aloft remembered he had done so, and hailed me to come down, a colder and wiser boy. What a way to spend a birthday ! However, I have never been late for a morning watch since.

II

Pacific Station

MY stay on the Mediterranean station was very short, as my knee again began to give me considerable trouble, so I was obliged to have an operation to have the cartilage removed. At that time the removal of a cartilage was rather rare, and I was advised that it would be better to have it done by a London specialist, so I had to sign a certificate to say I had been offered naval medical attendance but had refused it, which meant my father had to pay my expenses for me. He sent me £15 for the journey, and I came home via Tunis and Marseilles, arriving in London with exactly 6d. in my pocket, which was just enough to get me down to Sydenham.

My eldest brother, whom I had never known, came to meet me. He was some twenty years older than I, and had gone out to the Far East when I was a baby in arms. I had, of course, seen photos of him, but his appearance was not much like them— I suppose I too had altered somewhat from being a baby in arms to a full-blown midshipman. In consequence we failed to recognise each other. I duly went home, and as I was walking up the steps of my mother's house, I saw another fellow doing

the same thing, and on getting into conversation
we discovered we were brothers.

The operation was performed by a well-known
surgeon, but even then my knee had to be cut open
twice, as a result of which my leg got hardened and
could not be bent.   Two more operations took place
to try and bend it, both resulting in a broken tendon,
and eventually they gave me up as a bad job, and
told me I must face life with a stiff leg.   This was
too much for me, and at my mother's suggestion I
hired a masseur, who used to tie me down to a chair,
and then bend my leg a fraction of an inch at a time,
by force.   Eventually I got it right again, though it
has always handicapped me in playing games.

After my recovery I went to stay with my brother
on board the brig *Wanderer* at Weymouth.   One
evening I went out with some friends of his to
Buffalo Bill's wild-beast show, during which I was
taken suddenly ill with an abscess in my ear.   I was
taken to their house, where I remained laid up for
a fortnight, and was nursed by two charming
girls.   One of them, M., took particular care of me,
and nearly succeeded in killing me in the process,
as she had two medicines to give me, one morphia
and the other a tonic.   She made a mistake, and gave
me a tumbler of morphia and a teaspoonful of the
tonic mixture, which of course nearly snuffed me out,
and my parents were sent for in a great hurry from
London.   M. showed me a horoscope she had had
written by a certain lady at Southend, in which
this nursing incident had been foretold.   I wrote

to the lady at Southend, and had an amazingly true horoscope sent me in return, which not only gave me the age at which I should marry, but a description of my wife and father-in-law. I guessed at once who it was, and as her mother would not have approved of so young a girl having her horoscope told, I got her to write on the sly to the horoscope lady, and she received a reply giving her the date on which she would marry and a description of me. Events turned out exactly as foretold.

On my being returned to duty after over six months' absence, I was appointed to H.M.S. *Flora*, and arrived to join the ship at Esquimalt. I was, of course, furnished with a railway pass, etc., and my father gave me £5 for incidentals.

I sailed from Liverpool in one of the old Allan Line steamers. The first night on board I was invited to make a four at poker with three other men I had never met before. I very soon found I had lost £3 out of my £5—anyhow, it was a good lesson for me which I have never forgotten.

On arriving at Montreal, I offered the steward at my table a tip of 10s. He brought it back to me, and said he could not possibly accept it, as nobody else at the table had given him less than £1. I replied, " Thank God for that," and took back the 10s. We found we had to spend a day and a night in Montreal waiting for a train, but luckily I discovered my father had an agent there, and was able to borrow some money from him to get me across to the other side.

We had a very small gun-room in the *Flora*, and our number in the mess was only thirteen. Two kitchen chairs were all we had room for, the less fortunate having to sit on settees. We managed to squeeze in a cottage piano, and many a gay evening and sing-song we got out of it. The chairs were, of course, reserved for the " Sub " and senior midshipman, and I was glad when the day came for me to fill the post.

Our Captain—C. J. Baker—was a fine old sailor whom we, as midshipmen, used to think rather a severe old gentleman, as he was always chasing us around—but he had a kindly nature, and we always used to think that we could foretell if he was going to get angry, by the way the hairs on his nose began to stand on end.

We were what is called a " happy " ship, and all aboard worked together. The Gunner, now Lieutenant Sandover, was the particular friend of the snotties, as he was always ready to lend us money when we were hard up.

Shortly after joining this ship, my first dream of " shipwreck " came true. We were coming down the narrow waters between Vancouver Island and the mainland when we ran into a dense fog. The particular channel we were coming down was not very wide, and we were on the look-out for a buoy with a sort of cage on top of it. I was midshipman of the watch, and was on the bridge when the look-out reported a buoy with the cage on top ; the helm was put over to alter the course of the ship, when alas ! the " cage " flew away, as it was a sea-gull, which in the fog had looked like a cage. The mistake could not be remedied, as by altering course we had headed straight for the rocks, and with a grinding noise we ran right up on them.

The Captain ordered the engines to be put " full astern," but it was too late, and we bump-bump-bumped over the rocks. We finally got held fast, with a rock protruding through the ship's bottom. The ship began to fall over and took a heavy list. " Close water-tight doors ! " " Out collision mats ! " " Hoist out all boats ! " came from the Captain in rapid succession, as the men rushed away to obey his orders. In the meantime it was obvious that the ship was held fast, and the stern and after-part of the vessel had filled with water. There was no wireless in those days, and it was a long time before any message could be got through for assistance.

When the fog lifted, it was found that we were on an island called Denman Island, very sparsely populated, and chiefly consisting of thick woods.

We set to work to try to get the ship off, but it was obvious this could not be done till the water in the stern was got out and the ship lightened. The ports round the stern were all open, and so a party of men were sent ashore to cut down trees, and then fashion plugs to fit into the ports to make them more or less water-tight. This also meant that the divers had to put on their helmets and go down inside the ship. This was a most dangerous piece of work,

[*Jones (Esquimalt, B.C.).*

THE " FLORA " ON THE ROCKS, SHOWING STERN AND QUARTER-DECK COMPLETELY
SUBMERGED.

as so many things were floating about between the
decks that the divers were liable to have their air
pipes squeezed, and so be unable to get air. Our
gunner volunteered for the job, and in spite of the
great risk, got down inside the ship, and, together
with the men working outside, was eventually
able to get the after part of the ship more or less
water-tight. In the meantime lighters had arrived,
and we now had to get everything which would
lighten her out of the ship. This meant working
day and night. Guns and things on the upper deck
were fairly easy to get at, but with the ship heeling
over, even these were difficult to move, and an anchor
was laid out with a wire to the masthead to prevent
the ship falling right over. All the coal, the only
kind of fuel at that time, had to be dug out of the
bunkers and passed through small holes in the deck
and then through the port-holes.

The Flagship of the Squadron, H.M.S. *Grafton*
(Captain Keppel, who is now Admiral Sir Colin
Keppel, the Sergeant-at-Arms at the House of
Commons), had arrived in the meantime, and several
attempts were made to tow us off, but without
success, and it was not till a week later, when the
ship had been gutted and trees had been cut down
to make wedges under the fore-end of the ship,
that the *Grafton* eventually pulled us off.

We, as midshipmen, felt very pleased with ourselves at having had such an exciting week, and I
remember thinking I should never see a ship so
much under water again—but it was really quite

tame to what I was to encounter later on in the
Great War.

The old *Flora* was safely brought to Esquimalt,
and put into dry dock. There she remained many
a month, and we midshipmen had the time of our
lives. The gun-room where we lived had been kept
dry, but the Captain's cabins and the Wardroom,
where the senior officers lived, had been under
water for several days and were badly damaged, so
that they had to be accommodated ashore, leaving
us the ship to ourselves—and we made the most of
it. Our chests (with all our belongings) had also
been under water, and our clothes ruined, so that
we all got money compensation for our loss—*some*
of which went on getting new clothes.

Much jealousy was caused because I was the only
snottie who happened to have his journal (a diary
which all midshipmen are required to keep) in his
chest, the others having theirs in the gun-room. Of
course mine was badly damaged by the water, and
the Captain gave me a certificate to that effect, which
I reckoned would help me to get " full marks " when
I produced it before the examiners, when the time
came to pass the " Subs " exam. The others
thought this a splendid notion, and so one afternoon
all the journals were tied together and towed across
the harbour by a cutter, so as to get a thorough
soaking. But alas ! the skipper hadn't been born the
previous day, and saw through the whole performance
—the result being that, instead of getting certificates
of accidental damage, they all got their leave stopped.

After the *Flora* was repaired, we did some delightful cruising in the waters between British Columbia and the mainland. Some places we visited were only roughly charted, and so we would hoist our own little steam cutter, and this would be sent ahead to take soundings. Most of the places we visited were sparsely inhabited, and the conditions of living were very rough-and-ready. Some of the last of the Red Indian race were frequently seen with their strange-looking " totem " poles.

Comex, a small fishing village, was one of our favourite places, and here we lay for some months tucked away in the heart of British Columbia. It was from here that a pal and I decided to bike to Victoria during a spell of leave. It was over a hundred miles, chiefly through very thick forest, either with no track, or only a faint one, but it was very thrilling, especially one evening when darkness was falling and we heard the wolves howling, and never were we so thankful as when we finally sighted a tiny light, which proved to be a lumberman's cottage, and got food and a hard floor to sleep on for the night. Our adventures were not at an end, however, as the following day we ran into a forest fire, and it was a question of trying to get through, or of turning back ; we decided to go on, and I well remember charging down a steep hill with flames on either side. I narrowly escaped colliding with a tree which had fallen across the road and was invisible in the smoke ; my pal was not so fortunate, and came an awful cropper—but we eventually got through with nothing worse than a singeing and a smoking.

When the summer came, we were ordered to cruise in South America, and set off full of enthusiasm at the thought of seeing yet new places, a never-failing source of pleasure, as each place has something of interest in it. After fourteen days at sea, we anchored right on the Equator, in the centre of the Galapagos Islands. We were supposed to be looking for someone who had been marooned there ; and a large party of men were ready to land to make a search, and we also kept blowing our siren to attract attention, but it was obvious that they were islands on which no human being could live for long, as they chiefly consisted of lava from hundreds of volcanoes. A few of us landed with rifles to see what it was like, but found it very heavy going and very hot, till we came to a little sandy beach, and were amazed to see hundreds of what looked to us like large rats running about. Their bodies were much bigger than those of rats, and their tails much longer. We were a little scared at first, as there were so many, and we thought we might be attacked, but after we had shot a few, *they* were the ones to become frightened. We found out afterwards they were iguanas.

Whilst we were ashore, those aboard were catching fish, as our larder was very low, and we found when we got aboard that the catch included three sharks and hundreds of a sort of red mullet, which had been got by exploding a small charge of gunpowder in the water.

From here we had another ten days' run to Co-quimbo, in Chile. On our arrival we fired a salute of twenty-one guns, and our Captain was righteously indignant when the *Capitan Pratt*, a Chilean ship in harbour, failed to return the salute. However, an officer soon came over to apologise and explain that they had neither crew nor ammunition aboard, but that if the Captain would give him time, he would secure both. Whilst lying here peacefully, one Sunday, we had our first thrill of war, as what was known as the Dogger Bank incident had occurred, and relations with Russia had become strained. Long cipher messages arrived by telegram for Captain Baker, and we all waited on the *qui vive*, whilst they were being deciphered, hoping to be sent to China, or wherever the nearest Russian ship might be. But the whole affair blew over, and beyond coaling ship on a Sunday and taking in provisions, we had no excitement, barring a thrill and a sudden order to abandon our cruise and return to England, much to our disappointment.

We midshipmen had great fun passing through the Straits of Magellan, as the Captain had been an old surveyor in those parts, and he would frequently ask us the name of this peak or that headland ; and as long as we answered " Mount Baker, sir," or " Baker Point, called after the famous surveyor," he was perfectly satisfied.

We next called at Montevideo. I have a brother buried in Buenos Aires, and wished to go and see his grave. Having no money, I borrowed £2 from

Mr. Sandover, and set off on my mission, arriving at
Buenos Aires at seven in the morning, with only a
few shillings in my pocket.   I had no idea where my
brother was buried, so made my first call at the
British Consulate.   This was not open, so I then
called at the British Club, to find that the Secretary
had died the day before.   I then tried the British
Chaplain ; he was away on holiday.   Eventually I
went to the British Bank of South America, to find
that all the clerks had come out subsequent to my
brother's death.   I waited till noon, when I was
able to find the manager, Mr. Im Thurn, who
very kindly entertained me for the rest of the day,
which enabled me to have a good lunch and fulfil
my mission.

Then we called at St. Vincent.   Owing to the
sudden recall of the ship we had a large surplus of
cigarettes on board, which we sold to the Eastern
Telegraph Co., but the difficulty was to get them
landed.   Luckily a cricket match was arranged, and
we took a couple of cricket bags ashore.

We eventually arrived at Plymouth to " pay off."
That was in December 1904.   I suppose I did more
misdeeds in the *Flora* than in any other ship, but the
worst one was right at the end of the commission, at
Plymouth.   The Captain was giving a farewell
dinner-party to all officers and wives, and we midshipmen heard that the champagne was to be reserved for the senior officers, so one or two of us got
hold of the Captain's steward, and entertained him
in the gun-room in generous fashion, the result being

that we shared with the senior officers at the dinner-party. The following morning, about 10 a.m., the steward came along and said he would like to return our hospitality, and invited us to the Captain's cabin. We demurred for a long time, but eventually we cautiously went in, and whilst the Captain was walking up and down the poop overhead, monarch of all he surveyed, two bad midshipmen were drinking his whisky, out of his tantalus, with his steward. The other midshipman gave his life in the War, and I therefore refrain from mentioning names, but had we been " bowled out " I doubt if either of us would have remained in the service. Anyhow, bold actions often come off successfully—and this one, although very stupid, has often enabled me in later years, when I commanded cadet ships, to remember the folly of youth.

After paying off the old *Flora*, I arrived at my mother's home about eight o'clock in the evening, to find a youthful party in progress, and after embracing my mother, I went straight up and kissed the prettiest girl in the room, under the mistletoe ; she eventually became my wife. I had met her before when she was ten years old—she was the girl who fitted into the picture of my horoscope.

After a short leave I was again appointed to the *Irresistible*, and went out by P. & O. to join her at Malta in January 1905. Admiral Sir Sackville Carden, K.C.B., who was our Captain in the *Irresistible*, was the finest handler of a ship I have ever known. On one occasion, while coming into

Malta Harbour at about 12 knots, he put the helm hard over to go into dry dock. Owing to a mistake in signals, we found a cruiser moored in our way. Admiral Carden at once ordered full speed astern. Alongside the cruiser was a copper punt with three men on it painting the ship's side. However, in a perfectly calm manner, he shouted through his megaphone, "Copper punt, get out of my way, I am going to ram you," and he brought the ship up dead alongside in the exact place where the copper punt had been. We had been busy closing the water-tight doors, as it looked to us as if nothing could stop us ramming the cruiser, but we didn't touch her, the Captain having judged his distance almost to an inch. We had, as Commander, Horatio Colomb, who had been frequently wounded in the Boxer Rebellion and suffered from ill temper. We discovered that whenever he came out of his cabin at eight o'clock in the morning, the first two midshipmen he met had to go to the masthead, one to the fore and one on the main. Being senior midshipman, I arranged for two of the junior midshipmen to take this duty each morning.

A very short time afterwards I became due for the examination leading to promotion for Sub-Lieutenant. As the ship was at sea on the day on which I was due to pass, I was examined provisionally by a very stiff board of ship's officers, and, as one of them had been brought up under sail, I was thoroughly examined in sailing-ships, and they awarded me a provisional first-class certificate. On my return to

Malta, I was re-examined by a board consisting of officers from other ships, and, in spite of this being a much easier examination, I was only awarded a second-class certificate. One of the questions I was asked by the President of the Board was, What was the price of Welsh coal per ton ?—which hardly comes under the heading of seamanship ! Anyhow, having passed, I was made an Acting Sub-Lieutenant, entitled to wear a frock coat and sword, and sent back to England in the old battleship *Centurion*, which was on her way home from China.

III

Destroyers

ON arrival at my parents' home, near the Crystal Palace, my thoughts turned to love, as it so happened that the parents of my girl, who was still a flapper, had settled down only a few minutes' walk away.

The leave passed all too quickly and I had to go to Greenwich College for the usual Sub-Lieutenant courses, but it was easy to get to and from the Crystal Palace, so that I got home nearly every week-end, and not only did it keep me out of the temptations of London, but also enabled me to make headway with my courting ; though this did not particularly help me in my studies, as not being an x chaser at the best of times, the love feeling kept my mind preoccupied.

During the summer vacation I spent part of the time with my future " in-laws " (as it turned out) at Felixstowe. One night, whilst there, I succeeded with some difficulty in getting permission from Mrs. Davids to take her daughter out in a boat, with the intention of pulling out as far as the Cork Light Vessel, about three miles distant. We had to take the governess, a Miss Bradley, with us. We left about 8 p.m., and promised to be home by 10. All went well till the wind suddenly sprang up fresh from the shore. I should have turned back at once, but I didn't. By the time we got to our destination it was dark and blowing still fresher—the light vessel crew hailed us and told us to come aboard, as we wouldn't get ashore that night. I didn't dare risk staying out all night, in spite of the chaperone, so we started to pull for the shore. I have never had such a pull in my life. I had two oars, and Miss Bradley one, whilst Mary, who didn't know the first thing about it, tried to steer. The lights in the town were all out, and we had nothing much to steer by— I was thinking of the suspense our lateness and the state of the weather would be causing ashore. The coastguard had been communicated with, and had replied that it was of little use to launch their whaler on a night like that, but they patrolled the coast. In the meantime I was getting dead beat, but the helmsman never turned a hair, and kept encouraging me to go on; it was then that I thought to myself, "Well, if ever I marry a girl, it will be you." I have never seen anyone of that age so calm when in a tight corner.

Eventually we fetched up on the beach in the early hours of the morning, to find anxious friends and others waiting, and all that was missing was a parson to say, "For better for worse, for richer for poorer."

A photo of the Cork Light Vessel, mounted in a lifebuoy, has hung in my cabin ever since.

My time at Greenwich passed all too quickly. The only part of it I didn't like was the inadequate

pay, which was only £7 a month, and as the mess bill
was generally £8 it was a question of " 8 into 7
won't go—borrow 1." I didn't want to be an
additional burden on my parents, so I did what most
other subs did, and pawned my sextant, telescope,
and scales (epaulettes). In due course I was
appointed to a destroyer, where I found myself very
wealthy, as not only did I get an additional 1s. a day
messing allowance, but also 1s. a day " hard-lying "
money. So, as soon as I was able, I wrote to the
pawnbroker to redeem my goods. Unfortunately I
forgot to enclose the postage, and he sent a letter to
say the goods would be returned when the postage
was forwarded. The letter had the wrong initial
on it, and was addressed to my mother's house.
Consequently it got opened, and I received a letter
from my mother asking me why I had disgraced the
family by pawning things. I pleaded guilty, and
was summoned home for the week-end for a sort
of court of enquiry. I tried to explain the situation,
and was told that they were quite certain my elder
brother, Jim, then a Lieutenant, would certainly
not have done such a thing. On his arrival home
that evening he was asked if he had pawned anything, and his reply was : " Yes, everything, except
a monkey jacket and a pair of pyjamas." I was
therefore acquitted, and my father allowed me £2 a
month for the remainder of the period that I was a
Sub-Lieutenant—the only time during my service
career that I received any private allowance.

I also disgraced the family whilst at Greenwich on

the Trafalgar Day Centenary. It happened to be a
Saturday, and I had gone home to lunch, to find that
the family were attending a Mothers' Meeting of the
Missions to Seamen, of which my sister Emmie was
Secretary. Like a good boy I promised to go, and
walked to the house with the Padre who was going to
hold forth. I told him I had recently returned from
the Pacific Station, and had visited Buenos Aires,
etc. I found myself the only man at the meeting,
and luckily sat close to the door, because at the
conclusion of the Padre's address, he said in a very
clerical voice :

" You will be glad to know that we have amongst
us this afternoon an active service naval man who
has had the privilege, which has been denied to most
of us, of travelling round the world, and, after a little
prayer, I will ask him to say a few words on the good
work the Mission does in the great foreign ports of
South America."

Well, as a matter of fact, I hadn't even heard of the
existence of the Mission till that day. I blushed all
over, and during the prayers was thinking hard what
to do. At the end of the prayers he said :

" I will now ask for a few minutes' silent prayer,
especially remembering our active service naval
man."

This was too much for me, and as I saw everyone
deep in prayer I crawled quietly out of the door, got
my hat and stick, took the first train to London, and
went to the Empire Music Hall. I learnt afterwards
that there was much consternation when the " active

service naval man " was missing, but luckily my mother had a sense of humour, and I was soon forgiven.

After leaving Greenwich I went through the usual routine of gunnery courses in H.M.S. *Excellent*, really Whale Island, and torpedo courses in H.M.S. *Vernon*, being accommodated in the Navigation School. To the uninitiated these arrangements may seem strange, but H.M.S. *Excellent* corresponds to much the same as H.M.S. *President* lying off the Embankment, which is frequently used for Admirals to hoist their Flags on, many officers who have never stepped on board her being borne on her ship's books.

Whale Island is the actual island on which the gunnery establishments are built, and where a large number of officers and men are accommodated. It is connected to the mainland by a small bridge, alongside of which is a guard-house manned by bluejackets, where the usual guard duties are carried out.

The island is famous as the place where everything is done " at the double," and one is supposed to be thoroughly " shaken up." Many of our most distinguished Admirals have either been Captains, Commanders, or Staff Officers of this Gunnery establishment. It is the essence of smartness, and boasts of its efficiency, but my stay there as a Sub-Lieutenant, and subsequent visits I have paid there, have left me with the impression that there is too much of the " super " atmosphere about the place, which I am sure has led to many an otherwise promising officer being spoilt, or forgetting that the Navy does not consist of gunnery alone.

On completion of my courses, I was appointed First Lieutenant of the destroyer *Arun*. We were a most happy little ship, and the experience one gained as Sub-Lieutenant of a destroyer, with the important title of First Lieutenant, was invaluable, as it gave one a great opportunity for getting to know the men, not only at their work, but to some extent in their private circumstances. We had a most charming Lieutenant-Commander as Captain. He was at times rather eccentric, but a better destroyer Captain would be hard to find. He taught me many a lesson which helped me when my turn came to command a destroyer. On one occasion, off Lamlash, we had to pick up a target. Our destroyer was one of those with a high forecastle which easily caught the wind. I was standing on the forecastle with a party of men ready to hook the target, and the skipper steamed up and missed it three times running. I sort of shrugged my shoulders, inferring that I thought the Captain was making rather a mess of things, and that the job was an easy one. My attitude was of course improper in the presence of the men, and it also showed my youthful inexperience. The skipper had witnessed the incident, and calling me on to the bridge, quietly said : " You might pick up that target for me, I'm going down for some cocoa " ; I said : " Aye, aye, sir," and ordered " Full speed ahead," thinking I would pick it up at once. After

I had missed it three times the skipper returned to
the bridge and remarked, " Oh, haven't you got it
yet ?   I thought it was such an easy matter, and the
men are so tired of waiting on the forecastle."   I
never forgot that lesson, and thanked him for it
afterwards.

A rather curious row I had with the skipper ended
in a tragic way.   My cabin was just opposite the
skipper's, so that he could hear everything I said.
One morning, when we were lying in the basin at
Devonport, the Petty Officer came down to me about
7.15 a.m. and reported that Stoker " X " had overstayed his leave by ten minutes.   In due course I
saw the man, and after hearing his defence, let him
off with a caution.

When the skipper saw his " defaulters " later on in
the forenoon, he wanted to know why " X " was not
amongst them.   I told him that I had let " X " off.
He then gave me orders that any man who was not
on board exactly at 7 a.m. was to be brought before
him.   I protested that it was an unreasonable order,
and that I should be given at least some authority,
up to, say, fifteen minutes.   But it was no good—I
received the order in writing.   The following morning I was on deck with a stop-watch, and found that
about twenty men, including the Coxswain, had all
broken their leave for periods between one second
and two minutes.   Much to their amazement I
placed them all in the Captain's report.   At 10 a.m.
I went to the skipper and told him I thought there
was discontent in the ship, and showed him the

charge sheet against twenty men. He was furious,
and said of course he didn't mean that sort of thing,
to which I replied that he had given me a stupid
order and I had obeyed it in a stupid way to em-
phasise the fact. After many words, I asked him
if he would get a new First Lieutenant. This was
not the only time during my career I asked to be
relieved when I thought my superior was in the
wrong. Anyhow, peace was made, and I got my
way.

That night about midnight there was a splash—
the Quartermaster woke us up to say a man had
missed the gangway, and fallen between us and the
destroyer lying alongside. As it was a pitch-dark
night and bitterly cold (January), there would be no
chance of the man living, but we set to and grappled
for the body for several hours. The skipper and I
were personally working one grapple, and whilst
working he said, " I wonder who it is ? " I replied,
" Why—Stoker ' X,' of course," and sure enough,
as daylight was breaking, and we eventually hauled
the body out of the water, there was Stoker " X "
staring us in the face.

The Captain had a brother who was equally
eccentric. He once came down to stay with us at
Plymouth, and they spent most of the week-end dis-
agreeing—with very good humour and much wit.
One afternoon the two of them were up in Plymouth
at the once famous Jones's Oyster Bar. They
decided to drive back to Devonport in a cab, and
discussed with Mr. Jones as to whether it should be

open or shut. They couldn't agree, so Mr. Jones suggested they should have it half open and half shut. This arrangement met the case, and off they started, but after proceeding about half a mile they discovered that the brother who wanted the cab open was sitting in the half that was shut, and the one that wanted it shut in the half that was open, so back they went to Jones for further advice on the matter, and after more discussion, it was arranged that they should drive half-way with it shut, and then stop and open it for the remainder. This they eventually did.

During one manœuvres we were resting at Harwich on the Friday night till Sunday afternoon. The Chief and I got leave to go to London on Saturday, and we thought we would have a good day together, without my going to my parents' house. Of course the first person I met in London was my father, so like a good boy I *had* to go home, and it was only by very desperate lying that we succeeded in getting off in the evening to the Empire. That night we slept at the annexe of the Cocoa Tree Club, of which I was then a member. The valet failed to call us at the proper time, the result being we woke up to find we only had a few minutes to catch our train. Dashing out, we were lucky in getting a hansom-cab, and dressed in it on our way to the station, just catching the train in the nick of time.

The skipper and I were both very fond of dogs, and eventually we got two beautiful bull-terrier pups. His was called Sam and mine Nelson—the former

came to a bad end through taking to worrying sheep,
but Nelson lived through the Great War and fell
overboard in Plymouth Sound from the *Cumberland*
which I commanded in 1919. By that time he was
stone deaf and stone blind, and could only follow
the smell of my finger. I could almost fill a book
with yarns about Nelson. By orders of the skipper
he and Sam were brought up under strict naval
discipline—each had a kennel on deck. But they
used to sleep down in our cabins. As pups, they of
course used to eat people's slippers and so on, and
I had to bring them up before the skipper as
defaulters. He would then order them " confine-
ment to kennel for so many hours," or deprivation
of half ration of beef, as the case might deserve.

On one occasion we were exercising " Abandon
Ship," and when the abandoned crew were in the
boats, I reported to the Captain " Ship Abandoned."
He asked me what arrangements I had made for the
saving of the dogs (I had not thought about them),
and I told him I proposed putting them in his boat.
He ordered me to have lifebelts made for them,
which I proceeded to do, and next time we abandoned ship, I had the dogs paraded with their lifebelts on. The skipper ordered me to throw the
dogs overboard. The lifebelts, unfortunately,
slipped up their tummies, and all we could see were
their little tails wagging on the surface of the water.
Luckily a boat was at hand to save them from
drowning.

I shall be referring to Nelson again, as he had an

4

extraordinary character, and took much part in both my joys and sorrows. He served in many of H.M. ships, I might almost say with distinction, as he never bit anybody, and was always popular, yet faithful only to his master and missie. His only trick was a " hoax," which took in scores of people. If I held up a bun or biscuit, he would bark till I put it into his mouth. His trick was as follows. I held up the biscuit and said, " Three cheers for the King," and promptly slipped the biscuit into his mouth; then " Two cheers for master "—in went the biscuit; then " One cheer for missie (my wife) " —in went the biscuit; then " No cheers for the Kaiser "—this was the most difficult of all, as the biscuit had to go in mighty quick. It was extraordinary the number of people who were taken in.

My good time in the *Arun* came to an end in October 1905, when I was promoted to Lieutenant. I thought this a good opportunity to get on with my matrimonial ideas, and so I suggested to my future father-in-law, Mr. H. V. S. Davids, late Consul in Batavia, that I would like to marry his daughter. It was rather cheek on my part, as I had no private means, and no prospect of them, with only 10s. a day to live on. My father-in-law practically told me to go to h—— out of it, and so I applied for a China Squadron ship, and was appointed to H.M.S. *King Alfred*, the flagship of Admiral Sir A. W. Moore, G.C.B. I asked Mary Davids if she would look after Nelson during my absence, which she did, but my mother warned me that I would be unlikely to get my dog back without having to take my girl with it. On returning from China in May 1910, my parents, Mary, and her father met me at Southsea. My brother tactfully put me in a cab with Mary, having given the driver strict instructions to drive me about three miles round to the hotel, which was only a hundred yards away. I was so thrilled that I forgot all about proposing. The following day a big luncheon was held on board, and the rumour leaked out that I had got engaged, which was untrue. Anyhow, at the luncheon, an officer got up and proposed the healths of my fiancée and myself. My father-in-law, full of excitement, dashed off to the post office to telegraph the news to my mother-in-law, so we decided not to go through the formal process of proposing.

We arranged to get married in October, but on my joining the *Impregnable*, when the Captain, the late Rear-Admiral Savory, C.B., found I was engaged, he told me he would not have any married officers in his ship, and that if I got married I should have to leave. I pointed out that I did not consider that the Navy had any claim on one's private life, and that, provided my being married did not affect my duty, there should be no objection about it. He told me not to be hasty, and to take a fortnight to consider the matter. My reply at the end of it was the same, but I thought it advisable not to ask for marriage leave, and so we waited until the normal period of Christmas leave. On leaving the church

I told the driver to stop at the Vet.'s. There Nelson was waiting for us, with a big bow on, and he drove in the carriage to the reception. He insisted on sitting on my wife's train, which was laid out in the usual fashion, with a very superior air of " I am responsible for this."

CHAPTER IV

China

A FEW weeks after leaving H.M.S. *Arun* I was ordered to join the cruiser *Hawke* at Chatham, for passage to China, to recommission H.M.S. *King Alfred*, the Flagship on the Station.

Our ship was not exactly a happy one, though we pulled through pretty well. Our Captain was Owen F. Gillett, a very kindly man, whom we looked on as rather old-fashioned ; anyhow, he used generally to come on the bridge during the First Watch each night and relieve the Officer of the Watch for half an hour, to enable him to go down and have a smoke in the smoking-room. One night, when in the Indian Ocean, time was passing, and there was no sign of the Captain. I ordered the signalman to blow the siren, and the Captain promptly came rushing up as if we were on the verge of collision. When he came up, he said :

" What's the matter ? "

I said : " Sorry, sir, but somebody tripped over the siren lanyard by mistake."

He said : " Oh, is that all ? Would you like a relief ? "

I said : " Thanks very much, sir," and never

enjoyed a whisky and soda more. I have often
wondered whether he realised that he had had his
leg pulled.

I think on the whole we were all pretty thankful
to arrive at Hong-Kong on January 13th, 1908, and
to find all the Squadron there. We joined the *King
Alfred* the following day, to spend two and a half
happy years in her. She was flying the Flag of
Admiral Sir A. W. Moore, G.C.B., and the Captain
was G. F. Thursby (now Admiral Sir G. F.
Thursby).

We only had a few days to settle down when the
Commander-in-Chief took us to Penang. I had
hoped we would extend our cruise to Batavia in
Java, as my eldest brother, Don, was Vice-Consul
there, and he had invited the Admiral down ; but
we hadn't time to go, and we only visited Singapore
and Malacca before returning to Hong-Kong, the
Headquarters of the Station, where we used to receive
visits from men-of-war of all nations. I particularly remember the coming of the Japanese
Squadron, consisting of ships captured in the Russo-
Japanese War. Other visitors included the German
Flagship, *Fürst Bismarck*, followed later by the
Scharnhorst. We became very friendly with the
latter ship, and although she had a better armament
than ours, we reckoned we could have seen her off
in a fight in calm weather. We were both crack
gunnery ships, and often used to discuss the question
in a friendly way. Of course, at a later date, when
the *Scharnhorst* met the *Good Hope* at Coronel, the

chances weren't so even as they might have been—
the *Good Hope* was unable to use her main-deck guns
owing to the sea—and they had not had the time to
work up to a high state of gunnery efficiency such
as we attained with Rear-Admiral W. F. French,
C.M.G., as our Gunnery Officer.

In the middle of March Admiral Moore sailed for
England, and we hoisted the Flag of Vice-Admiral
the Hon. Sir Hedworth Lambton, of Ladysmith
fame, who later became Admiral-of-the-Fleet Sir
Hedworth Meux. Our new Captain was Clinton
Baker (now Admiral), and our new Commander was
F. O. Lewis, who had been our First Lieutenant
in the *Flora*. Each one was a personality, and as
Admiral, Captain, and Commander they made a fine
trio to serve under, with the result that from that
time on we became a really happy and efficient ship.

The Admiral hated being disturbed during the
night, and, to my horror, during one Middle Watch
the Captain's dog, Sarah, walked over the Admiral's
cabin and started barking. I crept along as quietly
as I could and removed Sarah back to the Captain's
cabin, stupidly forgetting that the cabin had two
doors, with the result that in a few minutes Sarah
was back over the Admiral's cabin barking again.
I heard the Admiral's bell ring, and, in due course,
I received a signal from the Commander-in-Chief,
saying, " Indicate the name of the dog barking and
the officer of the watch," to which I replied, " Sarah
and Campbell."

Another time, at Saigon, I was again officer of

the Middle Watch when the Admiral rang his bell
and sent for me about two in the morning.   He
was in a very bad temper, and wanted to know why
the h—— he had been bitten by a mosquito ; he
ordered me to make investigations and report in
the morning.   I made careful enquiries to find out
whether by any chance the Admiral's cabin fan
could have stopped, but finding that the dynamo
had been running regularly, there appeared no
solution in that direction.   It so happened that the
Captain came out of his cabin in the early hours of
the morning, and I told him what had occurred.
He asked me what I proposed to do, and I told him
the only thing I could think of was to put the
sentry under arrest for allowing the mosquito to
enter the Admiral's cabin without his permission.
This apparently satisfied the Admiral, and I heard
no more about it.

During our commission we spent many good
weeks visiting Japan, one of the most beautiful
countries in the world, and populated by a most
attractive race, especially in the inland spots.   Our
stay at Yokohama was a round of festivities.   The
Commander-in-Chief was received in audience by
the Emperor, and we were entertained in turn by
the British Ambassador, the Japanese Admiralty,
and the Mayor of Tokio, at whose dinner we had to
sit on the floor with chop-sticks, each of us attended
by two Japanese girls.   After that dinner we saw
some of the most beautiful dancing I have ever seen,
done by Geishas.

At the various functions we went to, the personage that appealed to me most was Admiral Togo, the victor of Tsushima. He left a great impression on me after our short talk, and I was very pleased when he gave me his autograph both in English and in Japanese.

Whilst at Yokohama, a big fire broke out at twelve o'clock one night. A large party of sailors was landed. I remember one party of about fifty men fallen in behind a wall adjacent to the house which was burning, and they got rather bored with the wait, so one of the sailors suggested knocking the —— wall down, and they proceeded to do so with a great charge.

Being the Flagship, we visited all the best places, covering nearly the whole of the station from Manchuria down to Singapore and Penang. We also went up the Yangtze River, but were too big to visit Shanghai, except from Woosung.

During our visit to Nanking we had an opportunity of visiting the Ming tombs, and we rode out there on donkeys with wooden saddles, which had a very painful effect the following day.

I happened to lunch one day with the chief engineer of the railway, and he asked me if I would take his wife for a ride in the afternoon. I told him that I had never ridden a horse in my life, and did not know the first thing about it, but he did not believe this, and said all sailors could ride. Eventually, very foolishly, I agreed to go, and mounted his very fierce steed ; we started by knocking down

some of the wooden palings in the backyard. I
eventually got the animal out into the road, and it
bolted with me all the way to Nanking, a distance
of about three miles. I luckily managed to hang
on, but I am afraid I was not much of a gallant
escort to the lady.

Amongst other places we visited was Tsingtau,
at that time under German control. We had a
great *entente* with the German Flagship, the *Fürst
Bismarck*, and other German ships. We also had a
very good time on shore, and the German Commander-in-Chief, Admiral Ingenohl, and his charming wife, were most kind to us. The town was
beautifully kept, and the whole place smelt of good
organisation. I, together with another watch-
keeper, challenged two German Lieutenants to a
beer-drinking competition—but the beer was so
light that at 4 a.m. we gave up the contest and
called quits.

Another place of great interest was Saigon, the
capital of the French possession in Cochin China.
It is well built, has fine buildings, and is a mixture
of the East and " gay Paree." The heat there was
terrific, the temperature in the cool season being as
much as 80°. The town is situated about fifty miles
up the river, which narrows to about four hundred
yards—so that to turn round we had to put our
nose on to the mud. We lay practically alongside
the main street, close to the French Flagship
Montcalm, with which we had many *ententes*.
We had what was called a free gangway, and the

men were allowed to walk on board at any time of the night.

It being Christmas time, everything and everyone was very gay. We watchkeepers had been given instructions to turn a blind eye, as much as possible, when men returned on board a little the worse for wear, provided they were quiet. I was on watch about three o'clock one morning, when I saw a Marine returning in rather a zigzag fashion ; anyhow, he wasn't disturbing anybody, so when the Sergeant-Major reported, " Private —— returned from leave," I said, " All right, tell him to turn in." The Sergeant-Major returned to say the man wished to see me, and in spite of my twice saying I didn't want to see him, he insisted on it. I asked him what he wanted, and he replied :

" Permission to go ashore, sir."

I said : " Well, you have come on board of your own free will when you needn't have done, so what on earth do you want to go ashore for ? "

He said : " Well, sir, I have just remembered that on my way down I met three Frenchmen. I knocked two of them down, but one of them ran away, and I want to go back and see if I can find him."

I asked him what he wanted to knock them down for—he said because they were —— Frenchmen.

The officers generally used to go ashore after dinner, as it was too hot to go before—the rig was generally black trousers, white mess jacket, and a stiff shirt—the latter usually suffered greatly from the heat. One evening I told my old Marine servant to put out my evening clothes for going ashore, and I was rather taken aback when he said :

" Are we going to get drunk again ? "

I said : " What the h—— do you mean ? "

He said : " Well, sir, we are running short of stiff shirts, and we can't afford to come on board with them crumpled up each night."

We spent many months in Wei-hai-wei, a spot we became very fond of. It was one of the most ideal places I have ever been to for the purpose we had in hand, namely, gunnery exercises, Fleet Regattas, and all kinds of sports and exercise. Target practice in those days was far more interesting, in a way, than at the present time, as one was close enough to the target to see the actual hits. One of my 12-pounder guns' crews created a record by scoring fifteen hits out of seventeen rounds in fifty-five seconds.

The Fleet Regattas were preceded by much practising, and I am afraid a good deal of betting used to go on, while a selling sweep used to take place on board, previous to the regatta. I was one of the four who took part in the officers' skiff race. In order to save weight we had no coxswain, and an arrangement was fixed up for myself as bowman to steer with my feet, which was no easy job. It was blowing pretty fresh, and the language going down the course was fresher, each one of the crew turning round and telling me in plain language what they thought of my steering. It was a great race ; the finishing line was between the *King Alfred* and the *Monmouth*, both of which ships were crowded with cheering crews—as the finish was between our two boats. By a gigantic spurt, at the last minute, we won by a stroke. I collapsed at the bottom of the boat at the finish. I have never been in a more exciting race. A few years ago I was walking in the gardens at Plymouth, beneath the Hoe, when I ran across the park-keeper, a naval pensioner and old shipmate of mine. He had been in the *Monmouth* at the time. We got talking, and this race came up. I remarked what a narrow win it was, and he said :

" Go on, sir ; you never won that race—the Flag-ship ' Navigator ' was the umpire, that's the only reason you won."

The gunnery exercises would go on all day long, and in the evenings there were no attractions ashore except a canteen, a naval club, and a golf club, so that the men came on board early at night and were ready for work early each morning. The *King Alfred* was one of the smartest and most efficient ships I have ever been in—the Commander-in-Chief gave us two very thorough inspections and couldn't find any fault. The mess-decks and spaces down below were a picture, thanks to our First Lieutenant, now Vice-Admiral H. J. Tweedie. But sports weren't overlooked, and, in addition to winning regattas, we had good football and cricket teams.

I used to run seining parties, and we got good sport, especially off the Korean coast. I remember arriving in harbour one Sunday, and we had great difficulty in getting permission from the Admiral to allow the men to go away seining. I wonder what he would have thought of the modern Sunday Entertainments Bill. Anyhow, we eventually got permission, and not only had a good haul, but we had great amusement when the bosun, who was in the centre of the net, and was pretty fat, suddenly disappeared, a garfish having had its nose through the net and given him a good bite in the tummy.

We had on board several Chinese midshipmen, who were under my special care. One of them became Commander-in-Chief of the Chinese Navy at a later date. One night they entertained me to a real Chinese dinner at Hong-Kong, with bird's-nest soup, eggs which were green with old age, and other delicacies which would probably have made me sick but for the fact that we were well fortified with some delicious Chinese samshu, which tasted strongly of rose water. Unfortunately, one of the English midshipmen, who was also of the party, did not realise that it was intoxicating, and we had an awful job getting him back on board.

Towards the end of our time on the station, while I was walking round the Island of Hong-Kong, a twenty-five mile walk, my knee suddenly got locked, and I could not open it or close it, with the result that I had to hobble back on one leg. The following day it suddenly unlocked itself, and the P.M.O., thinking I might have tuberculosis, put it in plaster of Paris, in which condition I had to go home. While the ship was in dry dock the Admiral very kindly sent

me to hospital. The P.M.O was a very strange old
fellow, who was apparently working for promotion
by keeping his expenses down, and as I was feeling
perfectly well except for my knee, I rather grudged
the lack of food ; but luckily one of my nurses had a
kind heart, and used to buy me food from outside.
When I went home the Admiral gave me his upper-
deck cabin, as I was confined to my bed the whole
time, and it enabled me to have plenty of fresh air
and comfort.

When we sailed from Hong-Kong for England, the
question arose as to flying a paying-off pennant as
well as the Commander-in-Chief's flag. We eventually got his approval to do so, and when we left the
harbour we were flying an enormous Admiral's flag,
and flying a paying-off pennant as well, which was
a thousand feet long and fouled two steamers on the
way out. As we sailed from the buoy, thousands of
Chinese crackers were fired, and we were cheered out
of the harbour by all ships. We proceeded to
Penang to turn over the command to Admiral Sir
A. L. Winslow.

We arrived at Portsmouth in the middle of April
1910. It had been a wonderful commission—the
Captain became an Admiral; the three of the
Lieutenants have already reached Flag rank, and
nearly all of them either got to, or are, still on the
Captain's list. The midshipmen haven't done quite
so well, but then, the Navy always *was* " going to
the dogs."

I left the ship before paying off. I have already

described the greeting I received from my family on landing.

It was soon discovered that I required a further operation on my knee, which was done by Sir Alfred Fripp, at the King Edward VII Hospital, started and run by Sister Agnes (Miss Keyser), one of the greatest personalities I have ever met in my life. She ran her hospital with a rod of iron, combined with such charm and sympathetic understanding that she held the affections of everybody in the hospital. Her smoking rules were very strict ; one pipe or two cigarettes after each meal. I remember her coming up one morning about 7 a.m., and smelling smoke. The offender, an officer of high rank, owned up to the offence, and got a real, full-blown dressing-down. It was whilst I was in the hospital that King Edward VII died—I shall never forget the picture that Sister Agnes looked when she came in, dressed in black, to announce the death of a great King and an old friend.

V

Boys' Training Ship

On completion of my sick leave and foreign service leave, I was appointed to H.M.S. *Impregnable*, the boys' training ship at Devonport. At that time the establishment consisted of the old *Impregnable*, one of the last of England's wooden walls, and joined to her was the *Inconstant*, an old cruiser ; later on the *Black Prince* was added. The Captain of this establishment was generally a very senior Captain, who received his Flag during his period of command. As already related, H. W. Savory was the Captain, and on my persisting in getting married, he applied for me to be relieved, but by the time that a relief was appointed, some months later, Captain Savory had left the ship on promotion, and I had sufficiently justified my existence in the eyes of the Commander and First Lieutenant to be asked to stay on. I eventually stayed over my two years' appointment, which shows that the fact that an officer is married does not necessarily interfere with the efficient carrying out of his duties. On the other hand, when I commanded, I had frequently to tell an officer that he spent too much time at home instead of taking an interest in the welfare of his ship, not

5

only during working hours, but also in the recreation
of the men in the evening. This latter is especially
important in a training ship.

The training service at that time was looked upon
as one of the most important and selective appointments, and so it should be at all times. We had
over 1,000 boys on board, and the routine and discipline were severe, but not too much so. In a
later chapter I will give some further views on the
Training Service. One's work in a training ship is
never ended, no matter what rank you hold, for when
you think of about 1,000 boys coming straight from
all sorts of homes, and requiring in the shortest time
to be turned out ready for sea service, it can be
realised there is a lot to be done. It was extraordinary and very interesting to watch the boys
arrive, very often dishevelled, some of them joining
because they liked the smell of the sea, others
because their fathers had done so before them, others
of good birth and poor parents, and others because
their mothers used to want their remittances, which
was one of the attractions put forward in the Recruiting Office.

I remember one very dirty boy joining the ship,
and on his being given a disinfectant bath, the
Petty Officer asked him if he had ever been in the
water before, to which he replied, " No." In due
course he was given a card, on which the instructions amongst others were, " Never tell a lie,
and always go to your officers when in trouble, as
you will find them your friends." After reading

the card, the boy went straight up to the Petty Officer and said :

" Very sorry, sir, I am afraid I have already told you a lie by mistake. I clean forgot that I fell into a canal when I was seven years old."

Another boy, who was rather soft, after having been served out with his new kit, had his leg pulled by some senior boys, and he went to his Lieutenant and reported :

" Please, sir, my kit is all complete except for my umbrella ! "

At one time I had charge of what were called the new entries, and I used to ask them about their past. One boy, when I asked what he had been doing, replied, " On Lord Haldane's Staff, sir, at the War Office." I was somewhat taken aback, but on further enquiries I discovered that he had to open the door for Lord Haldane to enter his office each day.

In whatever condition the boys joined, they always left as smart as a sailor could look. At the time when the late Admiral-of-the-Fleet Sir John Michael de Robeck was our Captain, we were honoured by a visit from Mr. Winston Churchill, who had just taken over the position of First Lord. I think we were the first ship that he ever inspected. He made a thorough inspection, but I shall never forget the First Lieutenant's face when Mr. Churchill asked him if he was Adjutant of the ship ! The visit was at the time I was looking after the new entries, and I received orders from the Captain to keep ten of these as dirty as I could, and with ill-fitting clothes on. During the inspection these ten boys were fallen in alongside ten of the smartest boys who were just completing their training. The Captain drew the attention of the First Lord to the way he received the boys and the way he turned them out. The First Lord appeared greatly impressed.

Another duty I had was that of looking after the swimming instruction, in which the boys had a fairly severe test to pass, and on three occasions I had to dive in after boys who had gone down. But the worst case I had was a boy who had an epileptic fit in the water, and an old pensioner who had witnessed the scene from the Cremyll Heights wrote a very rude letter to the Press about it, referring to me as being inhuman. All he had seen was the boy being hauled on to a raft where he kicked about all over the place. The *Western Morning News*, which always treated me with great courtesy, replied that I was far from inhuman. (The reporter had been to see me at my house, and I think had enjoyed his cup of tea.) The swimming test was a most unnatural and absurd one. A boy was not allowed to go to sea until he had in his certificate " Can swim," which meant passing a certain test. The Admiralty at the same time did not like boys being kept in a training ship when they required them for training at sea, and in consequence, boys frequently passed their swimming test on the day when the tide helped them along, which did not mean that they were sufficiently strong swimmers to swim round their own ship if required.

Frequently complaints used to be received by the Admiral commanding the training squadron that boys had been sent to sea with " Can swim " on their certificates, and it turned out that they could not swim from the lower boom to the gangway. There does not appear to me to be any particular reason why a sailor should of necessity be able to swim.

One of my less pleasant duties was to take charge, during the quiet hours of the evening, of the backward boys. Some of them nearly broke one's heart trying to teach them to swim, and in some cases, where the inability to swim was due to fear, the only thing to do was to make the fear of the cane or punishment greater than the fear of the water. I remember in particular one ginger-headed boy, who was under my instruction for about three months, during all of which he had both his leave and pocket-money stopped. Eventually he passed the swimming test, and got his leave back. I happened to be ashore one Sunday evening, walking with my wife, and passed this boy returning to the ship. He stared at me very hard, but did not salute. The following day I sent for him, and reminded him that he was expected to salute his officers, whether in uniform or in plain clothes, and asked him what on earth he meant by passing me without saluting. He replied :

" I am very sorry, sir, but I didn't recognise you."

I said : " What ! You didn't recognise me, and you have seen me every day for the last three months ?

I should have thought you would have been as sick of my face as I am of yours," to which he replied :

" Yes, sir, but please, sir, I had never seen you smiling before, and I didn't recognise you ! "

I spent most of my time shaking the boys up in general. One of the ship's corporals, who had the same ideas as I had, used to work hand in glove with me. When he left the ship, he asked if he could come and say good-bye to me, which he proceeded to do, and in thanking me for the assistance I had given him, he said :

" What I have always felt about you, sir, was that whereas Lieutenant ' X ' is what I would call more of a gentleman than an officer, you have always been more of an officer than a gentleman."

One afternoon, when I was in charge of the gun battery deck, a very extraordinary accident took place. A party of boys were being exercised in target practice with a ·23-inch rifle fitted inside a 6-inch gun—the target being a cardboard one fitted to a small steel box at the end of the gun. The target had been shot away, and the instructor had ordered the bolt of the rifle to be removed whilst a new target was being placed. A small boy was leaning across the muzzle of the gun replacing the target, when suddenly he was shot through the neck with this ·23-inch rifle, and died almost immediately. I was on the spot in a few seconds, and at once interrogated all the boys in the class as to how the accident had occurred. Each made the same statement, namely, that they had seen the bolt removed, and that no one had touched the rifle. As the unfortunate lad could not possibly have shot himself, these statements were obviously not true, but in spite of a long Court of Enquiry, and a long Coroner's inquest, not a boy would say anything further than his original statement. And although someone obviously lied, the truth was never elucidated.

The boys sometimes used to write direct to the King with their complaints, and these letters would come down through the usual channels. They used generally to say they had been bullied. I had one such letter written about me concerning my treatment of the backward swimmers, and I at once asked for a full enquiry to be made, which disclosed that there was no truth in the complaint.

One of the worst things we had to deal with in a big training ship like this was infectious disease. We used frequently to have epidemics of nearly every disease under the sun. On one occasion a boy got scarlet fever, and the following morning all the boys, about fifty of them, in the mess next to him, came out in spots and a slight temperature. They were all sent to hospital under observation, while the ship was put into quarantine. They remained there some weeks, but none of them developed scarlet fever. In the meantime their clothes had been eaten by rats, so they not only had a holiday in hospital, but also got new kit in return. It was many months before I discovered what had really happened. I got it from a Roman Catholic priest. Apparently

the boys had eaten soap pills, which brought them
out in spots.

An amusing side of the picture was the passing-
out examination of the boys. Sometimes one had
several hundred to examine in one day, so the
examination could only be very superficial—but it
must be remembered that the boys at that time went
on to sea-going training ships to complete their
training. The absurd answers one got would fill a
book. I remember once asking a boy what lights
a ship " not under control " hoisted at night, and
he at once replied : " Two black lights."

It was hard work in the *Impregnable*, but I was
sorry when my time came to an end. During the
time I was there I had served under four different
Captains, the last one being a Commander-in-
Command, now Rear-Admiral Laurence Oliphant,
who was the first Captain to have married quarters
on board. None of us relished the idea of the
Captain having his wife and children on board ; but
at a later date I changed my mind on the subject.
As mentioned previously, I was already engaged
when I joined, and on getting married during the
Christmas leave, which happened to coincide with
the departure of Admiral Savory, who was relieved
by Captain, now Admiral, Pears, my wife and I
were fortunate in getting a small cottage right on
the sea front, below Admiralty House, and within
five minutes of the ship—which enabled me to get
on board generally before the other Lieutenants had
turned out. The cottage had an historical interest,

[*Photo ι Vandyk, London.*

MY WIFE.

in that it had originally been King William IV's bathing-house, but had been divided up into six cottages, and had a little boat camber of its own. We found out afterwards that the people who had left it had done so because the house was supposed to be haunted, and certainly on many occasions, when people stayed in the house, they complained of hearing strange noises during the night, and of doors being opened, etc. It was probably due, either to the age of the house, or to the fact that underneath the house were a large number of water-rats. Personally, I only heard the ghost once, when there appeared to be somebody walking upstairs in the middle of the night. Being a coward, I locked the door and told my wife that as far as I was concerned it could walk about wherever it liked so long as I didn't see it !

I had been brought up by an old-fashioned mother, who did all her own shopping, whereas my wife, having been brought up in the East, had never done such a thing, and my mother impressed upon her the desirability of going to do her shopping personally to see that she was getting the best value for her money. I went with her on her first shopping expedition and we visited the greengrocer. My wife, who happens to be rather short-sighted, pointed out what she thought to be apples, and asked the man how much these apples were ; she got rather flummoxed when the man replied : " They are not apples, madam, they are potatoes ! "

Our one and only maid was the daughter of a

coastguard. She was frequently assisted by my
Marine servant, who also used to take me to and
from the ship in the Wardroom motor-boat. One
evening, when we were having a small dinner-party,
and my Marine servant was coming to help to wait,
our guests happened to include the Captain of
Marines of the *Impregnable*. On my arrival home
about 6 p.m. the maid came and asked me to go into
the kitchen. She then showed me that one of the
cupboards was stocked with ship's tobacco, which
my servant had smuggled ashore to sell in the town.
I therefore had to telephone off to the ship, and ask
the Captain of the Marines to put my servant under
arrest. He was punished severely, but when I said
good-bye to him, he said, " Well, after all, sir, I have
been doing it for ten years, and I never thought a
girl would give me away."

My naval brother got married a month after me.
We were both terribly hard up, although we both
had fashionable weddings with long lists of presents.
I arranged with my brother that he should send me a
cheque for £2, which appeared in the list of presents,
and I returned it to him with 2s. interest on his
wedding day, which also appeared as " Brother to
brother—cheque."

My wife and I used to spend a lot of time fishing
in a small boat I had, called the *Demon*. One evening
we happened to row past the *Impregnable* just about
dusk. The boys were all looking out of the port-
holes, and as they did not recognise me or my wife,
who was sitting in the stern, she was greeted all the

way along with—" Hullo, Queenie ; hullo, Duckie."
I never let them know the truth of the case, but took
an early opportunity later on of warning them not
to shout at boats passing the ship, as one never knew
who was in them.

Nelson lived partly on board and partly at the
house, and became a well-known figure. On one
occasion I saw a photograph of him in a photo-
grapher's window taken with a girl I did not know,
in evening dress. On making enquiries, I found she
was a girl from one of the shops, where Nelson used
to go on his own for a bun. He made friends with
everybody, though he only had one master. When
in a destroyer, I generally used to call in at a well-
known lounge in Devonport on my way home at
7 p.m. Nelson invariably went there by himself
and waited for me. There was a hansom rank outside the lounge, and occasionally if I was late I took
a hansom home. One night I went straight home
without calling at the lounge, and half-way through
dinner the maid came in to say that a hansom had
arrived with Nelson in it. He had apparently
waited as long as he thought fit, and then jumped
into a hansom ; the driver was too much afraid to
throw him out, as he looked very fierce, so had to
drive him home, and it was not till Nelson was
satisfied that I was really at home that he would
get out.

I was very lucky on leaving the *Impregnable* to be
appointed to the command of the destroyer *Ranger*,
belonging to what was known as the Port Flotilla,

which consisted of three destroyers and about six torpedo-boats. Most of them were commanded by Warrant Officers, and I found myself Second-in-Command of the Flotilla and Senior Officer of the destroyers. It was not a large command, but as I happened to be one of the youngest officers commanding a destroyer at that time, I not only considered myself fortunate, but also, as with a picket-boat, relished the idea of being in actual command of something ; and as, thank goodness, there was no wireless in those days, once one got clear of the Signal Station one was monarch of all one surveyed ; though I had a rather amusing incident in this connection.

My chief duty was to tow targets for the Gunnery School firing ships. I was doing this one day for a sloop called the *Rinaldo* commanded by a Warrant Officer, but on board of which was one of the Gunnery Staff with his gaiters on (why Gunnery Officers thought it necessary to wear gaiters at sea whilst other naval officers didn't, I have never discovered). I had ordered signal exercises to be carried out. The said Gunnery Officer objected, not realising that it was nothing to do with him, and that the command of the ship devolved on the Captain of the *Rinaldo*, even though he was a Warrant Officer, and no one else. I eventually had to make a rather peremptory signal to the *Rinaldo* to carry out my orders. The following day I was ordered to attend at the Gunnery School (which was situated in the Naval Barracks) in a frock coat and sword to see

Captain G——. He demanded an apology for the
rude signal I had made to him. I pointed out that
I had made no signal to him, but that I had made a
perfectly proper signal to the officer commanding
the *Rinaldo*, who was junior to me, and pointed out
that, had I made a signal to the Captain of the
Rinaldo inviting him to dine with me, I would not
expect Captain G—— to turn up. He was very
angry, and said he would take me before the Commodore at 11 a.m., so duly at 11 a.m. I appeared
at the Commodore's office. Much to my surprise,
I found the Commodore was on leave, and that
Captain G—— was taking his place. He started off
by saying : " I hear you have refused to apologise
to Captain G——," so I expressed an opinion of
what I thought of Captain G——'s attitude, and
was threatened with being reported to the Commander-in-Chief. It flashed through my mind as
to whether this Gilbert and Sullivan affair was going
to end up in my finding the Commander-in-Chief
on leave as well. Anyhow, when I had expressed
my readiness to see the Commander-in-Chief, the
Commodore, alias Captain G——, decided the
matter was closed.

The *Ranger* was one of the oldest destroyers,
and had no compass on the bridge—it took a Great
War to get one put there. It was very difficult at
times without a compass on the bridge, and I remember on one occasion, when returning from Fowey
with the Flotilla in a dense fog, I turned a complete
circle, and did not realise it till I found myself

cutting through the line and nearly having a collision. I then lost the Flotilla altogether, but it so happened I was the only one to hit the buoy off Plymouth : it was purely by luck, but I hit it literally. This enabled me to find my way to Plymouth and get into harbour, while the remainder anchored outside. The Senior Officer asked me next day how I had managed to get into the harbour, and I told him " thanks to my good navigation, I picked up the buoy at the entrance."

I was only in the *Ranger* about six months before I was ordered to turn over to the *Bittern*.

Just previous to paying off the *Ranger* into a sale list, we were sent down to Falmouth to take part in some exercises for testing the Examination Services. One of the jobs allocated to me was to try and enter harbour under a flag of truce. It so happened that the weather was bad, and all operations were cancelled, but the trip gave me a lever in two directions. In the first place, I was able to keep steam in eight boilers, so as to burn the coal instead of having to " get it out," my orders being that the ship was to be gutted and all stores returned. Secondly, I found on returning the stores that one Wardroom table-cloth was missing, and I inserted it in the list as having been lost overboard by accident. This was at once queried by a High Authority as to how a table-cloth could get lost by accident, to which I replied it had been blown overboard by a gale. A further question :

" How did it get blown overboard by a gale ? "

I replied : " When being used as a flag of truce."

A further question : " What occasion had the *Ranger* to use a flag of truce, as it had not taken part in any war ? "

I replied : " When taking part in exercises at Falmouth—a copy of orders attached."

A further question : " Why was a tablecloth used for this purpose ? "

I replied : " Because the only two white things on board suitable were the Captain's private sheets and the tablecloths, and the latter were selected."

The correspondence lasted over several months, but this last reply settled it. As the ship had been in commission for over twenty years, I thought the loss of only one tablecloth pretty good. At that time it was considered wrong to have any surplus stores on board, but needless to say, the ship having been in commission so long, we had a great quantity of surplus paint, etc. We gave away what we could, and threw the remainder overboard in the dock-yard, thereby wasting hundreds of pounds' worth of stuff. The ship having been gutted, on the day we were leaving, orders were received for her to be fitted out again and sent to Portsmouth. In the meantime I had taken over my command of H.M.S. *Bittern*, but I think the paying-off of the *Ranger* was typical of some of the methods of Admiralty organisation which I hope, but doubt, have now been removed.

The *Bittern* was a better class of destroyer, and we actually had a compass on the bridge. Our duties were the same as in the *Ranger*, except when we got sudden orders to go to sea to search for a Submarine of the A class, which was missing in Whitsand Bay. We were the first destroyer on the scene, and many of us searched for days, trying to locate the submarine : she was eventually located after many " false " locations had been made. It is a good thing to know that at last devices are going to be used to locate submarines which sink by accident in reasonably shallow water.

Beyond this experience nothing unusual happened in the *Bittern* till the outbreak of war.

VI

Early Days of the War

At the end of July 1914 it appeared obvious that war
was coming. My condensers were under dockyard
repair, but I urged the Captain of the dockyard to
speed up their completion, and got to sea on August
3rd, patrolling the English Channel. We were
warned to look out for enemy mine-layers, which it
was anticipated might lay mines previous to the
outbreak of war. During that night there was a
dense fog, and I found myself alongside of what I at
first took to be a suspicious vessel. I received no
reply to my hail, so I had the guns loaded ready for
firing, and I shouted out to the vessel that if there was
no reply I would sink it. We then got a reply in
broad Devon, asking what the h—— it was all about,
and the vessel turned out to be an innocent trawler.

On the outbreak of war the Commander-in-Chief
thought that the War would be a short one, and said
that the destroyers should change crews completely every week. We all protested against this, as
we preferred to run our own ships, and it was
arranged for us to work three weeks on and then a
week off. During the three weeks on, we had to
patrol at sea alternate days and nights, and when in

6   81

harbour remain in the Sound near the Fort with steam up. The Fort was the centre of the Port Control, and had a few soldiers there as sentries. I remember one night being sent for by the Captain in the Fort and went over in my small boat. On approaching, I was " hailed," and replied in accordance with the custom of the service—*Bittern*; luckily the beam of a searchlight swept the Fort at this moment, and I saw a Cameronian Highlander who had a fixed bayonet on his rifle pointed at me. He of course didn't know naval hails, and thought " Bittern " sounded a bit German. I yelled out " Friend " just in time.

It was not long after the outbreak of war that rumours were spreading of suspicious lights along the coast, and the destroyers were sent to investigate. The nearest we ever got was a flashing light near Dartmouth, which, on investigation, turned out to be caused by a tree blowing about outside a lighted room. On another occasion I was recalled to harbour to investigate a suspicious flashing light which had been previously seen in a vicinity where my wife and I had one of the six cottages, and which was on the shore overlooking the entrance to the harbour. It was thought that as I lived there, I should be the best person to solve the problem. On returning home about 7.30 and going in the smoking-room, which overlooked the sea, I asked my wife what on earth was the matter with the gas, as it was going on and off. She said it had been like that for several days, owing to there being water in the pipe. The window was wide open and the blinds not drawn—so that was the answer to the suspicious light on this occasion.

At the outbreak of war I had on board a Gunner whom I did not like, whilst a Gunner and old shipmate whom I wanted was in another torpedo-boat belonging to the same Flotilla. I tried through the usual official channels to effect an exchange, but failed to do so. I awaited an opportunity when we were at sea together, and then in my capacity as Senior Officer on the spot, ordered an exchange of Gunners to take place. Eventually I got another old friend with me, Mr. Sandover, who had lent me money in the *Flora*.

We had a variety of duties to perform in the Channel—escorting ships, looking for contraband, and in fact patrol duties in general. Quite early in the War I was sent down towards Land's End to intercept a Swedish ship which was carrying contraband. I found her, and after sending an officer on board to make sure she was carrying a cargo of resin and cotton, ordered her to follow me to Plymouth, but before reaching harbour I was ordered to release her, as at that time we adhered to the Treaty of London, and the cotton was allowed to go via Rotterdam to make gun-cotton for Germany.

Our usual patrol was in the vicinity of the Eddystone Lighthouse, which in foggy weather used to fire a gun. I had been down to the westward and was returning in a dense fog; I knew I was close to the lighthouse, and was listening for the gun, but couldn't hear it, so I luckily slowed down, as a few minutes later there was a shout of "Rocks right ahead." I ordered full speed astern, and found myself alongside the rocks with the lighthouse towering overhead, and the gun went off at the same moment. I was so close that one could have jumped on to the rocks. It was just one of those freakish tricks which sound very often plays in a fog.

This gun, incidentally, was a source of great annoyance, as during foggy weather, especially at night, some coast-watcher would report heavy gunfire to the southward or wherever it might be, and off we would be sent to investigate.

When the Zeppelins started coming over England, we had orders that if they approached Plymouth, we were to close the Eddystone Lighthouse and hail the keeper to put his lights out. I often wondered how it would be done in a howling gale.

The first few months of the War were rather monotonous. I had always had visions of a war meaning a fight almost at once, and here we were doing odd jobs, but nothing in a fighting way. Our first real thrill came when we received news that a submarine had passed through the Straits of Dover. When I say a thrill, it gave me one, but my crew didn't believe it, as they had got to the stage of just going on in a routine way miles from the North Sea. But now that submarines had entered the English Channel our work became more strenuous, and more precautions were taken over escorting ships. The first big convoy job we had was to escort the first contingent of the Canadian troops from overseas. They had come across the Atlantic in thirty-two vessels under an escort commanded by Admiral-of-the-Fleet Rosslyn Wemyss. Several of our destroyers went out to meet them at the entrance of the English Channel, and we were keeping an extra good look out, to make sure that no attack was made on this great Armada. Just as day was breaking on the morning we were due to meet them, our " look out " reported a mine in sight, and sure enough we saw this terrible-looking black object in the water. The sailors at once got up their rifles and started shooting at it to explode it, but several hundred rounds were fired without success. The situation appearing serious, and time being limited, I lowered a boat and sent an officer over to try and hook the mine ; he came back beaming all over and reported that our mine was a dead cow. I had in the meantime sent a wireless message, and when I eventually reported the cow, I received a message from the Senior Officer saying : " I hope the Bovine was not too strong."

It had originally been the intention that the convoy should proceed to Southampton, and we were to escort them as far as Portland and then turn them over to other destroyers, but owing to the reported presence of submarines off the Needles, they were diverted into Plymouth. No preparations at that time had been made to cope with transports at Devonport, but by a marvellous and rapid organisation the transports were got up harbour,

and in a few days all the troops had disembarked.
In the meantime they had some shore leave, and as
it coincided with my boiler cleaning, I had the
pleasure of meeting a lot of them.

One evening, whilst lying in Plymouth Sound, a
very heavy gale sprang up, and we were all ordered
up harbour to lie alongside the dock for the night,
with orders to come out again at 7 a.m. Berthing
alongside was rather difficult owing to the heavy
gale, and being the Senior Officer, I selected the
most difficult berth. I unfortunately bumped my
bows against the stone wall, knocked a hole in them
under water, and flooded my fore compartment. I
at once got a friend of mine in the constructive
department on board, and asked him if he could get
it repaired by daylight. He said it was not only
quite impossible to do so without docking the ship,
but also it was unsafe to go to sea as I was. I took
him down to my cabin privately and said, " Look
here, if you were in my place and wanted to go to
sea and take the risk, what would you do ? " He
said, " Fill it up with a mixture of cement and
ashes." So after dark I sent some scouts out to
steal some cement, and then carried out the mixing
and filled the fore peak. In the meantime I had
informed the Flag-Captain, Back (who lost his life
in the *Natal*), of my accident, but assured him I
would be at sea by 7 a.m., and I was. Luckily we
had fine weather, as my bows were like a breakwater
and wouldn't rise with the sea. In a few days,
when we docked for our refit, we found the hole was

much bigger than was ever realised, and I doubt
if I should have risked going to sea had I known.
The Flag-Captain was a very understanding man,
and said, in view of the fact that I had completed my
patrol, there would be no Court of Enquiry into
the accident.

The submarines, towards the end of 1914, came
right into the Channel and started sinking ships.
We went off on many wild-goose chases after them,
as people on shore spread all kinds of imaginary
scares. On one occasion, a whole crowd of us,
destroyers, trawlers, drifters, etc., had chased a
supposed submarine in Whitsand Bay. I happened to be Senior Officer, and was dashing along
at top speed when suddenly the starboard engine
stopped, and the Chief Engineer came on the bridge
to report that if he moved it, possibly the piston-
rod would go through the bottom. I asked him
how many men it would kill, and he told me three.
Thinking this a reasonable sacrifice, if necessary,
to obtain a submarine, I gave him a written order
that in the event of my putting the engine-room
telegraph to full ahead, he was to go full speed
ahead, and I would be responsible for the con-
sequences. It turned out that the submarine was
only a black fish. The Commander-in-Chief took
a lot of time to realise this, and issued a memo.
condemning me for prematurely abandoning the
chase, and what was worse, a favourable opportunity of destroying an enemy. I took strong
exception to this, and requested to be tried by

court-martial, which was refused, and the memo. was put away in a pigeon-hole.

The first ship I actually saw after its being torpedoed was the French steamer *Auguste Conseil*. We found her abandoned in the early hours of the morning. As there appeared to be a chance of saving her, I sent my First Lieutenant, Lieutenant Beswick, R.N.R., on board with a party of men, and in due course we got her in tow. I gave Beswick strict orders to see that there was no " looting." After we had been towing her several hours, she was obviously sinking, and I ordered Beswick to abandon the tow. They just got down into their boat in the nick of time, but not before I had seen them hurl one or two things into it, including, of all things, a ham.

The second torpedoed ship I ran across was also a French ship ; the crew were lying off in boats. I again sent Beswick on board, and he reported that she was capable of proceeding under her own steam, but it was some time before we could persuade the crew to return to her. I again happened to be Senior Officer of the escorting torpedo craft, and placed myself on the starboard bow, whilst on the port quarter was a torpedo-boat commanded by a Warrant Officer. We got the ship safely into harbour, but I was rather annoyed next day when I learnt from the Captain of the torpedo-boat that the ship had a cargo of brandy in casks, and they had been continually falling out of the hole in the ship's side during all the tow ; but he had been too

frightened to signal me.   Had we known, we might
all have set ourselves up for life.

One dark night I was sitting on the bridge as was
my wont whilst the Gunner, Mr. Ide, was on watch.
Suddenly he shouted : " Submarine right ahead."
I jumped up and saw a " wash " crossing my bows.
I at once ordered " hard a-port and full speed
ahead " when, to my horror, I found I was trying
to ram H.M.S. *Duke of Edinburgh*, a big cruiser
making for Plymouth at high speed, of whose
approach I had not been warned.   My hair nearly
stood on end, as we had indeed a narrow squeak.
The following evening I happened to be ashore in
Plymouth and met one of the officers, who told me
that the Captain was very annoyed at my coming
so close, and thought I was running an unwarrant-
able risk—he little knew how scared I had been.
The mistake had occurred through my not having
been given the proper information.   Secrecy was
often overdone.   For instance, I was out on patrol
one day when I got called into the Fort about 3 p.m.
in the afternoon.   The Captain-in-Charge gave me
instructions as to where I was to patrol at night, as
a certain ship was leaving harbour.   I said :

" I suppose it is the *So-and-so* ? " and he said :

" I am afraid I can't tell you, as it is too secret."

Well, even if I had wanted to, I couldn't have communicated to any enemy as I was at sea.   Anyhow,
that night H.M.S. *So-and-so* sailed, and was cheered
out of harbour by crowds of people on the shore
front to give her a send off !   It was the same when

the *Inflexible* and *Invincible* sailed for the Falklands under Admiral Sturdee, as it was the common talk of the town where they were bound for and what time they were sailing, but it was too secret to tell Commanding Officers.

I was extra careful never to tell my wife anything about movements of the ships and never to write anything. The only exception I made was when it so happened that my brother Jim came to Queenstown in H.M.S. *Albion* at the time of the Rebellion, and as he was returning to Plymouth a few days before me, I asked him to tell my wife that she might expect me on Thursday. On my arrival the Commander-in-Chief, Sir George Warrender, invited my wife and myself to lunch, during which, in passing conversation, Admiral Warrender said to my wife :

" You must be glad to see your husband back. I suppose you knew he was coming ? "

To which she replied : " No, my husband never tells me what he is doing."

He said : " But surely he must have told you he was coming to Plymouth ? "

She stuck to her lie, but she turned crimson, which rather gave the show away, and of course as usual the conversation took place during a lull in the talk.

In January 1915 my son David was born at Guildford. I was on patrol at the time, but on our return to the dockyard for refit I at once went up to see him. Before going on leave, I had assembled the Ship's Company and given them a special privilege as regards leave, telling them that in the

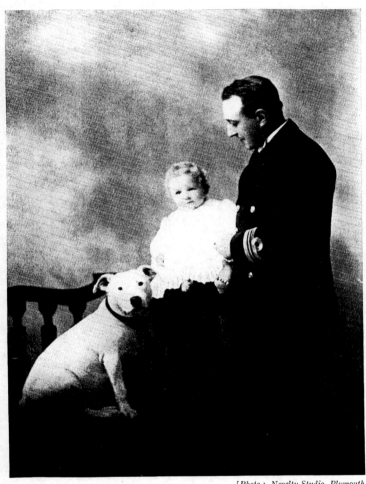

[*Photo : Novelty Studio, Plymouth.*

SELF, DAVID AND NELSON, 1915.

event of a single man abusing the privilege, I would stop the whole Ship's Company leave for a day. Whilst at Guildford a magnificent silver cup arrived for David, engraved, " To the son and heir of our Captain, from the Ship's Company of H.M.S. *Bittern*." It was accompanied by a very charming letter. On return from leave I found unfortunately that one man had abused the privilege given. This placed me in rather an awkward position. I realised I couldn't go back on my word, so I mustered the Ship's Company and, after thanking them as eloquently as I could on behalf of my son for their handsome and generous gift, I then proceeded to stop the whole Ship's Company's leave for a day. I think they were rather tickled.

My command of the *Bittern* came to rather a sudden end.

One afternoon when patrolling, I saw what looked like a suspicious vessel proceeding at high speed up the Channel. As she refused to answer my challenge, I wirelessed into the Commander-in-Chief that I was chasing a suspicious vessel, and I ordered my Chief Engineer to go faster than he had ever done before, with the result that he " bust " up one engine and damaged the other, so I had to go back to harbour at 4 knots on one engine. It meant a complete refit, and we were ordered to pay off.

On paying-off the ship I found the only thing that was missing on this occasion in returning the stores was an oilskin. My coxswain, who served me faithfully for some time, was nearly heartbroken that he should have lost anything, so I forgave him, and entered it in the register as " lost overboard by accident." This was queried, and I was ordered to give further details. I selected a suitable day when we had been chasing submarines, and reported that as there had been a submarine in the vicinity when the oilskin was blown overboard, I did not think it advisable to stop the ship and risk men's lives—no further reply.

It was at this time, in September 1916, that I was selected to fit out and command one of the mystery or " Q " ships. I have already written a book on mystery ships[1] and will not elaborate on them again ; but since writing it I have obtained a very good photograph showing the ship after she had been on fire for several hours when practically the whole of the poop had been burnt out, but the white smoke could still be seen coming forth.

I still meet people who believe the yarn that, dressed up as a woman and carrying a baby which was really a bomb, I threw the " infant " down the conning tower of a submarine and so destroyed it. There is not an atom of truth in this yarn, though, when I come to look at some of my cuttings and see how widely it was reported in the Press, I am not surprised at its survival.

I was sorry when my time came, greatly against my wish, to give up mystery-ship work. My officers and men said they wished to give me a parting present. This I pointed out was against the regulations, so the Officers made a very handsome

[1] *My Mystery Ships.*

H.M.S. "DUNRAVEN" ON FIRE, 1917 (p. 92).

U.S.S. "KIMBERLY" (pp. 140–145).

present to my wife and the Ship's Company one to my daughter. This was but the forerunner of many other similar presentations from other ships.

I did not mention in my book a rather amusing experience of Lieutenant Bonner, R.N.R., who was my First Lieutenant. After the sinking of the *Dunraven* Bonner was awarded a Victoria Cross, but owing to the secrecy he had not officially received it when he was about to go to sea in command of a dangerous-looking " Q " ship called the *Eileen*. I had fears that perhaps the same disaster might overtake him as had overtaken Sanders, who had won the V.C. in H.M.S. *Prize* and never lived to receive it. Bonner had a young wife at Plymouth, and I knew that the chief satisfaction in a person receiving honours was to hand them over to somebody else. I therefore got into communication with the Admiralty, and asked if it would be possible for Bonner to be decorated before he sailed, and Bonner was sent for the following day. The letter I received from him describes what took place, but the yarn he told me verbally contained more than he thought fit to put in a letter.

" Dear Captain Campbell,—

" I have just returned from Sandringham after spending the week-end at York Cottage and being invested with the V.C., and as I know you have been the chief cause of all this happening, I want to thank you right away and feel that perhaps you would like to hear all about it.

" On Friday at 10 p.m. I received a Naval Signal
at my digs in Saltash ordering me to report to the
Fourth Sea Lord at 10 a.m. on Saturday. I had
little time to spare, and thinking an investiture was
being held at Buckingham Palace, and that I would
probably travel back to Devonport on Saturday night,
took only a small despatch bag and sword, and proceeded by the midnight train. I reported myself to
the Fourth Sea Lord at 10 a.m. the following morning, and he told me I was to proceed to Sandringham
by the next train and spend the week-end with the
King. This rather staggered me, and I explained to
him that I could not possibly go, having no clothes
or luggage and no time to get any, but he said that
was quite in order ; I had got to go anyhow, and that
I should find everything O.K., and he finished up by
saying he had really no idea of the procedure, as he
had never been himself. I was given a letter of
introduction to Colonel Wigram, and started off.
At King's Lynn, unfortunately, I upset part of my
tea-basket over an elderly gentleman sitting opposite
me, who was naturally very annoyed, and did not
hesitate to say so. At Wolferton Station I was met
by two huge men in Green Liveries, one of which
seized my despatch bag and sword, and the other was
most anxious to empty the guard's-van to get out my
heavy luggage. I was then asked to step into the
Royal Brougham and was driven to Colonel Wigram's
residence, where I was met by the Colonel and Mrs.
Wigram, and also introduced to the only other guest,
the Dean of Norwich. About 6 p.m. the Dean and

myself were driven to York Cottage, and Captain
Fausset took me along to the King's study, where he
left me with H.M., who was awfully nice.   He gave
me my V.C., asked me a lot about you, and settled
down to tell me some of his own sea experiences until
dinner-time.

" As I left his study, I found the Queen and Princess Mary outside in the Hall, and was presented to
them, and then ushered into a room where the Staff
was waiting.   The first one in the line was the old
gentleman I had upset the tea over in the train.   He
was now in evening dress, smothered in orders and
decorations, and he turned out to be Lord Marcus
Beresford, the Master of Horse.   On seeing me, he
used some expression which sounded like a smothered curse, but told me to stand next to him, as I
needed someone to look after me, and during the rest
of my visit was most charming to me whenever I
met him.

" At dinner I sat next to the King, and my opposite
number, the Dean, next to the Queen.   After the
Queen, Princess Mary, and the ladies had retired, I
was turned over to the Duke of York, and later taken
into the drawing-room to talk to the Queen.

" About eleven our car was reported alongside,
and the Dean and myself were driven back to
Colonel Wigram's house, where we spent about an
hour in his study, and about midnight the Colonel
asked me to ring up the War Office to ask for latest
reports, then the Admiralty, and I must say I had no
idea anyone in the Admiralty could be so polite and

obsequious as the gentleman, whoever he was, who reported to me. I got to bed shortly after midnight, and was called at 7.30 by my servant, who brought me a tray of tea and toast, enquired what time I would like my bath, and what temperature. The only temperature I could think of was 32 degrees Fahr., and that seemed rather cold. The servant returned at bath time with a towel about the size of a turkey carpet over his arm and escorted me to the bathroom. After breakfast I walked about the grounds with the Dean, who flattered me by discussing his forthcoming sermon and asking for suggestions. Later I walked to Church with H.M., and was put in the front pew with Sir Dighton Probyn, V.C., he being the oldest and myself the youngest V.C.s at the moment.

" After Church the King asked me to walk over with him to see Queen Alexandra at Sandringham House. Queen Alexandra was most gracious, and patted me on the back, and I was asked to sign her autograph book. After that I walked back with H.M. to York Cottage, and after lunch said good-bye to them all, and was motored up to King's Lynn after a most enjoyable week-end, everyone from H.M. down doing their utmost to give me a good time, especially Colonel and Mrs. Wigram, and I shall always have most happy recollections of my visit there.

" I hope to see you again soon, and meantime remain,

" Yours very sincerely,

" C. G. BONNER."

In spite of the humorous side of the yarn, I know
Bonner felt that the King, by doing him so much
honour, was expressing his high appreciation of the
wonderful service of the Officers of the R.N.R.
during the Great War.

One of the best " Q " ship actions was with
H.M.S. *Prize*, commanded by the late Lieutenant
Sanders, V.C., when the German Captain and
three others were taken prisoners.   In 1930 the
Captain of the submarine wrote a book of his
experiences of the action, and I thought it extremely
nice of him to send a copy to me inscribed, " To the
famous ' U '-boat killer, Admiral Gordon Campbell,
from a lucky German ' U '-boat Kommandant
(lucky not to meet him). (Signed) Freber von
Spiegel." I sent him one of my books in return,
thanking him, wishing him good luck, and hoping
I would have the pleasure of meeting him one
day.

I had a short time of service at the Admiralty
between two of the " Q " ships I commanded, when
I was attached to a new department called the Anti-
Submarine Department. I used to be sent to
various places to inspect mystery ships which were
either being fitted out or about to be fitted out. I
wasn't at all popular when I came back and reported
that a ship was unsuitable, and got an especial rap
over the knuckles when it was discovered that I took
with me a Lieutenant and Engineer-Lieutenant
R.N.R. My chief asked me why I wanted to take
those damned R.N.R. fellows with me. I pointed

7

out that a naval officer didn't know everything, at least I certainly didn't, and that when inspecting merchant ships as to their suitability for warships, I liked to have the opinion of those who had expert knowledge of merchant ships. For instance, I would go on board a ship and send the Engineer down below to inform me of the state of the engines, the speed, where the donkey boiler was, etc., and in the meantime tell my First Lieutenant (now Captain R. N. Stuart, V.C.) where I would like to put the guns. He would advise me as to whether there was any possible way of concealing them, and without making the ship look conspicuous. I have little doubt that there would have been more successes with " Q " ships but for the conservatism of the Anti-Submarine Department of the Admiralty.

I remember in particular one ship they selected— a small canal steamer with a slanting funnel and baggage ports, neither of which could possibly be disguised—and incidentally the ship, which was supposed to operate out in the Atlantic, only carried two days' supply of coal. I could mention many similar cases.

I eventually came to blows over a ship which had been specially selected at Hartlepool, and which was in my opinion entirely unsuited for the job. To add insult to injury, it was being fitted out alongside a Norwegian steamer which was about to sail for Norway. On my making an adverse report, I was ordered out of the room, for which I was not sorry, and the Second Sea Lord gave me *carte blanche* to go and find a ship for myself, which I proceeded to do in the course of the next twenty-four hours, and having fitted her out, went off and sank a submarine. In my opinion the interference of the Staff at the Admiralty with those at sea in mystery ships was deplorable, and the " intelligence " which they could helpfully have given was too secret to give !

During the fortnight I was at the Admiralty, I was able occasionally to see my parents. My father, although getting on for the eighties, joined up in the Volunteer Training Corps, in which he served throughout the War. On one occasion my brother, E. T. Campbell, who had arrived home from Java on leave, joined the V.T.C. as a private. He had been serving in Java as Vice-Consul, and had been doing good and valuable service, for which he received no pay but the thanks of the Foreign Office. He had volunteered to join the Army, but Lord Kitchener had written him that he was doing more valuable work out there. I had been invited to go down to inspect the V.T.C. at Dulwich, and was received there by my father as Commandant and by my older brother, who was his Orderly. About this time my brother, Private Campbell, gave a big champagne luncheon-party at the Trocadero, consisting of my father as Colonel and another brother and cousin (both Colonels), myself as Captain, my naval brother as Commander, and various other relations of rank.

The family record of the Clan Campbell during

the Great War had not been a bad one. The total casualties in all services were 5,419, and the number of decorations received, 1,195. In my own particular family, apart from my father's service, my eldest brother Ian, although over age, had gone over to France with the Argyll and Sutherlands, and was wounded. He handed over command of his company to Harry Lauder's son, who was killed a few weeks later. My next brother Charlie, who belonged to the Indian Civil Service, became a Colonel in the Recruiting Service ; E. T. served as I have already mentioned ; Jim was Navigator of Ships at the Dardanelles and in the Grand Fleet ; and my youngest brother was unfortunately prevented by health reasons from serving, although he volunteered many times. My two sisters, Emmie and Rosie, were both hospital nurses. My old mother was of course very proud of her family and especially of her sons, whom she never stopped talking about. Her great wish was to have five minutes with the King in order to tell him exactly what she thought about me. Eventually her chance came. After the War, their Majesties invited all the V.C.s to a garden-party at Buckingham Palace, and each V.C. was allowed to take two next of kin. I arranged with my wife that I should take my parents, but my mother said, " No, your wife comes first, you must take her and your father." Well, in due course a special command came for Mother— which pleased her no end, and she told all her friends how she had got a special command of her own, whereas my wife and father were merely on my card as next of kin. Mother could talk of nothing else.

The day at last came, a splendid summer Saturday afternoon. We all mustered in Wellington Barracks, Navy, Army, and Air Force. The V.C.s were fallen in according to their date of award, so that Admirals and bluejackets, Field-Marshals and privates were all mixed together. In the rear came the wounded, driven in Royal carriages. That great sailor, Admiral-of-the-Fleet Sir A. K. Wilson, was the Senior Officer of the Navy, so fell in at the top ; then, led by the Guards Band, we marched out of the Barracks past Whitehall and down the Mall, through dense crowds. Some took off their hats in silence, some cheered, and others, thinking of their lost ones, wept. Personally, I felt ill at ease, and I am sure each V.C. was thinking, as indeed he always must, that for each living V.C. there are thousands who earned it far more, who died, the last man at the gun, or the last man on board. Then there are others who did noble things which were never witnessed, or which had occurred in great battles of such a size that individual gallant actions were looked upon as trivial.

My parents were at the gates as we passed through, accompanied by my wife and little boy David. After entering the Palace we were inspected by His Majesty and the Royal Family, and we marched by the King and Queen, who shook hands with each one of us. After that I witnessed one of the most democratic sights I suppose ever seen in the Royal

Gardens. We were told that their Majesties were taking their tea, and hoped we would do ditto. Of course Tommy Atkins had brought, not only his wife or sweetheart, but also the babies, who couldn't be left at home. There you saw little family picnic parties sitting on the grass thoroughly enjoying their tea—every man-jack of them appreciating the Royal kindness, and behaving as well as, if not better than, a Society garden-party. After tea, their Majesties came and mixed with us all. The Queen had a word for all the women and children, while the King spoke chiefly to the men. An Equerry came and told me that the King wished to see my parents and wife. I thought, now is Mother's chance. On being presented, she curtsied so low that I thought she would fall—then the King said :

" You must be very proud of your son, Mrs. Campbell."

Mother replied : " My sons are always ready to fight for their King and country."

I thought, this is a good beginning, but as the King turned to talk to my father, I noticed Mother for the first time in my life look a bit scared, and suddenly without any warning, and much to the astonishment of those around, she curtsied again and said to the King :

" Well, I won't detain Your Majesty any longer."

I imagine the King must have been a little taken aback at thus being dismissed. Mother had had the ambition she wanted, to shake hands with the King, but the general scene and occasion had been too

much for her to say all she wanted to, especially as
when H.M. the Queen had talked with her, they
had talked as mother to mother about their sons in
H.M.S. *Renown*, as my brother was Navigating
Commander in the *Renown*, when she took H.R.H.
the Prince of Wales round the world. It was a
great day in Mother's life and in mine, too.

VII

Queenstown in the War

On one of my short leaves, after getting torpedoed, I got permission to go over to France with three other naval officers, and we had a visit I shall never forget.

We landed at Boulogne, and saw over one of the great Military Hospitals, after which we went to the Château de Grandcourt, which was our head-quarters, and where distinguished or, in our case, undistinguished visitors were entertained. Amongst the distinguished visitors there the night we arrived was General Smuts, a genial, far-seeing man, and we listened to him telling yarns of the South African War. I particularly remember one remark of his, namely, that in the South African War he fought against England, as he believed he was fighting for his country in the interests of civilisation, and now he was fighting for England because again he thought he was fighting in the interests of civilisation. He left the impression on me that had he been in active command in France, he would have been far more ruthless, and would have employed German prisoners in a far more active manner. We received great hospitality at the Château, and two Staff cars were placed at our disposal, which enabled us to go all down the line from Ypres to Péronne.

On approaching Ypres I happened to be sitting in front with the chauffeur and shelling was going on on either side of the road. I was particularly struck by the fact that the fatigue parties, which were working in the so-called fields, were taking no notice of the shells that were exploding in close proximity to them. I remarked to the chauffeur that things looked fairly warm, and that possibly a shell might hit our car. His reply was :

" That don't matter much, but it is a nuisance if a shell falls in front of the car and makes a hole in the road, as it would take a long time to get the car out of it."

On arrival at Ypres we were taken into the Square and shown the ruins of the famous Cloth Hall. Our guide was a corporal in the Dorsetshire Regiment, and he spent most of his time explaining how superior his regiment was to the Northants Regiment, referring to them as the Dots and Nots. Just before twelve he advised us to take cover, as he said the enemy invariably dropped a shell just where we were standing at that time. We therefore went to the Provost-Marshal's dug-out, and stayed there until a shell exploded just where we had been standing. During our visit I was invited to give a lecture about how I had won the V.C., to which I replied that I was ashamed to wear the ribbon of the V.C. in

France, and I felt that if I had earned it, every man in France had earned it twice over.

We had many discussions comparing the hardships of the fighting between the Army and the Navy. The soldiers very generously seemed to think that those in the North Sea facing winter gales and steaming about amidst mines, etc., had a far harder time than those in France, but I pointed out that sailors' warfare was comparatively comfortable compared with that of the troops in the trenches. I have never altered from this opinion, as in a ship you always have hot water available to enable you to get a hot drink, and you can invariably get a shift of clothes if you get wet to the skin, whereas a Tommy has to go for days without either.

At Arras—it was just after the Second Battle of that town—we left our car in the streets and walked towards the trenches. Just after we had crossed the railway line, a shell exploded immediately behind our backs. It rather disturbed our guide, who had strict injunctions to look after our safety (the reason being, I believe, that if we were killed in France when not on duty, there would be a question as to who would be responsible for our pensions). One of the things that impressed me on approaching the second line of trenches was the sight of the Padre carrying out the burial of the dead, whilst the shells were passing overhead, and an aeroplane battle was taking place in the air. We were not allowed to go into the front-line trenches, and came back by the so-called main road, which was crowded with transport going up on one side and troops coming down on the other.

I happened to be dressed in a rather extraordinary rig, consisting of a tin hat, a naval monkey-jacket, grey flannel trousers, and puttees. Two Tommies turned round and looked me up and down, and just as I passed I heard one say to the other :

"What the 'ell is that —— Tar doing over 'ere ? "

Another example of Tommy's sense of humour came when we got back to our car, and found that the house across the road had been hit by a shell and demolished. On my remarking to the chauffeur that he appeared to have had a pretty close shave, he merely replied :

"That's all right, sir, it's the other side of the road."

We then went south to Péronne, which was the part that appeared to me the most devastated. The inhumanity and stupidity of war faced one in all directions. A road map for guidance was useless. Villages had ceased to exist. Trees had been withered, and even graveyards had been used for trench lines and the vaults as dug-outs. I think if more people had seen some of these sights, they would realise the desirability of trying to avoid future wars ; but in spite of war's disgustingness, I have at the same time a great deal of sympathy for France in the attitude she has taken up since the War, as being strong in her endeavour to prevent her country from ever being invaded again.

Just before leaving France I got a message to say
that General Charteris, the Head of the Intelligence
Department, would like to see me at Montreuil, and
I went to his headquarters.   Much of our conversation I am unable to repeat, but he, like many
others, firmly believed the yarn about the baby and
the bomb (referred to on page 92).

We returned to London, not only lost in admiration for our magnificent troops, but also with a grim
determination to support them in any way that lay
in our power.

After losing my ship the *Dunraven* I was kept unemployed for a month or so, and was never so miser-
able in my life.   I spent the time at home in Saltash,
Cornwall, turning the lawn into a potato patch.   In
the autumn of 1917 I was approached as to taking
command of a light cruiser in the Grand Fleet, or,
alternatively, going to the Mediterranean as a sort of
adviser on mystery ships, but the Commander-in-
Chief, Admiral Sir Lewis Bayly, under whom I had
served for two years, asked me to come as his Flag-
Captain at Queenstown in the light cruiser *Active*, an
offer I could not refuse.   Although I realised that
the chances of a scrap weren't very great, yet I
wanted to serve under the man I admired more than
any other, and I had already learnt how valuable and
important the work at Queenstown was.   I had to
proceed to Dover to take over command of the
Active.   She belonged to the Dover Patrol, and I
remained in her at that port for about a week, the

condition of the moon requiring the Admiral to have his Patrol at full strength in the event of an attack on the shipping in the Downs or elsewhere in his command.

I then took the *Active* to Queenstown, and hoisted Admiral Bayly's flag.   Soon after my arrival, the wits of the harbour produced certain " poems," two of which—with due blushes—I am tempted to quote :

> " There's a certain ' active ' Captain
>   In the Navy whom we know,
> Whose quest for hidden dangers
>   (Which he scents out down below)
> Must seem, almost, to strangers
>   On the verge of the insane ;
> For no sooner he's in harbour
>   With fresh letters to his name,
> Than he's wishing like the dickens
>   To be out at sea again.
> Death seems to dodge the footsteps of
>   Some fearless men who court her,
> For this man takes to peril like
>   A spaniel does to water."

" 10 little ' U ' boats setting out in line,
    1 bent her hydroplanes, then there were 9.

" 9 little ' U ' boats sang ' The Hymn of Hate,'
    1 sang too loudly and then there were 8.

" 8 little ' U ' boats thought they'd get to Heaven,
    1 found he'd missed it, then there were 7.

" 7 little ' U ' boats, full of nasty tricks,
    1 met an airship, then there were 6.

" 6 little ' U ' boats did a record dive,
    1 burst his ' innards,' then there were 5.

" 5 little ' U ' boats tried to make a score,
1 attacked a convoy, then there were 4.

" 4 little ' U ' boats, busy as could be,
1 sighted Campbell, then there were 3.

" 3 little ' U ' boats, feeling rather blue,
1 ran himself ashore, then there were 2.

" 2 little ' U ' boats' cruise was nearly done,
1 found a minefield, and that left 1.

" 1 little ' U ' boat staggered back to port,
Said that strafing England was not so easy as he thought."

Despite these poetic prophesies my job at Queenstown did not prove a very exciting one, and I had to spend far more time in harbour than I cared about ; but a cruiser always had to be at hand to take the Commander-in-Chief to sea, in the event of a further rebellion in Ireland, and also to try and intercept any German raiders or gun-runners that might come down the Irish coast.

Queenstown was both a naval and military port, and one of great importance, as the Commander-in-Chief had to arrange for the safety of the large mass of shipping approaching the English Channel, Irish Sea, and North Coast of Ireland, though he had a Rear-Admiral at Lough Swilly to assist him in the latter part of the work.

Queenstown was the first base used by the Americans when they came into the War. A flotilla of destroyers came over with a depot ship, U.S.S. *Melville*, under the command of Captain J. R. Pringle, U.S.N. He became in effect Senior Officer of the American forces at Queenstown, but all forces were under Admiral Bayly.   We worked absolutely as one force.   If I happened to be at sea with an American officer senior to me, I would be under his orders or vice versa.

Admiral Sims, U.S.N., who was in command of all the American Naval Forces in European waters, was a frequent visitor to Queenstown.   He was a delightfully charming man, very tall, and with a very commanding presence.   I often heard him referred to in the States as the most " British " Admiral in the American Navy.   He certainly had his whole heart in winning the War, and quickly brushed aside any difficulties that might arise—and there were a few, as although the officers of the two Navies got on splendidly, the same cannot be said of the men, I think, chiefly because the American sailors had more money.   However, there was very little actual friction ashore, and each Navy used to frequent its own set of " pubs," which reduced the chances of drunken brawls.

The *Active* used to lie half-way between the *Melville* and the naval pier, so that I was in daily contact with Captain Pringle, who would call on his way to and from Admiralty House, ostensibly to discuss " affairs of State," but somehow his visits generally coincided with cocktail times, the American ships being dry.

During my time at Queenstown we used to get frequent visits from distinguished visitors such as Lord Jellicoe, Admiral Wemyss, the late Dean of Manchester, Mr. G. Paine (the American writer), and Mr. Pollen. They came over ostensibly to visit the American ships stationed there, but I am not at all sure that white bread, grape-fruit, and unrationed butter and sugar were not part of the attraction. I was often invited to stay at Admiralty House to help entertain the guests, though Admiral Bayly and his niece, Miss Voysey, were hosts in themselves. Admiral Bayly had a dry house, following the example of H.M. the King, but I am afraid we were not all quite so conscientious, and when staying at Admiralty House, I generally made an excuse to go down before dinner and have one at the Club. When I got back Admiral Bayly invariably said to me : " What has it been to-night—gin or sherry ? " The Club was generally full of officers of both Navies, and it was noticeable how far more incautious the Americans were than ourselves, in talking about matters of a secret nature. As Ireland was a country which harboured many German sympathisers, this was particularly deplorable, and one felt bound to attempt to check it.

One of the visits of Admiral Sims coincided with the time when I had just been fitted with a new type of paravane, which was towed over the stern for catching submarines. The expert who came over to advise me in the technical part of it was a Lieutenant R.N.V.R., who by profession was a parson ; he didn't disclose this to me till he had heard all my after-luncheon stories ! He used to keep a surplice in his kit, ready to read the burial service if anybody was killed whilst on trials.

When I had completed the fitting of these paravanes, I went to sea for trials. Admiral Sims and
Admiral Bayly came on board to witness them. As
it was necessary for the ship to be either stopped or
only moving at a slow speed whilst the paravanes
were being hauled in, I ordered everybody on board
to put their lifebelts on, as there was a danger of the
ship being torpedoed while we were so stopped.
Admiral Bayly absolutely refused to put a lifebelt
on, and of course Admiral Sims followed suit.   I
felt a great responsibility in having on board these
two great Admirals who would not take reasonable
precautions. I therefore sent for the Sergeant-
Major and my biggest Petty Officer and, unknown
to these distinguished Admirals, had the two men
standing below the bridge all the time we were at
sea, with orders from me that, in the event of the
ship being torpedoed, they were to seize the two
Admirals and put lifebelts on them by force.
Luckily we got through the trials without any unfortunate incident.   Now that I had these paravanes,
I looked forward to more time at sea, and was very
disappointed when the Commander-in-Chief told
me he couldn't let a light cruiser go dashing about
on its own, as the risk of being torpedoed was too
great. I felt inclined to ask to be relieved and go to
a more active part of the War area. The Commander-in-Chief obviously knew what was in my
mind and sent me to sea the next day to embark
some guns at Pembroke, then to Berehaven, and so
on.   In fact, he kept me on the run till eventually I

had to ask permission to return to harbour to clean the boilers. When I went up to see him, his only remark was : " *You* asked to return to harbour, I didn't call you back "—very subtle.

Admiral Bayly used occasionally to come to sea in the *Active* himself, and I always had to be ready for him at very short notice. One night he signalled down to me about 11 p.m. saying he was coming on board at midnight to go round to Berehaven. It so happened there was an ebb-tide running, and very little room for me to turn the ship. On one side of the harbour was a line of trawler moorings, which unfortunately on this night were all unoccupied. I therefore had great difficulty in seeing the moorings, and on completion of my turn, thinking I was clear, I went ahead down harbour, but unfortunately found myself on top of this long line of moorings. I stopped the engines and drifted down with the tide right through them, making a signal to the Captain of the dockyard in case I had damaged any of them. I clean forgot that the Admiral, who had already turned in, would feel the bumping of the buoys under the ship. On arrival at Berehaven the following morning, Captain Nasmith (now Rear-Admiral, V.C., C.B.) came on board to breakfast. Admiral Bayly casually asked me whether I had had any difficulty in getting out of harbour the previous night.

I said : " No, none at all, sir."

He turned round to Captain Nasmith and said, " You know, Nasmith, the trawler moorings at

Queenstown are rather annoying when they are un-occupied."

The Admiral took Nasmith and me for a walk, and said : " Look here, you are the two youngest Captains in the Navy, and I am an old man. Tell me, how am I going to deal with the submarines ? " And Nasmith and I aired our suggestions, whilst the old man said nothing. When we had finished, he tore nearly all our schemes to pieces. I always remember this incident, because it has taught me that, although young ideas may be worth listening to, and may be made use of, it generally needs a level-headed man of experience to hold the balance.

Having had our walk we left Berehaven, and I took the Admiral up to Galway, where the Sinn Feiners had given a certain amount of trouble. I went ashore with the Admiral in uniform, and we went for a walk through the low parts of Galway for obvious reasons. Having done that, we returned to Queenstown. We were due to arrive at Queenstown about midnight, and the Admiral had given me orders that he did not want to be called until 7 a.m. I had informed Queenstown by wireless of my arrival, asking them to keep the patrol drifters clear of the approach, and proceeded towards the entrance of the harbour at 25 knots. Suddenly, to my surprise, I saw a drifter dead ahead of me. I put the helm hard over and went full speed astern on one engine. I thought I was bound to sink her. She grazed right down our side, but in response to my signal, she informed me she was undamaged.

As I saw the Admiral over the side the following morning, he told me he had been awakened by the ship going astern, so I told him what had happened ; he asked me if any damage had been done, and I said, " No."

As he got clear of the ship, he shouted out to me and said : " If no damage has been done to the drifter, you might as well remove that large chunk of her side which is jammed in your boat's davits."

On enquiry it turned out that I had ripped the best part of her side out, but as she was in no danger of sinking, and the Captain knew he was in the wrong, he intended to try and bluff it through, and get the repairs done privately in the dockyard. Unfortunately, the piece he had left in my davits let the cat out of the bag.

When the late *Vaterland* made her first trip across the Atlantic under the name of *Leviathan*, with about 10,000 American troops on board, four American destroyers were sent out into the Atlantic to meet her, and Admiral Bayly decided to go to sea in the *Active* to meet her at eight o'clock the following morning. We were at the rendezvous at the appointed time, but there were no signs of the *Leviathan*. On communicating with the destroyers, I discovered they had lost her during the night, owing to the *Leviathan* having altered course without signal. The Admiral came on deck in not too good a mood, and accused me of not being at the proper rendezvous. We spent an anxious forenoon trying to find out where the *Leviathan* was, and it was not until late on in the day that we discovered that she was well up the Irish Channel, and there was no chance of overtaking her.   I was therefore ordered to return to harbour.   The sea being very calm, I decided to save time by not zigzagging and to get the Admiral back in time for dinner at his house. As an extra precaution, I placed a Lieutenant at each end of the bridge to look out for periscopes, as I felt certain I could see one if there was one about. The Admiral came on the bridge and asked me why I wasn't zigzagging, so I told him that with the calm sea and extra look-out, I could make sure of seeing a periscope.   He left the bridge without a word. About three days later we received a report from a British submarine, who, unknown to me, was in the vicinity, that she had passed the *Active*, flying the Commander-in-Chief's flag, about 300 yards distant, and had been in a favourable position to torpedo us had she wished to do so.   Admiral Bayly, in forwarding the report to me, merely remarked on it : " We live and learn."

During our time at Queenstown an epidemic of influenza broke out.   I was the first to get it on a day on which we had been ordered to proceed to Berehaven for torpedo practice.   Although I had a high temperature I refused to go on the sick list ; the First Lieutenant went up to inform the Commander-in-Chief, who came on board and gave me a direct order that I was to go to hospital.   I, of course, had to obey, but particularly requested that the ship be allowed to proceed to sea with the First

Lieutenant Colville, in whom I had every confidence, in command.   I was such a thorough nuisance to everybody in the hospital that after four days they discharged me, and I went by car to Berehaven to rejoin the ship.   The ship picked me up at Glengariff, and on arrival on board I found over half the ship's company down with influenza, but Colville still carrying on the exercises.   I suggested it was asking a bit too much, but he replied it was the first time he had had command of a ship, and he was not going to miss his opportunity, for which I did not blame him ; but as soon as I took over command, I anchored the ship until the crew recovered.

One day, when lying at Queenstown, a message was received from the Admiralty ordering the Commander-in-Chief to send a representative to attend a conference at the Admiralty, presided over by Captain W. W. Fisher.   Admiral Bayly ordered me to go at once.   I only had an hour or so in which to catch the train, and told my Secretary to send a telegram to Holyhead reserving a sleeper for me.   This he sent " O.H.M.S. "   I went to London to attend the conference, with which I was not impressed, and returned to Queenstown.   As nothing practicable came out of the conference, as far as we were concerned, I forgot the whole show. A few weeks later I received a letter from the Admiralty saying that telegrams reserving sleepers were not allowed to be sent " O.H.M.S.," and ordering me to send forthwith 1s. 3d. in stamps in payment for the said telegram.   I replied regretting my breach of the regulations—in fact, I had not read them. I enclosed 1*s*. 3*d*. worth of stamps, and requested their lordships to be good enough to furnish me with a receipt for same, which in due course I received from the Secretary of the Admiralty. Thus was the War won !—when we were spending about nine million pounds a day.

A reorganisation of Flotillas took place in the early part of 1918, and Captain, now Rear-Admiral, E. R. G. R. Evans, famous for his Antarctic exploits and as Captain of the *Broke*, was ordered to relieve me in the *Active*, and to be employed on convoy work. He came to Queenstown for the purpose, but Admiral Bayly, with his usual thoughtfulness, arranged for the transfer to take place at Plymouth, as my home was there. Although Evans was senior to me, he waived his seniority, and I took him to Plymouth as a passenger, and there turned over the command to him. After a couple of days' leave, I proceeded to Grimsby to take over the command of the light cruiser *Patrol* from Captain, now Rear-Admiral, R. A. Hornell, D.S.O.

Although I had not seen any fighting at Queenstown, a lot of useful work had been done, and we were a very happy base under a man whom the whole command trusted. He ruled us with a rod of iron, absolute justice, but with a human touch. Everybody knew exactly where they were. A destroyer returning from patrol would be able to let fires die out and have a complete rest ; if it was necessary for her to be shifted from a buoy to the dock, a tug

had to do it.   Admiralty House was an open house
for all Commanding Officers, and not only that, but
a portion of the garden, which happened to be
walled in, was turned over for officers and their
wives, to use for tea-parties and so on without
being disturbed.

VIII

Holyhead in the War

AFTER completing the transfer at Grimsby, we sailed for Holyhead, which was to be our new base. As we were coming down channel, we got a sudden wireless message from the Admiralty to anchor in St. Helens Road for the night, I presume so as not to cross the transport service from Southampton. We had no war chart of the approaches to Portsmouth, nor did we know any of the local war arrangements, and we had great difficulty in finding our way in. When we did eventually get in, we found the anchorage crowded with ships, and narrowly averted collision with one without any lights before coming to our anchorage, where we remained for only a few hours before proceeding on our journey. I was wishing I had remained at sea all night, as it had been rather a nightmare.

On arrival at Holyhead, we moored to a buoy close under the breakwater, and near to Soldier's Point. The situation at Holyhead was rather a curious one. The Irish Sea came under the orders of Commander-in-Chief Queenstown, and I was his representative at Holyhead, and in direct charge of the vessels employed. Yet the Senior Naval Officer at Holyhead and the base, coaling station, etc., were not under Admiral Bayly's orders. In spite of various protests from Admiral Bayly, no change was made, the yarn being that the L.N.E.R. objected. The arrangement did not lend itself to efficiency. As far as I was concerned, I held the dual capacity of Flag-Captain to Admiral Bayly and also Captain D. It led to many curious situations, as I frequently had to write letters to myself. Perhaps as Flag-Captain I would order a Court of Enquiry over which I might myself preside as Captain D., and then in forwarding the findings to the Commander-in-Chief, would add my remarks as Flag-Captain. I was faced with a similar situation, which I will relate later, in South Africa. I remember one of my uncles telling me of a similar experience in India, where he had to forward a confidential report on himself.

When I first took over the command of the Irish Sea, I did not like the way the base at Holyhead was run, as I had great difficulty in getting cypher and coded messages dealt with expeditiously ; and since my orders were to " clear up " the Irish Sea and reduce the sinkings of merchant ships which were taking place, I had my work cut out.

Admiral Bayly paid an early visit to Holyhead, and a change in Senior Naval Officer took place. The new one, who was full of beans, told me he had never seen such a place in his life, and asked me where I suggested he should start his " shake up." I recommended his looking into the Coding

Office, where the Women's Royal Naval Service
worked, about 9 p.m.   He replied that if he had his
way he wouldn't have a woman within a hundred
miles of any naval base.   Stringent orders were
forthwith issued concerning Women's Royal Naval
Service and offices, etc.   I thought we were at last
going to get a move on, but alas, in a few months
the new Senior Naval Officer succumbed and married
one of the W.R.N.S. on his Staff.   He had to go,
and we got yet a third Senior Naval Officer who was
junior to me.   When the King's Messenger came
through with secret mails, instead of giving the
password, he would say : " Is this the base where
the S.N.O. married a W.R.N.S. ? "

I had under my direct orders a Flotilla of old
destroyers, a yacht, a drifter, about twenty motor-
launches, four airships, and a squadron of aeroplanes.   In addition to these, all destroyers, patrol
boats, etc., passing through the Irish Sea, which
normally came under the orders of Queenstown or
Milford Haven, automatically came under my orders
whilst in the Irish Sea, provided they were not
actually escorting a convoy.   For instance, perhaps
four American destroyers would be coming up to
Liverpool with a convoy, and as soon as they had
fulfilled their convoy duties, I would give them
routes by which to return.   It was an extraordinarily interesting job.

The *Patrol* herself was chiefly in harbour, as I had
direct telephones to the base and Admiralty, and
could receive messages and information which were

too secret to pass by wireless. I always had steam ready for short notice, and each morning at daybreak I had steam for full speed ready, as the upper works of the *Patrol* showed over the breakwater, and I always visualised a submarine coming up one morning and shelling us, without our being able to reply effectively, unless I was in a position to slip my moorings and get to sea. The submarines invariably entered the Irish Sea by the North Channel, and after a careful study of their movements from the time they left Germany onwards, I was generally able to tell within an hour what time they would enter, as they usually came in with the tide, and so by stopping or greatly reducing speed, could not be heard by our hydrophones. Their average speed after entering was easily worked out, and I also found by observation that they generally worked down the lee side of the Irish Sea (i.e. if an easterly gale was blowing, they would come down the Welsh coast), but I had to be ready for all emergencies. The submarines generally proceeded to the south of the Isle of Man, off Liverpool or off Dublin, so I had a destroyer waiting in each place.

One morning I knew a submarine had entered the Irish Sea, and she appeared off Dublin about 7 a.m. to attack a merchant ship ; the destroyer went after her, preventing the attack, and dropped two depth charges. The day went by and I received no further news of this submarine (I was expecting all day to get an S.O.S. from some ship or some report which would give me a clue in what direction she was

working, but as I received none, I could only assume
that she had either gone out of the Irish Sea or was
still round about the same place), so the following
morning I had two destroyers lying off Dublin.
The submarine appeared again at the same place at
the same time, and both destroyers dropped about
eight depth charges. It may be wondered why the
destroyers didn't get it—but if a submarine is
sighted, say three miles away, it takes a little time
for the destroyer to get there, and by that time the
submarine may have gone a quarter of a mile under
water in any direction. Again the day went by
without further news, and the third morning I had
three destroyers off Dublin—two British and one
American. The submarine appeared in exactly the
same place at exactly the same time, and the destroyers dropped about twenty depth charges. I had
by this time got rather annoyed with this fellow, and
took it as a personal insult. I slipped my moorings,
steamed across the Irish Sea, and circling over the
place where she had last been seen, I dropped sixty
depth charges, which I always carried on my quarter
deck. The submarine left the Irish Sea that night,
and returned to the Fatherland without having
attacked any ship.

Since the War, I happened to meet a fellow who
had returned from Hamburg : he told me this story
from the Submarine Commander's point of view—
how, whenever he put his periscope up in the Irish
Sea, he was received by depth charges, and how, one
morning while they were having breakfast, sixty

depth charges were dropped all round them. This was too much for the crew's nerves, and they wanted to go home.

This is a very good example of the effect of depth charges on the *moral* of a submarine crew. It is very difficult to score a direct hit, but one can picture the crew sitting inside a submarine hearing these explosions going on all round, and not knowing exactly how far off they were, and also wondering whether the next one would be a hit or not.

Although we didn't actually destroy any submarines during the five months I had control, yet we kept them under, thanks to the brilliant work of all the flotillas which were continually patrolling. (I had no great faith in hydrophones.) Only two ships under my protection were lost, the *Leinster*, and a small ship during the night. I was able by wireless to shift all craft about from place to place, so that whenever a submarine made an appearance, it could be pretty sure of an attack by depth charges. The airships and aeroplanes carried out their aerial patrols, the former extending all over the Irish Sea and the latter nearer the coast. I had a special wireless set for communicating with these craft, and had to relay their intelligence to the surface craft.

About the middle of June, some twenty United States chasers were sent to work under me at Holyhead. They were manned chiefly by what we would call Volunteer Reserves, being young men who had volunteered from the American Universities, etc. The Senior Officer was Mr. J. Robins. I had on my Staff a Lieutenant-Commander of the United States Navy—Walsh by name—who used to look after the discipline of these craft. I was much amused one time when it was reported to me that the Captain of one of these chasers had been untactful, so I sent for the Lieutenant-Commander and asked him to deal with the case, and happened to mention that I assumed it would necessitate asking Admiral Sims for a court-martial. In a few days' time I asked him if there had been any developments. He told me he had fixed the whole thing up all right by making the First Lieutenant of the boat the Captain and the Captain the First Lieutenant.

The young officers and crews in these chasers deserve all the praise they can be given, as they were enthusiastic to the backbone, and ready for any job.

I sometimes had as many as fifty or sixty patrol vessels of all sorts working under me at one time. I generally made a point of going to sea in one or other of each class of craft, including the airships and aircraft, so as to get a first-hand knowledge of the strain I was putting on the personnel, as I used to keep them pretty hard at it. As an example of this, the twenty motor-launches under Lieutenant-Commander Colin Campbell, R.N.V.R. (no relation, but a charming and enthusiastic fellow), spent three thousand seven hundred and ninety-three hours at sea, during which they steamed fifteen thousand nine hundred and fourteen miles. This was in the month of October, when the weather was bad, and Admiral Bayly referred to this excellent performance as being almost incredible. In the better month of August, they steamed twenty-four thousand nine hundred and fourteen miles. Two things must be remembered when considering these figures : the first is, that when at sea they were sometimes stopped for several hours at a stretch, hydrophoning, though I didn't encourage too much of this; and secondly, I have left out the times the boats were laid up for repairs or normal rest. In other words, one could let the figures look even more imposing than they are.

Of the destroyers permanently attached to my command, the total mileage steamed by eleven of them was over eighteen thousand miles in a month. Except for the two Senior Officers, Lieutenant-Commander Kennedy in the *Kestrel* and Lieutenant A. Grant,[1] D.S.C., in the *Griffon*, they were all manned by officers of the Royal Naval Reserve, and most of the men were R.N.R. or R.N.V.R., or "joined for hostilities only."

One hears so much about the Navy that I am glad to have this opportunity of giving some small idea of the splendid work done by the Royal Naval Reserve and Royal Naval Volunteer Reserve. When inspecting the ship's company of one destroyer, I noticed a particularly youthful lad who told me he

[1] Grant had risen from the lower deck, and had been especially promoted to Lieutenant for his gallantry in action in H.M.S. *Lion* at the Battle of Jutland.

was nineteen. I happened to meet him a year or two ago, and he told me the whole truth. He had joined the Army at sixteen, but was bowled out, and discharged, so he joined the Navy at seventeen, and gave his age as nineteen. Such is the spirit of the British youth.

As regards the aircraft, the airships, or blimps as they were more commonly known, were under the command of Major Elmhurst, who had been a Sub-Lieutenant, R.N., in the early days of the War. They were greatly hampered by weather conditions, but did yeoman work, and flew, between April 1918 and the Armistice, over three thousand one hundred hours. The aeroplanes, which were of an old type, and were not required in France, were under Major Probyn. At first they had no bombs, but the moral effect of flying and swooping down on periscopes was great, and of course the Germans didn't imagine we were so stupid as to employ aircraft with no bombs on board. We had one or two crashes with the aeroplanes, but no lives were lost, and the patrol craft were generally quickly on the spot to rescue and if possible salve them. Taking the aircraft as a whole, they attacked and damaged two submarines, bombed three periscopes and eighteen oil patches. In the month of April, ten ships were sunk in the Irish Sea, and in the month of October, when more submarines were operating, only two—both on occasions when the weather was unsuitable for aircraft.

Although I had no direct control of the convoys in

9

the Irish Sea, yet I was kept well informed of their movements, and was expected to clear the path of submarines before their approach. At night-time I also had to see that the dangers of collision between the cross-Channel steamers and the convoys were reduced to a minimum.

A rather exceptional incident took place on one occasion when a convoy was coming into the North Channel. A ship of the convoy somehow or another got lost and was torpedoed and sunk off Dublin. Apparently without being observed, she had broken away from a convoy which was bound for Liverpool. Some of the crew fetched up on the Welsh coast, and this was the first intimation I had either that the ship was one of the convoy or that she had been torpedoed. After making arrangements for the survivors, I informed the Admiralty. A few days later the Admiralty sent a letter which inferred that I was to blame for her being torpedoed. I was very indignant, as I had nothing to do with it directly or indirectly, and therefore wrote requesting either that a Court of Enquiry might be held, or, if it was inferred that I was in any way to blame, that I might be tried by a court-martial. However, neither took place, and I have never heard to this day how the ship came to be lost from the convoy. I have already referred to the work done by the Flotillas, and although I was always ready to serve out blame and admonishment where or when it was necessary, this particular case could not be attributed to any neglect on their part.

One evening at Holyhead about 9 p.m. I received a signal from the *Olympic*, which was going up the Irish Sea full of troops, saying " S.O.S. Torpedoed." I at once ordered every ship in harbour to proceed to sea to her assistance, and made a signal to the *Olympic* informing her of what I was doing, and asking for her exact position. I waited many anxious minutes before I received a reply, in the meantime imagining that she had probably sunk, but was relieved to get the answer : " Have not been torpedoed." It appeared that one of the escorting destroyers had seen something in the dark and dropped a depth charge for luck. The wireless operator of the *Olympic* had felt the ship shake, and, thinking she had been torpedoed, had sent out an S.O.S. without informing the Captain, who knew nothing about it until he got my signal. The Captain was that very distinguished sailor, Sir Bertram Hayes, K.C.M.G., Commodore of the White Star Line. On one of his voyages he rammed and sunk a submarine, which was, if not the only, one of the very few cases of the kind during the War. I have seen a good deal of Sir Bertram since the War, and although getting on in years, he devotes all his energies to the interests of the Merchant Navy. He looks what he is, a real sailor of the Bulldog breed.

The mail steamers between Kingstown and Holyhead used to cross at about 23 knots, unescorted, both day and night, but for some reason the Dublin Mail Steam Packet Company suddenly got the wind up about the danger of crossing at night-time for fear of collision with convoys. I pointed out that I would always be able to warn mail steamers of a convoy being likely to pass through their route during the night, and I further mentioned that they had been going on for four years without any accident. In spite of my strong protest against the stopping of night sailing, it was agreed that they should be stopped, with the result that all sailings took place in the daytime. This meant that there were four ships from Dublin each morning at about the same time, so that a submarine could have four shies for a penny. I was not a bit surprised when a week later I received an S.O.S. about nine o'clock in the morning to say the *Leinster*, which had over 1,000 passengers on board, a large number being soldiers on leave, had been torpedoed. Every available ship was sent to her assistance, but unfortunately the S.O.S. had been sent by a ship who had witnessed the torpedoing and not by the *Leinster* herself, and the position given was therefore several miles wrong. This reduced the number of lives which we were able to save ; in fact, only about two hundred people escaped.

Admiral Bayly had given strict orders that all messages were to be placed on his table and not brought to him personally. On this particular morning he was just leaving his house for a two hours' walk round the dockyard. The officer on duty, realising that the loss of the *Leinster* would be a national disaster, thought it a case for breaking rules, and rushed up to the Admiral with the signal. The Admiral told him to put it on his desk and went on his way to spend the forenoon in the dockyard. On his return, he sent for the duty officer and told him that in future he was to obey his orders; that he had placed Campbell in charge of the Irish Sea, and that if he didn't trust him to deal with all emergencies, he wouldn't have put him there. No wonder we all liked serving under a man like Admiral Bayly.

A few days later I received a wireless message to say that the *Ulster*, which was due to leave Dublin at three o'clock in the afternoon, had refused to sail without an escort. The Commodore of Kingstown sent one of my destroyers to escort her. On the *Ulster's* arrival at Holyhead in the evening, I telephoned to find out whether they would sail at seven o'clock the following morning, and received a reply that they would refuse to sail unless given an escort. I pointed out that escorts were a matter of policy, and no one ship could demand an escort. In the meantime I mustered my crew and called for sixty volunteers to sail the *Ulster* if required, and needless to say, practically the whole crew volunteered (sailors as a rule love doing somebody else's job for a change). I informed the remainder that we would go to sea ourselves short-handed, so as not to give the *Ulster* a chance of saying they had demobilised a cruiser. I then informed the *Ulster* that, if they refused to sail, I would place a naval crew on board. Shortly after this, I received a further notice to say that if I placed a naval crew on board, the officers

would refuse to sail.   My reply was that in that case
I would place naval officers on board.   I did not keep
the Admiralty informed of my action, as I knew they
were too near the House of Commons.   During the
night I received a message from Dublin asking me on
whose authority I was acting.   I replied : " On my
own."   About 2 a.m. I was informed from Dublin
that if I placed a new crew on board there would be a
general strike of all transport in Dublin.   I informed
them that this did not interest me, and I was merely
responsible for seeing that the King's mail left in
the *Ulster* at 7 a.m.   At 6 a.m. I proceeded to the
wharf with my Chief Engineer and a party of sixty
men.   I went on board the *Ulster* and asked Captain
Newton, a most charming man, what the situation
was.   He told me that the crew still refused to sail,
and asked me if I would go and talk to them.   This
I declined to do, and pointed out to him that he was
Captain of the ship.   He asked me if I would give
him a written order to sail without escort, which I
promptly did, as I had one in my pocket ready for
such an emergency, and the crew then decided to
sail.   I suggested to the Captain that he should sail
very promptly, as my own crew were simply itching
to have the novel experience of sailing a mail steamer.
The *Ulster* sailed at 6.55 a.m. without an escort.

I made a point of crossing in the *Ulster* a few days
later in the hope of giving confidence, and I was
received with great kindness on all sides—I might
almost have been the Governor-General ; in fact,
whenever I crossed from Queenstown to Dublin after

that I received special attention—even the so-called
Sinn Feiners who formed the crew used to touch
their hats to me in the street. I had kept the Commander-in-Chief, Queenstown, informed throughout
of what I was doing, but except for saying that I
personally was not to take command of the *Ulster*,
he didn't interfere. In due course the whole proceedings were reported to the Admiralty, and they
told me that I was a good boy, or words to that effect ;
but what I appreciated most was a telegram from
Admiral Bayly, which read as follows :

" I congratulate you on the ability, tact, and
patience with which you have dealt with a very
difficult situation. I interfered as little as possible,
feeling that I could trust you who were on the spot.
Thank you."

He was following his usual custom of trusting the
man on the spot, a thing that Higher Authority
frequently finds it so difficult to do.

In due course the Admiralty, to allay fear, arranged
a sort of half-hearted escort for the mail steamers,
but in spite of that we narrowly escaped another
disaster, as one of the mail steamers which was being
escorted by an airship, an aeroplane, and a destroyer
was hit by a torpedo, which luckily didn't explode.
What did as much good as the escorts, was a message
from Admiral Bayly to all the captains, officers, and
crews of the cross-Channel steamers, expressing his
great admiration of the pluck, seamanship, and
ability they had shown for nearly four years of war,
and pointing out that this great feat of keeping the

cross-Channel traffic going was entirely due to the devotion to duty of the officers and crews of the ships.

The sinking of the *Leinster*, together with the submarine activity, necessitated my working the flotillas absolutely to the utmost of their strength, and on October 20th, 1918, I issued the following memo. to the flotillas :

Memorandum.

H.M.S. " PATROL,"
October 20th, 1918.

" The Commander-in-Chief has expressed his appreciation of the way the Irish Sea Flotilla has met the situation during the past ten days.

" The loss of the *Leinster* (giving rise to a certain amount of uneasiness among cross-Channel traffic), an unusually large number of submarines using the Irish Sea, bad weather, full moon, and a lot of defects, necessitated an extra call on the resources of the Flotilla.

" I have had no hesitation when necessary in keeping the boats out when they were due to ' stand off.' I knew they would answer the call cheerfully.

" Our Armies are advancing towards Germany, and need all the reinforcements and supplies they can get. It is up to us to do what we can to back them up by keeping the enemy under, and allowing as many ships as possible to arrive in safety.

" You have all done well, and more difficult situations may yet arise, and we must be ready to meet them.

" (*Signed*) GORDON CAMPBELL,
" *Flag-Captain.*"

The loss of the *Leinster* was undoubtedly a national disaster. I fully anticipated that either a Court of Enquiry would be held, or that somebody would be court-martialled, but it was not so. I cannot help coming to the conclusion that when big disasters take place, such as the loss of the *Formidable* on December 31st, 1914, with over 500 lives, the loss of the *Leinster* with nearly 1,000 lives, or even more recently the " unrest " at Invergordon, and no Court of Enquiry or court-martial takes place, then it is reasonable to assume that the blame must rest either with the Board of Admiralty or some higher authority, who imagine themselves immune from trial. The theory of such immunity is very mistaken, as sooner or later the mass of people in the country will not tolerate it.

IX

Holyhead in the War *(continued)*

It may be remembered that the Press at one
time labelled me " The Mystery V.C." This
really had nothing to do with the fact that at
the time I was serving in mystery ships : it was
entirely due to the Admiralty's desire for special
secrecy, and to the fact that my name therefore
appeared in the Court Circular as having received
the decoration at the hands of H.M. the King, before
any announcement had been made in the *London
Gazette*. On the night of the award, a reporter got
hold of my parents' address, and came down to
Norwood to interview me. When I declined to be
interviewed, he tackled various members of my
family, but luckily only learnt that they knew no
more about it than he did himself. I telephoned to
a sub-editor of the paper concerned, and, on grounds
of official secrecy, extracted a promise that nothing
should appear in the Press ; nevertheless, there were
the headlines the next morning about a " Mystery
V.C."

This " mystery," thus started as a newspaper
stunt, attracted the attention of the Germans also ;
they connected it with another episode altogether,

and I understand put a price on my head. From that moment I repeatedly received information from various sources that they intended to " get me."

One day at Holyhead my First Lieutenant told me that it was rumoured in the town that an attempt was to be made on my life : it also appeared that the ship's postman had been stopped on one or two occasions, and asked at what time I came ashore and where I landed.

My First Lieutenant begged me to alter my routine, but I declined to do so.   Nevertheless, it so happened that I was late going ashore one evening, owing to having had to board one of the mail steamers, and the shore boat went without me.   As the boat was approaching the pier, a little boy hailed it and asked the crew to pick up his dropped fishing-line. The boat stopped, and the two men in the bows started to haul in a piece of wood with a fishing-line attached to it.   At the end of the line was a bomb, which exploded in the boat, hurting one man's hand very severely, another man less seriously, and doing a certain amount of damage.   The boy, who had a Russian name, stated, on being questioned, that a strange man had come down and thrown this thing into the water, had then given him a shilling and told him that when the steamboat came in at 6.45, he was to ask the officer, who would be standing in the stern, to haul the line out of the water.

I at once communicated with the Secret Service, who took the matter in hand, but to this day I have never heard the whole truth of it.   In the meantime, many rumours went round, and by the time I got ashore to dinner about 8 p.m., my wife had heard that I had been torpedoed !

Whilst lying at Holyhead I one day received an urgent telegram from the Admiralty ordering me to proceed to Pembroke to embark the First Lord of the Admiralty, Sir Eric Geddes, and Mr. Roosevelt, Assistant Naval Secretary of U.S.A. (now Governor of New York State and Presidential Candidate), together with their staffs, amounting to six in all, and take them to Queenstown. It was further intimated that I would be escorted by U.S.S. *Kimberly*, commanded by the Senior American Commander, Captain Johnson. The idea of this visit was to increase the *entente* between the two Navies, though it was everything that could be desired already ; however, it enabled the authorities to see at first hand how things were working, and no doubt they enjoyed some white bread and grape-fruit. I was very disgusted at the order, as it upset the organisation of the Irish Sea for which I had quickly to make temporary arrangements.

Anyhow, orders are orders, and I left the following morning at 8 a.m. Attacking submarines appealed to me more than embarking distinguished visitors, and I made a signal to *Kimberly* to keep three miles on my beam as we proceeded down the Irish Sea in order to increase our chances of sighting a submarine. It was very thick weather all the way down, and we neither saw anything nor heard any fog signals. About four o'clock in the afternoon, I

estimated that we were six miles south of the Smalls
Light Vessel, and due to turn due east for the
twenty-mile run into Milford Haven. I ordered
the *Kimberly* to close, and asked her what she made
our position. The Captain reckoned we were about
thirty miles south of the Smalls. On looking at the
chart I saw that whether six or thirty miles south of
the Smalls we were quite safe in steering due east,
so I told him to take station astern of me, and proceeded in an easterly direction at 10 knots. The
Kimberly's sounding machine had broken down, so
I had to do all the sounding myself. Shortly after
this the *Kimberly* asked permission to steam ahead
at 20 knots and look for land. As luck would have
it, I replied, " Not approved " ; and a few minutes
later the look-out on the forecastle shouted out,
" Rocks right ahead." We both went full speed
astern, and I narrowly avoided going aground. The
fog lifted a little, and we found ourselves in a big
bay where there were no landmarks we could recognise, only a few farm-houses. We steamed up and
down the bay for several hours, trying to make out
where we were. I had already signalled to Pembroke that I expected to arrive at about 5 p.m., I then
said 6 p.m., then 7 p.m., and eventually made a
signal that I did not know when I would arrive.
When darkness was approaching, about eight o'clock,
I made an official signal to the *Kimberly* : " Close
the land—send a boat ashore, and enquire at the
farm-house where we are," and I made a private
signal, Captain to Captain : " I am ashamed to give

you such an order, but I think it is better than keeping the First Lord and Secretary Roosevelt waiting."
The *Kimberly* lowered her boat, but as luck would
have it the fog lifted before the boat got ashore and
we found ourselves in St. Bride's Bay, north of the
Smalls. What would have happened if the boat
had ever got ashore and reported that the American
and British Navies had lost themselves, I hate to
think. We eventually got to Milford Haven in the
early hours of the morning, to receive a signal that
the First Lord and party were embarking in the
Kimberly at 6 a.m. I signalled over to the *Kimberly*
and asked the Captain if he had enough food with
which to entertain the distinguished visitors, as I
knew he had already been at sea for several days.
He replied " No," so I sent him over a leg of
mutton.

On leaving Milford Haven, as the *Kimberly* was
able to go at over 30 knots and I was limited to 25, I
did not see that I could be of much use as an escort,
and asked permission to return to Holyhead so as
to get on with the War. This was not approved of,
and I was ordered to follow the *Kimberly* to Queenstown. I knew there would be a big dinner-party
that night at Admiralty House, so I reduced speed
in order to avoid having to attend it, but Admiral
Bayly, probably knowing what would be in my mind,
made a signal to me, ordering me to dine with him
at 7.30. I therefore had to increase speed again so
as to get there in time. After dinner, Sir Eric told
me he would dine on board the *Patrol* the following

night, and then he wanted me to take him to Newport, Mon.   I suggested there would be no need
to sail until 10 p.m., and that he would get a better
dinner at Admiralty House, as my cabin was only a
small one and most of it was taken up with charts
of the Irish Sea, but in spite of Admiral Bayly's
backing, the First Lord was insistent on dining on
board the *Patrol*.   I wondered whether the fact that
U.S.S. *Kimberly* and Admiral Bayly's house were
both dry had anything to do with the necessity of
dining on board the *Patrol* ; private enquiries rather
strengthened this idea ; so I took the precaution of
sending a Lieutenant on duty to Cork (which was
out of bounds) to purchase some champagne, and I
was able to give the party a first-class dinner, of
which Mr. Roosevelt reminded me when I had the
honour of dining with him as Governor of New
York State, so I was able to tell him the secret
history of the dinner-party.

About 11 p.m. Sir Eric came on the bridge whilst
the *Kimberly* was just ahead of us.   I was smoking
my pipe, as was my custom, when the officer on
watch told me the First Lord was coming up.   He
kept on repeating this information and eventually
said :

" Had you not better stop your pipe, sir ? "

I said : " No, I am Captain of this ship, not the
First Lord."   I pretended not to know that the
First Lord was just behind my back, till he said :

" I see you smoke, Captain."

I said : " Yes, sir, all day long."

He then asked me where the escort was, and I showed him, and remarked that, as far as I was concerned, I would much sooner travel without an escort, as with sixty depth charges on my quarter deck I thought I would have a sporting chance of getting a submarine if attacked. He thought for a little while, and then said :

" If you care to put the destroyer ten miles astern, you can do so, provided you give her orders that in the event of your getting torpedoed, Mr. Roosevelt and I are to be saved first."

This struck me as rather extraordinary at the moment, but I quickly realised he was perfectly correct, as we could never have lived down the fact of the First Lord of the Admiralty and the Assistant Secretary of the American Navy being taken prisoners. We arrived at Newport at 6 a.m., and having discharged my distinguished visitors, and having thanked God for letting me see the last of them, I returned to Holyhead to get on with my job. Before parting company, the following signals were exchanged—showing the happy feeling between the two Navies. Long may it continue :

" August 25th, 1918.

" From ——, Naval Secretary,
    To ——, H.M.S. *Patrol* and U.S.S. *Kimberly*.

" First Lord is proud that he should have had the privilege of taking passage in the U.S. Destroyer *Kimberly* with the Assistant Secretary of the U.S. Navy on board from Pembroke to Queenstown, and also, that whilst on passage in H.M.S. *Patrol*, *Kimberly* should have been the escort.

" Mr. Roosevelt joins with Sir Eric Geddes in appreciating this unique instance of two warships of kindred Navies being so intimately associated.

" Knowing that both of them will render the best service during this war, the First Lord and Mr. Roosevelt tender the Captains, Officers and Ships' Companies their thanks for personal services during the last two days, and also wish them good luck and every success."

" From ——, H.M.S. *Patrol*,
    To ——, Naval Secretary.

" Captain, officers, and men of H.M.S. *Patrol* respectfully thank the First Lord and Mr. Roosevelt for their kind message. They were proud to share with the U.S. Navy the honour of taking them to sea."

" From ——, U.S.S. *Kimberly*,
    To ——, Naval Secretary.

" Captain, officers, and men of U.S.S. *Kimberly* are proud of having the opportunity of serving the First Lord and the Assistant Secretary of the two English-speaking Navies, and thank them for their message."

October 1918 was our busiest month, and then we realised that the Armistice could not be long delayed. Although we had to continue all precautions till the last moment, yet the submarines had been withdrawn to Germany to take part in the final attack on Britain's naval strength.

On the night of November 10th, I had ordered the wireless operator to switch my aircraft wireless (which was not used at night) on to the Eiffel Tower in order to get the latest news. About 6 a.m. on November 11th he came rushing to my cabin saying, " The Armistice has been signed."

I said : " Are you sure ? "

He said : " Yes, I have intercepted it direct from Marshal Foch's headquarters."

I at once sent wireless signals to Queenstown and to Milford Haven, and heard them sending out wireless messages to cease hostilities immediately and for patrol craft to return to harbour. In the meantime I had fired several guns, and I passed the news to all ships in Holyhead. I mustered together all my crew to give them the news, and called for three cheers for the King. We also hoisted the White Ensign over the German Ensign reversed at the masthead. All ships were dressed with flags, including the motor-launches, which were then in Menai. The life-boat station started firing guns, and the U.S. Chasers let off rockets and Very lights. When I had seen this outburst, I went down to my cabin about seven o'clock for a cup of tea, and told the signalman to fetch me a copy of the original signal—which was in French—and instead of reading " The Armistice signed," it read, " Hostilities will cease on all fronts at eleven o'clock," which was of course entirely a different matter, and might merely mean that the peace delegates were passing through the lines. I have never had such cold feet in my life. I shuddered as each gun went off, and I had visions of ships still being sunk at sea, whilst the patrols had been withdrawn. I at once rang up the duty Captain at the Admiralty and asked if the Armistice had been signed. In a curt voice he replied, " No." My feet got colder and colder. I walked up and down the quarter-deck by myself, pretending I was intensely happy, but wondering whether I could get on board a ship as a stowaway to the Argentine if a mistake had been made.

To add insult to injury, the airships flew out about nine a.m. and asked permission to drop bombs to celebrate the occasion. I had to keep it up, so I approved their suggestion, and they dropped their bombs ahead of the approaching mail steamers. At 10 a.m. I couldn't stick it any longer, and decided to go ashore to see if the Senior Naval Officer had any news. Just as I was landing, I met the Senior Naval Officer with a long telegram from the Admiralty, not only saying that hostilities would cease at 11 a.m., but giving detailed instructions as to how the day was to be spent. As far as I can recollect, the men were to be enjoined to take part in concerts and bands were to play. The order definitely stated that no salutes were to be fired, and ships were not to be dressed with flags. The first part had already been carried out, and I hadn't the heart to order the ships to haul down their flags, so I made a general signal : " Owing to it being a fine day, ships may take the opportunity of drying their flags."

At noon I assembled all the Commanding Officers, both British and American, and we celebrated the occasion in a suitable fashion. In the meantime the following signals had been exchanged between me and the Senior Officer of the U.S. Chasers. I always think that these sort of messages should not be forgotten, as they were made in great sincerity, and the good spirit should be fostered and maintained.

" November 11th, 1918.

" From ——, the Flag-Captain, H.M.S. *Patrol,*
" To ——, Senior Officer of U.S. Chasers.

" On the occasion of the cessation of hostilities, I should like to express to all the officers and men of the United States Navy under my orders, the pride I have felt and the pleasure I have had in being allowed to command them for a period of the War. Their loyal co-operation, their efficiency and zeal have helped in our common task of making the sea safe and free for the legitimate commerce of the world."

" November 11th, 1918.

" From ——, the Senior Officer of Chasers,
" To ——, H.M.S. *Patrol.*

" Your message has been passed to all Chasers and a copy mailed to Detachment Commander.

" The officers and crews of all Sub-Chasers who have had the pleasure of serving under your orders consider it an honour to have served under your

command and to have earned your unmeasurable
admiration for their loyal co-operation in our
common task of making the sea safe and free for
the legitimate commerce of the world, and until
further orders for the final cessation of hostilities
are received we will endeavour to give the same
co-operation while serving under your command."

The time immediately after the Armistice was a
very trying one, as naturally the " hostility only "
men expected to be able to go home at once to try
and recover their civilian jobs. This, of course,
could not be done, as an Armistice does not necessarily mean peace, and until the German Fleet and
submarines were surrendered or destroyed, they
might at any time come out again.

I arranged a big Thanksgiving Service on the
breakwater, which was attended by the forces of both
Navies, the service being conducted by the Rev.
C. W. Barlow, who, as a temporary chaplain, had
been of great assistance to me in many ways. The
sailors marched through the streets of the town with
the White Ensign and Stars and Stripes flying, and
headed by the band of the training ship *Clio*. The
whole service was most impressive.

The Commander-in-Chief made a special visit
to Holyhead and Menai to express his thanks and
appreciation to all officers and men. The visit
was not an entire success. After he had addressed
all the men from the Flotillas on board the *Patrol*,
I took him by sea in the destroyer round Anglesey

to visit the aeroplane stations, the motor-launch base, and the airship station. It was blowing half a gale, and his hat blew off and could not be recovered, so I lent him mine, and I, in turn, borrowed a Lieutenant's hat, so that when it came to his making various inspections, with guards of honour paraded, they were all rather taken aback at seeing the Admiral arrive in a cap of Captain's rank, and me with no brass on my hat at all.

The job now was how to keep the men occupied without getting them too restless, pending their return to their home ports. I used to take the destroyers to sea for ordinary peacetime tactics, as most of the crews had never seen such exercises, and it gave them a certain amount of interest. At the week-ends, I sent them to the Isle of Man and other ports to dance or otherwise enjoy themselves, and eventually they got orders to return to their home ports.

When the destroyers left Holyhead, Lieutenant A. Grant, now Commander Grant, C.B.E., D.S.C., who was Senior Officer of the Flotilla, led the Flotilla round the *Patrol* and cheered the ship—a graceful act which I very much appreciated.

In the meantime the *Patrol* was ordered to run a sort of ferry service between Holyhead and Kingstown to bring back U.S. sailors who were returning to the States to be demobilised. This was a job my crew didn't relish, as they thought they ought to be demobilised first. Anyhow, I got them to see the humour of it, and in order to keep their spirits up,

I used to arrange our sailing to coincide with that of
the mail steamers, and then we would race them
across the Channel. My officers entered into the
spirit of it, and used to go down to the stokeholds
and give a hand at shovelling, as we were a coal
burner.

It was shortly after the Armistice that I gave a
series of parties on board, the first one being to
all the W.R.N.S., as during the War I had never
allowed any woman on board under any circumstances.

Another party I gave was to the Air Officers.
During the War, I had been up with Major Probyn
in one of his aeroplanes and Major Elmhurst in
one of his blimps. The former had given me a
terrible time, looping the loop and doing special
dives, and had finished up by flying under the Menai
Bridge. He was boasting about this feat after
dinner, and pulling Elmhurst's leg that he couldn't
fly under the Menai Bridge in one of his rotten airships. Elmhurst accepted the challenge, and the
following day came to me for official permission to
fly under the Menai Bridge. He showed me the
plan, and how he would have four feet to spare, two
above the ship and two below. It struck me as
rather a foolhardy stunt, but the Armistice spirit
was on us, and I agreed, provisional on my being
one of the crew, as I thought it too risky a stunt to
approve of without going myself.

So three of us started off in the blimp. We had
a lead line carefully measured, and as long as the

lead was just touching the water, we knew we were clear above. Elmhurst made a dummy approach to try out the lead line, and then we made the final attack ; and much to the consternation of hundreds of witnesses, we flew clean under the Menai Bridge. I think I was as much surprised as anyone when we got through—but it was undoubtedly a very fine feat on the part of Elmhurst, though possibly a stupid one, for which I was responsible. He was so excited at having got through, that he put his helm hard over and nearly hit the people who were standing on the bridge. An account of this incident appeared in the Press the following day, and I quite expected a rap over the knuckles, but at that time the Air Force and Navy were somewhat mixed up, and perhaps no one knew who was responsible.

I found towards the end of, and after, the War that as a result of my services in Mystery Ships, when I was three times torpedoed and once set on fire, I was unable to sleep without dreaming of the incidents, resulting in insomnia and later on a sort of nervous breakdown.

So when early in December I was offered the command of H.M.S. *Cumberland*, which was to be fitted out to take cadets for a cruise, I asked to be allowed to refuse it, although it was of course an ideal job. But apart from the expense which I imagined would be incurred, I had had a very strenuous six months in the Irish Sea, and I felt I needed a complete rest. But I was persuaded to accept, and accordingly turned over the command of the *Patrol* to Rear-Admiral Archdale just before Christmas.

On leaving Holyhead, the R.N.V.R. officers invited me to a big dinner, and told me they would make me a presentation. I declined, as it was contrary to the regulations, but they pointed out that if I did not take it then, they would be in a position to send it to me when they returned to their civil jobs. I saw the point of their argument, and so agreed to accept it at the dinner-party. It was a magnificent silver bowl, which has stood on my table ever since, as a reminder, if such were necessary, of the very pleasant time I spent in command of and in association with the officers of the Royal Naval Volunteer Reserve.

X
West Indies

ON January 1st, 1919, the " Post-War Navy " may be said to have started. A very true remark which I made at that time in a speech was, that the officer would have to come down a certain extent and the rating would have to go up a certain extent, and the person who could adjust the proper line would be a very exceptional person. In some ships the officers tried to continue the pre-War Naval discipline, somewhat of a martinet character; others went to the opposite extreme, and went ashore while their men danced on the quarter-deck.

The Board of Admiralty had great difficulties ahead of them. They were tied, I imagine, by traditions, customs, and favouritism which had been going on for years. They had to make big reductions in both the personnel and the matériel of the Navy. It was common knowledge after the War that there was a great deal of discontent in the Service over the scales of pay. These were adjusted by telegram. A Welfare Committee was instituted by the Admiralty, which in itself undermined the position of officers both in command of ships and in divisions. The reduction of officers which had to take place, instead of starting at the top of the tree, started well down the list, and even then was not done sufficiently widely to reduce the Navy to its post-War scale, thereby causing ships in command to change their Captains or Commanders two or three times in the course of a year, in order to enable Captains to get sufficient sea time to qualify them for Flag rank. Limited expenditure no doubt handicapped the Admiralty in schemes which they would have liked to put into force, but the fact remains, as far as my observation went, that during the period from 1918 to 1928, more attention was paid to the matériel than to the personnel, the eventual result being the unfortunate incident at Invergordon.

There was a great cry that the Navy lacked a Naval Staff. We proceeded to produce one, which, in my opinion, was greatly overdone. Even on the small stations there were a large number of staff officers who went out of their way to make unnecessary work and to interfere with the proper functions of the executive officers in charge of ships.

In the following chapters, I can simply relate some of my own experiences, and even these must of necessity be restricted, owing to the fact that many good fellows with whom I served are still on the active list.

I held, throughout, a rather strange position, in that although the youngest Captain in the Navy, I held some of the best commands, which enabled me to dine with Commanders-in-Chief, etc., and hear their views. At the same time, the fellows of my

own seniority were chiefly Commanders or Lieu-
tenant-Commanders, which kept me in touch with
the feeling in the lower ranks of the Navy ; and I
had (and always have) a natural inclination to
associate myself with Warrant Officers and men of
the lower deck.

Thus I had a great field of opportunity for review-
ing the situation from various points of view.   And I
must say that my confidence in the Board of Admiralty steadily decreased throughout the ten years.
Again and again I was protesting against some policy
or other ; and if I often did not press those protests sufficiently to ensure their reaching the Admiralty, that was only from a desire to get things done
by other methods than an appeal to the Admiralty,
whenever that was possible.

My leave was only a very brief and rather distracted
one.   My wife and I went for a few hurried days to
Queensferry to visit the Grand Fleet, as throughout
the War I had never come in contact with it.   It
was a magnificent sight, spreading for miles on
either side of the Forth Bridge, and one little thought
that in the course of a few years most of it would be
in the hands of the shipbreakers.   The Grand Fleet
had saved the British Empire—Jellicoe at Jutland
was the only man who stood between Germany and
the world.   Much has been written about Jutland,
and I have no wish to add to the many things that
have been said, except that if Jellicoe had lost the
battle, the British Empire and its Allies would have
lost the War.

The controversy that took place for many years
after the War was neither a credit to those in high
positions, who took part in it, nor beneficial to the
moral and well-being of the Service.   It was Jellicoe
who had trained the Grand Fleet, brought it to a
high state of efficiency, and who had issued the
Battle Orders, which had the general approval of the
Admiralty and the Flag Officers who served under
him.   After the Armistice, Jellicoe was sent on a
" mission " round the British Empire, whilst Beatty,
who had only been a junior Flag Officer at Jutland,
received the Freedom of various cities and headed
the Peace Procession in London, a position which
only Jellicoe should have taken.   The matter was
freely discussed in every Wardroom, and in consequence on every lower deck, and one had to be either
a Jellicoite or a Beattyite.   I should have been proud
to have served under either, but it so happened that
I hadn't, and I was therefore able to listen to the
controversies with an unbiased mind—having great
admiration for both men, as great leaders in different
ways.

Anything more detrimental to the discipline of the
Service than this controversy can hardly be con-
ceived.   It extended farther afield, as in both South
Africa and Canada I was asked about the Battle of
Jutland ; I replied that I wasn't present and knew
nothing beyond what had been published.

On returning from Scotland, I set off for Plymouth
to take over the command of the *Cumberland* from
Captain Blackett.   She was in a filthy state, having

done convoy work across the Atlantic Ocean since June 1917 in all kinds of weather, and having also had a serious influenza epidemic on board. During the War she had steamed 150,012 miles, and consumed 76,489 tons of coal. No wonder she was in a dirty state.

It was essential that the first impression the cadets should have of a man-of-war should be one of smart appearance, so no time was lost in getting her as ship-shape as possible. The " term " of cadets waiting for sea training was over a hundred, so they were divided between us and the *Cornwall*, commanded by Captain Kitson. We submitted independent cruises to the Admiralty, and both selected the West Indies for the main portion of our cruise, arranging to meet once or twice during our six months' cruise. Our only orders were that two-thirds of the time should be spent in harbour and one-third at sea. The programme I forwarded was approved, except that the then Second Sea Lord thought I ought to go to Trinidad, which I had omitted, owing to the heat, to enable the cadets to see the Pitch Lake, which he considered of great importance to their training.

We officially commissioned with a new crew on February 1st, 1919. The officers for the most part were specially selected, including at my personal request an officer from the Royal Naval Reserve and one from the Royal Naval Volunteer Reserve. The crew were a very mixed crowd : as most men were on " war leave," I got men who had been released from the Detention Quarters on the signing of the Armistice, and a lot of young men. However, in due course they gradually settled down to peace-time routine.

Our first job was to take in 1,500 tons of coal, which was a good shake-up to start with, and then I ordered all officers to wear frock coats (which had been laid aside during the War) on Sundays, which was a shake-up too.

My wife had arranged to come to Plymouth to see me off, but at the last moment I had a telegram saying she had pneumonia. I was unable to leave the ship, as there was so much to be done in the way of altera-tions in order to make suitable accommodation for the cadets, both as to their messing and sleeping, and also for their instruction. On the way down harbour on February 12th I received a telegram saying my wife had double pneumonia. On anchor-ing in the Sound, I felt the strain was too much, as I had had practically no leave after a rather strenuous war, and my insomnia was getting worse ; my wife had double pneumonia, and my boy was in a nursing-home recovering from mastoid. I knew there were plenty of Captains who would be only too pleased to have such an ideal job, so I girt on my sword and went ashore to see the Commander-in-Chief, Admiral Sir C. Thursby, and asked to be relieved of my command for private reasons. He asked me to state them, which I did, and then with the most generous consideration, he got into telephonic communication with the Naval Secretary, Admiral Sir Rudolf Bentinck, and arranged that I might have four days' leave, and further that, if I wished, the ship could sail under a temporary Captain and I could join her later in the West Indies. It was one of the rare cases in which I have run across real humanity in the Admiralty. I took my four days' leave and no more, and with rather a heavy heart stepped on board my ship in the Sound to be told that my faithful dog, Nelson, who was stone deaf and blind, had fallen overboard and been drowned.

Our first port of call was Queenstown, where I went for no other reason than to pay my respects to my late Commander-in-Chief, and to invite him and Miss Voysey to luncheon, after which we sailed for Gibraltar.

General Sir Horace Smith-Dorrien was Governor at the time, and entertained myself and several officers, and was also very kind to the cadets. He looked a typical soldier, and I instinctively felt he was a man I should have liked to serve under. Our stay at Gibraltar was much the same as that of other ships, and the cadets climbed the rock and saw all the sights that were to be seen. I found out that it had been customary in cadets' training ships for all cadets, when visiting such places as Gibraltar, to have a day off *en bloc*. I put my foot down about this, and insisted on a certain number being always on board for duty, so as to teach them that duty comes first, and that in every ship, however great the attractions are ashore, some of all ranks and ratings have to stay on board.

On leaving Gibraltar, we sailed for Madeira, which

we reached on February 23rd. On the evening
before, I got the Padre to give a lecture about the
place. This was a custom I invariably followed, so
as to enable the cadets in particular, and any others
interested, to know the history of the place before
reaching it. Our next stretch was eight days across
the Atlantic to St. Lucia. The weather had now
become hot, and after satisfying myself from the
various " books of the words " that no sharks had
been reported in the vicinity, I stopped the ship at
four o'clock in the afternoon and ordered " hands
to bathe." A life-boat was lowered as a usual precaution, and the bathing commenced. The cadets
jumped in from the quarter-deck and the sailors from
the forecastle. Now a ship may seem pretty big
when you are living on board, but when you are in
the Atlantic Ocean it looks terribly small and much
farther away than it really is. I was standing at the
end of the fore-bridge watching the bathers, when I
saw the sentry on the after-bridge throw the lifebuoy
into the water. I at once realised something had
gone wrong, but what had really happened was that
one of the cadets had got cold feet, as he didn't
realise we were in several thousand fathoms of
water, and thought he was in the shallow end of a
swimming-bath. He was soon rescued, but unfortunately the word " shark " was started, and it
spread like wildfire. There were several hundred
men bathing from the forecastle, and when the word
" shark " reached them, something in the nature of a
panic nearly ensued, a good many of the men starting

11

to shout for help and splashing about furiously.
For some reason I have never been able to explain, instead of swimming towards the ship and coming on
board, they started to swim away from the ship.   I
quickly got another life-boat into the water and every
available lifebuoy was thrown overboard.   I was
thankful when the last man was safely on board, as
I had had visions of losing a lot of them.   I decided
not to stop again for bathing, sharks or no sharks.

My Instructor-Commander was F. M. Broadbent,
a man much older than myself.   He might well have
objected to serving under anyone so young ; in fact,
I felt when he joined that he didn't quite relish the
situation ; but he turned out to be one of my best
friends, and I shall never forget all the loyal assistance,
and I might say guidance, he gave me throughout
the cruise.   He was a born leader and set a noble
example to the cadets, taking a personal and fatherly
interest, not only in their work, but also especially
in their cricket and other recreations.

In the hot weather, he pointed out to me that he
found the cadets were not much good for afternoon
instruction after a long dinner hour.   So I made the
following arrangement.

At 2 a.m. each morning the clocks were put on an
hour, as no one misses an hour's sleep in the hot
weather.   Breakfast was served at 7, though the
clocks showed 8, the forenoon and afternoon work
was combined, and they worked on till 1.15 by the
clock.   I had to apply this routine to the ship's
company as well, so at one o'clock I put the clocks

back to noon, and this enabled the sailors to have their dinner and rum at eight bells, to which they were accustomed. When I assembled the ship's company and told them what I intended to do, they were a little bit sceptical, but when they found that they had a " make and mend " (half-holiday) every day, and the clocks ashore were the same as they were on board, they thought the Millennium had arrived, and that instead of a six-day working week they only had four !

In due course we reached Castries, the capital of St. Lucia. Lying in harbour was the yacht *Eileen*, which had been in command of some of the patrol motor-launches during the War. She had on board one of those intensely patriotic retired Admirals, Admiral Simpson, who had given up his rank and become an officer in the Royal Naval Reserve. I called on him immediately after breakfast. He was rather surprised to see me, as he said it was his duty to call on me first, which he had intended to do at 10 a.m., and he told me of an unfortunate snub he had received from the Captain of one of H.M. ships for not calling. My reply was, " Once an Admiral always an Admiral," and that I desired to pay my respects to a man who had surrendered his rank. He returned my call, and I received him with an Admiral's Guard while the band played " Rule Britannia "—quite irregular, but suitable for the occasion.

The Administrator of St. Lucia was Lieutenant-Colonel Davidson-Houston, a most popular and firm administrator, and a man I got to like immensely. I had the pleasure of staying with him, and not only was he a perfect host to me, but he also let the cadets have the run of his tennis-courts. I remember being up at his house one afternoon when he had all the cadets to tea—he had an enormous repast laid out, which I think he had intended should last for two " does," but it all disappeared in one fell swoop. No one has any idea of what a cadet's appetite is like till it is put to the test.

Our stay at St. Lucia was a delightful one ; we had several cricket matches, in which I took a feeble part, and the officers were entertained, as indeed was the case everywhere, right royally. The cadets were not forgotten, and had several good picnics to the Hot Springs, etc.

We had a very snug anchorage at St. Lucia—so snug that we had to use our picket-boat to push the bows of the ship round, as there was no room to turn. We were all sorry to leave, and I left behind as a gift to Colonel Davidson-Houston a little pup, whom he christened " Mystery." I had on board one of Nelson's " flirts," a beautiful little Sealyham terrier, which had been presented to me by one of my officers in " Q " ships. She had a litter during our passage to the West Indies, and I distributed some of the offspring to the various Governors.

After leaving St. Lucia, we made a short run to the island of St. Vincent, and then went on to spend a day at Grenada, where the Governor and Commander-in-Chief, Sir G. B. Haddon Smith, made me a present of a beautiful parrot, which I intended taking home. Unfortunately, I hung it up in a cage on a part of the deck which was allocated to the cadets, and I discovered that in a few months the parrot's language was so dreadful that I did not dare take it home, and had to give it away.

After leaving Grenada, we went to Port of Spain, Trinidad, where we had a continual round of festivities, one of the special attractions being the Club, where dancing went on till the early hours of the morning. Luckily the Commander was a keen dancer, and so the officers could rely on a boat off at 2 a.m. every morning.

Incidentally a rumour came to my ears that no less than twenty-five ladies came on board one afternoon to enquire for the Commander.

As one of our chief reasons for visiting Trinidad was to see the wonderful pitch-lake, I invoked the aid of the Governor, Colonel May, the Chief of the Police, and Mr. Fuller, and they made all arrangements with the necessary authorities for us to visit not only the pitch-lake but also the oil-wells. I gave all the cadets a day off, and a good many officers came as well. We left at 7 a.m. in a variety of cars, and drove fifty miles to La Brea, where the pitch-lake is situated. The pitch-lake, although reckoned to be one of the wonders of the world, is not much to look at, appearing merely as a large expanse of asphalt of about fourteen acres. There are various theories as to how it came to be there, one being that it comes from an inexhaustible store at the bottom of the sea, and, in support of this theory, the local niggers will sell you shells filled with pitch.

From the pitch-lake we drove to the oil-wells at Siparia, where we had a delightful picnic lunch put up by the Company's Staff at their " Club House." The oilfields were much the same as any others I have seen. Then we went to a sugar refinery. In fact, the hospitality we received throughout the day could not have been surpassed, and it would be impossible to mention the names of all the people who escorted us, fed us, and took us round. The only contretemps was when one of the cars full of officers collided with a car containing a nigger wedding party, and both capsized, but luckily no one was hurt, and the officers seemed highly amused at the incident, though unfortunately the nigger party couldn't see the humour of it.

Lying alongside the wharf at Port of Spain were several of H.M. Motor-Launches, which had been used for patrolling during the War, and which were under the command of a Commander R.N.V.R. They were awaiting orders from the Admiralty as to their disposal. One of my very zealous Lieutenants, who was in charge of the ship's boats, thought he saw a good opportunity of obtaining some loot which would help to smarten up our own boats, such as boat-hooks, ventilators, etc. He decided to make a night raid. Unfortunately, various items were observed to be missing after we left, and sufficient evidence was forthcoming that somebody from the *Cumberland* was the culprit. A letter duly followed to one of the other islands we were visiting, and I was obliged to take official action. The Lieutenant concerned admitted the deed, so I had officially to reprimand him, and ordered him to pay for the freight of returning the goods (I imagine he arranged some cheap passage). I sent for him afterwards and commended him on his zeal for the good of the ship, but pointed out that when I had committed similar deeds, I had taken the precaution not to be bowled out.

We eventually sailed from Trinidad towards the end of March. I think many cadets, and even officers, left their hearts behind, but this happened at nearly every island we visited. At most of the islands, we happened to be the first man-of-war to pay a visit after the Armistice, so came in for an extra round of tea-dances, dinners, evening dances, mixed bathing parties, etc. Unfortunately, although I was younger than several of my officers, I had to watch them dancing with the sweet young things, whilst I had to do my job as Captain.

The next island we visited was Barbados, where we anchored in Carlisle Bay off Bridgetown. The Governor at that time was Sir Charles O'Brien, and he together with his wife and daughters kept open house for us. Barbados is a comparatively flat island, and does not appeal to the eye like St. Lucia or Grenada, but there are many beautiful spots on the island, and I remember the cadets being very upset one day when I wouldn't let them have leave for a night bathing picnic in one of the pretty bays. But if the island does not look particularly attractive at first sight, the same cannot be said of the inhabitants.

Whilst staying there I went out one night to dine with my friends, the Camerons, at their Sugar Plantation. On arrival back at Government House I tripped over something at the front door, and discovered it was the A.D.C. who had received orders to receive me when I returned, and feeling very sleepy, had laid himself full length on the door-step to make sure he would not miss me. He didn't !

During our stay here four American battleships arrived, together with destroyers. The rumour at the time was that the United States Government had eyes on the West Indies in exchange for the War debt, and nearly all the islands received visits from U.S. ships. I decided only to land picked men to ensure that there were no unfortunate incidents. It did come to my ears that one of my stokers, walking down to the boat and smoking a cigarette, happened to meet an American sailor who, having had one over the eight, said to him : " Who won the War now, Jack ? " The stoker, without taking his cigarette out of his mouth, just landed him one under the jaw and knocked him flat. On the following day, when I went to see the Governor, he asked me if I had heard of the incident. I said : " No, sir." He said : " Nor have I."

The U.S. Flagship gave a big dance on board, and

the American ensign was hoisted at the masthead of all ships. I decided to go one better, and when we gave our dance, I invited the Governor and his wife to dine with me. Although it is not the custom to fire a salute after dark, I found there was nothing in the regulations to say you were not to. At that time Governors were not entitled to the National Anthem, but I arranged with the Governor that he should leave the ship at eleven o'clock when the dance concluded, and when naturally the National Anthem was played. At the same instant all the illuminations were switched off, the red ensign was hoisted at the masthead with a searchlight turned on it, and I saluted the Governor with seventeen guns. As an American officer said to me : " You treat your Governors in fine style."

Our dances invariably ended punctually at 11 p.m. It was pointed out to me that this was a bit early, and that the cadets felt they were being treated rather like children, but in view of the fact that they had to do work in the early morning, I declined to alter my decision, and told them they could start earlier if they wished to. At each dance the same thing would invariably happen : one of the officers would come up to me and ask if I would mind being introduced to Miss So-and-so ; off I went to be introduced to a most perfect-looking fairy with lovely eyes, who after a few minutes' conversation would say : " Don't you think, Captain, we could dance till twelve to-night ? The cadets are enjoying themselves so, and they are so nice," etc., etc. I had to harden my heart and say : " I'm afraid the dance will finish at 11 p.m."—of course, I knew some cadet had put her up to it—also that she would trot off and say : " What an awful man your Captain is."

There were many sad hearts when the time came for us to sail—I softened my heart sufficiently to arrange to sail after " Prep." (i.e. after the cadets had come on board at 6 p.m.), though I don't think love is much of an inducement to do Prep. It was dark when we sailed, and so we gave a searchlight display as we left the harbour to bid farewell to our many good friends. We steamed up past St. Lucia and Martinique, so as to see the famous Diamond Rock, hauled in towards St. Pierre to see Mont Pelée, and then proceeded to Dominica and anchored off Roseau, the capital. There a cricket match was arranged, the *Cumberland* versus *Dominica*. It was a large cricket ground, and there were crowds of people, and also a band. As I went in to bat, a distance which seemed like several miles, the band played " See the Conquering Hero Comes," which made me more nervous than ever, with the result that I was out first ball and had to walk back in silence.

XI

West Indies *(continued)*

AFTER leaving Dominica, our next official port of call was Jamaica, but I decided to anchor for a few hours off Antigua, in order to enable the cadets to see Nelson's dock, which he used during the wars against France. I had one cadet on board who appeared to have relations in every place we visited, but I thought that as our visit to Antigua was unexpected, and it was a very small island, I should at least be spared requests from his relations at this port. But not a bit of it! There was a letter waiting for me on our arrival, asking for special leave, and on landing, there was quite a fleet of cars full of young fairies to greet us—or him. We almost thought we were back in Barbados again. Even when we got back to Oban I found this fellow had relations there, but by this time I was thoroughly suspicious.

After visiting the Nelson dockyard, which is now no longer in use, and chiefly consists of cobbles with overgrown moss, we continued our voyage to Jamaica, and anchored off Kingston, which we reached on April 8th. The Governor of Jamaica was Sir Leslie Probyn. The chief interests to the

cadets in Jamaica were the crocodiles and the bathing, but although they sound rather a funny mixture,
the former could be seen and the latter carried out in
safety.

During our stay here, the S.S. *Remuera* passed
through *en route* to New Zealand with returning
troops on board. They had a great reception on
shore, so much so that some of them missed the
boat, but luckily our picket-boat was able to pick up
some of the stragglers and get them on board as the
ship was leaving harbour.

After a few days at Kingston, we went down to
Port Royal to coal, which was done by native labour.
I landed half the crew in the forenoon to go to see
the Nelson relics, and had proposed landing the
other half in the afternoon, but on going ashore
shortly after the men had landed, I was astounded
to see most of them lying about in the streets, and
discovered that most of the houses had cheap and
dangerous rum. So on our second visit, I mustered
all the crew and told them I thought that Port Royal
had probably left a nasty taste in their mouths,
and had brought discredit on the ship. I therefore
landed practically the whole of the ship's company
under arms, and made them march through the
streets with a band at their head. They quite
appreciated the situation, and cocked their chests.

On leaving Jamaica we proceeded to Santiago de
Cuba. I had particularly wanted to visit this place,
because of the attack during the Spanish-American
War, when the Americans tried to block the rather

narrow entrance.   The approach is very impressive as, after going through the entrance and passing Morro Castle, you suddenly find yourself in a large open bay with the town at the head of it.

A big reception was given in our honour by the Governor, and I had to make a speech.   This was interpreted word by word, a very weary proceeding, which gave me an idea how terribly difficult some of the European Conferences must be.   We then assembled on the balcony to listen to our ship's band, which was playing in the square below.   The whole of Santiago de Cuba seemed to be assembled there, and their smart cars, with very chic ladies inside them, were driving round and round.   At this time everyone in Cuba appeared to be very rich and the ladies' dresses seemed chiefly to be the same colour as the cars ; I don't know whether the dresses were bought to match the cars or whether the cars were repainted to match the dresses.   At the end of the band performance, the National Anthems of our country, Cuba, the United States, and Spain were played.   The first was received with great applause, the second with rather less, the third with none at all, but the last received the greatest applause of the lot.

I found that the German propaganda had been very deep, and they were surprised to see a British ship arriving, as they understood they had all been sunk.   Our visit was a very pleasant one, and in addition to the many official calls, we were well entertained ashore.   Mr. William Mason, the British

Consul, took some of us for a beautiful drive round the island, and he presented me with a unique walking-stick, which had been subscribed for by the English inhabitants to be presented to one of the great Admirals who commanded the Grand Fleet. I was, therefore, very lucky to receive it in my humble position.

The Governor of Santiago invited me to go for a drive round the town with him, accompanied by the Mayor and an interpreter. After a good drive in the country, we returned to the town, and drove round and round a very small square full of what appeared to me to be painted ladies. I conveyed, through the interpreter, how much I appreciated the beauty of the various buildings, but the Governor asked me whether I did not admire the ladies also, so I had to reply that, as they were so beautiful, I could not find words with which to express my admiration.

Another interesting day we had was when a distinguished Frenchman gave a big luncheon party on his estate, at which there were present, in addition to myself and some of my officers, some American Air Force Officers. The discussion during the cocktails before luncheon concerned the visit of President Wilson to Europe, where he was at that time, and it was heartily condemned both by the Frenchmen present and the Americans. After luncheon the loyal toasts were drunk, and then, to my horror, our French host got up and proposed " the speedy return of President Wilson from Europe." I nodded to my officers who were present to keep their seats, and the Frenchman turned to me and said :

" I see you don't take part in this toast," to which I replied :

" No, sir—I am a naval officer, not a politician."

On leaving Santiago, I broke my usual custom of refusing all interviews, and arranged to receive the two leading Press representatives, as I thought it desirable not only to express the great honour the Governor had done us by visiting the ship, and our thanks for the generous hospitality we had received, but also to refer, in no boastful way, to the work of the Allies in overcoming the German Empire, and the help that Cuba, as one of our Allies, had also given in helping to patrol the seas against the possible raids of German submarines.

We left Santiago bound for Bermuda, but in the middle watch a wireless message was received from the Commander-in-Chief of the West Indies, Admiral Sir Morgan Singer, ordering us to return to Jamaica, where we eventually stayed for a month. Normally the *Cumberland* was a " special service ship," and I received my orders direct from the Admiralty, the Second Sea Lord being the one we came under, but now I received orders to place myself at the disposal of the Commander-in-Chief of the West Indies. I wondered what it was all about, and on arrival at Jamaica at once reported myself to the Governor and then visited the Brigadier-General and Senior Naval Officer.

There was at that time a fear of a " rising " of the natives in the West Indies, and men-of-war were allocated to all the more important islands. The Native Labour Battalions, who had done good service in France, but had shown signs of unrest at the end of the War, were due to return shortly, and it was thought a possible rebellion might ensue, which would have been a fairly natural sequel to the course of events. The niggers had been taught to look with respect on the white man, but now they had been to France, and they had seen the white men fighting like savages, with poison gas, flames, and every instrument of destruction that could be thought of. The white women no longer had the respect that they had for years held, as the niggers had been to big foreign ports. Their whole outlook on life was changed. Communism had no doubt sown its seeds, and they had visions of that glorious and often misunderstood ideal, " Self-government."

In the meantime I had to get ready for every emergency. I sent the men ashore for regular route marches to get them thoroughly fit, and on board ship I kept the arms " piled " day and night, so as to be ready to land some two hundred men in a few minutes. They were to go under the orders of the Commander, and I myself intended to land with the second " flight," unless our big guns were required. I had arranged that the band was to go with the first landing party, unarmed, though of course I made arrangements for their safety. I still had great faith in human nature, and I thought a band playing patriotic tunes might well appease many of the natives.

In vain did I ask the Governor as to when I should " open fire " if such a thing became necessary—whether I should wait till Martial Law was declared or the Riot Act read. I never got an answer, so I gave a written order to the Commander to open fire at his discretion, and added that if he did so, he wouldn't be promoted, because the people in England would say he murdered innocent people, and if he didn't open fire he wouldn't be promoted, because people in England would say : " If only we had had a strong man in the place," etc. And so it will always be in any civil disturbances—the armed forces of the Crown can seldom rely on the support of the Government (I don't mind which one).

In due course the ship bringing the returning troops arrived. The streets were decorated with flags, ready to welcome the conquering heroes. The ship itself was anchored a good way off the town, and the Governor went out, not in state, to welcome her. I had suggested to him that he should go out in our smart picket-boat with his flag flying, while I paraded a guards' band and fired a salute for him, but instead he decided to go out in a dirty old dockyard launch. He addressed the troops, but received no cheers. The troops themselves were landed at daylight the following morning, and scattered about the island. All was peace.

Whilst in the West Indies, we had heard various rumours of unrest in certain ships and in parts of

12

the Army, due either to the pay, the impatience of
" hostility only " men, or even possibly Communist
propaganda, all of which had good ground in which
to sow their seed amongst war-weary people. One
day a man with quite a good record and two conduct badges was brought before me charged with
" refusing to obey lawful order and command to
place his boots on the boot-rack." On my question-
ing him, he explained to me that he was a man, and
that the days of obeying Petty Officers were over ;
in fact, he was as good as they were. I warned him
of the seriousness of his conduct, but he persisted in
refusing to obey. I therefore ordered him to prison
for ninety days with hard labour. As he was being
taken ashore with an escort I heard a lot of cheering,
and on going outside my cabin I found that practically the whole of the ship's company had manned the
side to cheer the prisoner. I had visions of a
mutiny, and at once ordered the Commander to
assemble everyone on the quarter-deck. When
they were all present, I proceeded aft, and standing
well above the men, I thanked them for the way
they had shown their appreciation of the punishment I had recently awarded to a man who was a
discredit to the ship and service. I then pointed
out that I was paid as Captain of the ship to administer with justice the Naval Discipline Act,
and that, in future, I didn't want any expression of
opinion one way or the other of the manner in
which I performed my duty. I never heard another
word, and there were no more refusals to obey.

Various other ships, the *Lancaster*, *Devonshire*, *Berwick*, and *Dauntless*, visited the island whilst we were there. The *Dauntless*, although the most up-to-date ship of the lot, was not looked on as of much importance by the natives, as she only had two funnels and no band ; whereas we (who were almost obsolete) had three funnels and a band.

During our stay I took the ship to sea two or three times to get a blow-through and do some exercises, but I found the rather trying heat was telling on the cadets, and they, together with some of the officers, came out with some extraordinary skin diseases, which we never fathomed. Thanks to the kindness of the Military Authorities, I was able to send all the cadets up to the barracks at Farm Ridge, Newcastle, several hundred feet above sea-level. Here they were able to get a complete change of air and routine. It coincided with the half period of our cruise and became a sort of additional half-term holiday.

Our " stand by " at Jamaica had upset our original programme, and when our presence was no longer required, I asked permission to visit Havana, Cuba. This was approved, and we sailed on May 18th. On the way we called at a rather unknown island called Cayman, and spent most of the time painting the ship ; then on to Havana, to find further trouble in store. I called on the Chargé d'Affaires, Mr. Cowan, and discovered that a general strike was in progress, and there was some talk of setting up a Soviet Government. I arranged to work in close conjunction with him, and take any steps that might be necessary to protect the lives and property of British subjects.

The following day I called on all the officials, including the Governor, the Prime Minister, the Mayor, the Ministers of War, Marine, etc. With a prearranged programme, their calls were returned the following day, and I fired in all one hundred and fifty-eight guns. The programme was well arranged, in that each personage as he called was received with a guard of honour and a band which played half the Cuban National Anthem, then came into my cabin, which was on the upper deck, for a drink and a Havana cigar, whilst the band played a suitable tune, and then left when half the Cuban National Anthem was again being played. The only slip was with the Governor, as my steward made a mistake and handed him a Jamaican cigar. He took it up, looked at it, and put it down again. His A.D.C. took one, lit it, gave one puff, and also put it down. I realised a *faux pas* had been made, and sent a message to the Commander to play the whole of the Cuban National Anthem. In the meantime I asked the Governor if I might have the honour of saluting him with guns when he left the ship, and how many would he like? He told me seven (the correct number to which he was entitled). I pressed him to allow me to give him a few more, but he was adamant, until I suggested that, if the Governor of Santiago got seven guns, surely the Governor of the magnificent city of Havana ought to receive more. This appeared to tickle him, and he said he would like to have nine.

The situation in Havana needed careful handling. I was continually in touch with the Chargé d'Affaires, and took the precaution of landing the officers in uniform and only the men with good conduct badges. There was a fear at one time that the strikers would refuse to run the lights of the town, and I was asked if I would undertake the job, but I pointed out that I could not interfere in a general strike unless the lives of British subjects were in jeopardy. When everything had quietened down, I asked permission of the Admiralty to sail, after consulting with the Chargé d'Affaires, but the Admiralty, instead of trusting the man on the spot, replied that I was not to sail until further orders. I therefore decided, in order to maintain the *entente* which had been set up between the *Cumberland* and the people ashore, to give a big reception and dance on board, and invited all the important people, and at the same time asked the Secretary of the British Club, which had kindly made me one of their life members, to invite fifty of the most charming ladies of the island. The show was a great success. It cost the Admiralty a lot of money, but eventually I got permission to sail.

At Cayman, as there was no chaplain on the island, we had had a christening on board, when I stood sponsor to six negro children. Here we had another, when I became godfather to a baby girl who was blessed with the names Alice Virginia

Cumberland Campbell. The Padre was a little nervous over the ceremony, and pronounced that she should renounce the devil " and all her works."

A small matter which greatly interested me whilst we were at Havana, was the fact that a Mexican gunboat was lying there. At that time, we had broken off diplomatic relations with Mexico, but the Commander in command of the Mexican gunboat came to call on me, and I received him with the honour due to his rank. I then had to think whether it was correct or not to return his call, and decided that I should do so, so I was in turn received with due ceremony, but I declined to accept any hospitality in the way of a drink or a smoke from the Captain when I went down to his cabin. I reported to the Admiralty what I had done, and requested that I might be informed if my action was correct for future guidance. I never received any reply.

On entering Havana harbour we had taken on board a Cuban pilot. I would much sooner have gone in alone, as I could not possibly understand what he wanted, especially when it came to the time that he asked me to lay an anchor down just before taking up my moorings. I protested for a long time, and eventually gathered it was some regulation, and so I complied, but took the precaution when we left Havana of giving the wrong time for my sailing, which enabled me to go to sea without a pilot.

XII

West Indies *(continued)*

On arrival at Bermuda, I called on the Governor, Sir James Willcocks. His A.D.C. returned the call, and had a couple of cocktails that my steward had made of a special brand. At dinner that night the Governor informed me that he intended to return my call the following day. When I pointed out that his A.D.C. had already returned the call, and that Governors do not call on anybody below Flag rank, he said : " I know that—but damn it, I hear you have the best cocktails in Bermuda." I expressed the honour I should have in receiving him, and asked him if he would address the cadets. On his arrival on board, I received him with the salute and ceremony due to the Governor, and he then addressed the cadets, after which he visited my cabin.

During our visit I sent the cadets to one of the small islands for camp. Much discussion was taking place on board as to whether these cadet cruises should be of six months' or three months' duration. The officers, chiefly the married ones, were in favour of three months, in order to enable them to visit their homes, but I stuck out for the six months, as I believe one of the defects of the Navy is that there is too much home leave, and I think that even a longer cruise than six months would have been desirable.

Whilst here, I attended the longest luncheon I have ever been to. It was the yearly luncheon of the Legislative Council, with the Governor, Commander-in-Chief, etc., present, and lasted from 1 p.m. till about 6.30 p.m.

On leaving Bermuda we were ordered to tow a Canadian submarine to Halifax. The tow parted, and so I let her go on her own. We then ran into a dense fog which lasted for several days. When I got into the vicinity of St. John's, Newfoundland, I stopped the engines, and waited for the fog to lift, and when it did so, about 9.30 in the forenoon, there were nearly a hundred icebergs in sight ; it was extraordinary how we had steamed through such a lot of them in dense fog without actually hitting one.

On our arrival at St. John's, the Governor, Sir Alexander Harris, told me he had received a deputation from the local fishermen requesting me to destroy, by gunfire, a big iceberg, which had run aground, and was interfering with the fishing. I pointed out that I might just as well throw peanuts at it, but he was so persistent in his request that I took the opportunity of carrying out some 6-inch gun practice. Of course it had no effect on the iceberg, but nearly led to what might have been a regrettable incident, as one of the shells ricochetted off and landed in a village about four miles inland.

How on earth it got there I do not know, as we were firing at point-blank range.

On leaving St. John's, we went to St. George's Bay, a big bay practically uninhabited. Whilst we were there we received news that peace had been signed at Versailles. The news arrived in the evening while a number of officers were ashore, and I hoisted the signal " Peace " at the masthead. We had orders to splice the main brace, fire a salute of a hundred and one guns, and dress ship overall. The Commander suggested that, as there was nobody to see us, it would be a great opportunity to give the whole thing a miss, but I took a different view, as I thought, and still think, that sailors like ceremony, provided they do not think it is done for the benefit of the officers' wives and friends.

That evening there was a concert party. I read to the ship's company the terms of the Peace, and we all sang " Rule Britannia." For the following day, I thought the best treat I could give the men was to allow all hands to lie in until 8 a.m. At 11.30 a guard was to be paraded, consisting not only of Marines but also of cadets, seamen, and stokers. The stokers were so keen to put up a good show against the Marines, that they turned out in the early hours of the morning to practise and let the Marines know they were not the only people who knew how to parade. The ship was dressed with flags at 8 a.m., and at 11.30 the whole ship's company mustered on the quarter-deck with various guards of honour and the band. For a quarter of an hour we had a Memorial Service, followed by a quarter of an hour's Thanksgiving Service, followed by a *feu de joie*, and then a salute of a hundred and one guns, during which all the Anthems of our Allies were played. I then called for three cheers for H.M. the King, and three cheers for the officers and men of the Navy and Royal Marines who gave their lives during the Great War. In the afternoon the Master-at-Arms asked to see me to express the thanks of the ship's company for the ceremony, saying how especially pleased they were that I had given three cheers for the dead, a thing they had never heard done before.

In St. George's Bay, the cadets arranged a paper chase, and there was much alarm when one of them was found to be missing. Six officers were at once sent ashore to look for him, as to lose a cadet would be worse than losing a ship, but luckily he turned up all right.

Next we proceeded to Halifax, our last port of call over the other side. By this time we were all a bit tired of our round of entertaining, but we especially enjoyed our visit to the famous Studley Quoit Club, which has a special punch bowl, the recipe of which is only known to a very few people. It tasted delicious, in spite of Halifax being " dry "—which reminds me of the man who was brought before me for being drunk. I asked him how he managed to get drunk in a prohibition town ; his reply was, " Boot polish," and I discovered you could buy solidified alcohol in the form of boot polish. As for the cadets, they spent their last pennies, banking on a fresh supply when they got to Scotland.

On leaving Halifax, we ran into a dense fog which lasted for four days. I maintained a speed of 12 knots. My navigator kept suggesting that I should reduce speed owing to the presence of icebergs, but on thinking the matter over, I decided that if we hit an iceberg at either 8 or 12 knots, we should rip the bottom out, and on the other hand, the high speed ensured our getting out of the fog more quickly. I do not think many of my officers agreed with me, but I still think the decision was the right one.

Incidentally, some months later, the Admiralty questioned me about coming from Halifax to Oban at 12 knots instead of at the economical speed of 10 knots, to which I replied that it was part of the education of the cadets—but the real reason was that I had my parents and my wife waiting for me at Oban, and I wanted to get there as quickly as possible.

On arrival at Oban we were received with cheers from the shore, chiefly, I imagine, from wives and sweethearts. I moored as close to the shore as I could, but when I paid my respects to the Provost of Oban he informed me that I would have to shift berth, as I was in the way of the steamers going to Mull, etc. I pointed out that there was plenty of room for the steamers to get round me, but he insisted on my shifting berth, and I finally replied that if he wished me to shift berth, I would do so, but it would mean taking the ship away from Oban and informing the Admiralty that His Majesty's ships were not welcome there. I further emphasised the fact that Peace Day was approaching, and it might be to the advantage of Oban to have a man-of-war present. This was too much for him, and he withdrew his request.

My first thought on landing was, " Why go to the West Indies, when you can get far more beautiful scenery at home ? " Of course the answer is that travelling broadens a man's mind, and he sees other people and other customs, and although we were at home again, I am sure a good many hearts thought of some pretty face or some pretty tune left behind in the West Indies.

I had my wife and parents at Oban, and was kept busy with a lot of social engagements, as most of my relations come from that part of the world. I think the cadets rather missed their whirl of entertainments, but there was plenty of golf for them, and several friends offered fishing. The men were not forgotten, and several of us got up an outing for the petty officers of the ship to Dunstaffnage Castle, by kind permission of my cousin, who owns the place. We allowed each petty officer to bring a girl with him, and my father, mother, and wife attended. We had the satisfaction of discovering later that my steward, Barnes, who had been with me in two ships already, and who was to follow me again, had popped the question and got engaged to a charming Oban girl—this was done in spite of the fact that the trip was made in the ship's boats and everyone was seasick on the way back.

Several dances were also given for the crew at the Memorial Institute.

The chief event during our visit to Oban was the official celebration of Peace Day. We were very honoured at receiving a message from H.M. the King in reply to one we had sent, and we also exchanged messages with Admiral Jellicoe, who was then in New Zealand, to let him know that, although so far away, he was not forgotten on this day of victory. Oban didn't particularly celebrate it, as they kept all their shops open for the Glasgow folk. We dressed the ship overall, and at noon the Provost and other officials came on board, and after the band had played the National Anthem, a *feu de joie* was fired, followed by a Royal salute of twenty-one guns. In the afternoon the ship was open to visitors, and thousands came on board, and with the band playing, the sailors were not backward in finding partners for a dance.

I went ashore for an hour or so in the evening. When I returned on board and went into my cabin I found it reeking with scent. As I had given strict orders that no one was to be allowed in my cabin without my permission, I sent for my steward to enquire who had been using it. Much to my surprise, he told me the Commander had. It then transpired that just as a small boat with a lady in the stern was coming alongside, a signalman who was standing on the rails round the quarter-deck to put up some decorations for the dance, lost his foothold, turned a somersault and landed in the boat alongside the lady, just as if he had quietly taken his seat there. His calmness, however, was hardly shared by the lady and other visitors in the boat, and the Commander very gallantly went to their rescue and took them to my cabin.

In the evening the officers gave a dance, the chief feature of which was an " eightsome," in which my old Father and Mother took part. The pipes were played by the Pipe Major of the Argyll and Sutherland Highlanders. The ship had been illuminated for the occasion, but at midnight the illuminations were suddenly switched off, while a firework display took place ; it incidentally set the bridge on fire, but that was quickly extinguished. The flag of each ally was hoisted at the masthead with a single searchlight on it, whilst the band played the appropriate anthem, and we finished up with a Royal salute of twenty-one guns, " Auld Lang Syne," and the National Anthem. I was told that the spectacle from the shore was most impressive.

So we came to the end of a memorable day, and when I went ashore with my wife, the strains of a jazz band reached me, so I imagine the officers continued the celebrations well on during the night. Anyhow, they were all up for Church in the morning, when my father read the Lesson, after which the officers invited my father and mother into the Wardroom.

After leaving Oban, to the strains of " Auld Lang

ONE OF THE LAST SNAPS OF MY PARENTS, OBAN, 1924.

Syne," we steamed up to Ballachulish to enable the
cadets to see Glencoe. The following morning I
decided to see what practical knowledge the cadets
had gained, and at the same time to let the sailors see
that the ship could go to sea without them. So at
5 a.m., before the hands had been called, I got under
weigh with the cadets only. One had been detailed
to act as Captain, another as Commander, and so on ;
a party of cadets were assembled on the forecastle to
weigh anchor by themselves, others were in the
chains heaving the lead—in fact, all the essential jobs
except the engine-room were done by the cadets.
When we got to sea, I let go a lifebuoy, and made the
cadets man and lower the life-boat to pick it up. As
it took a hundred men to hoist one of these life-
boats, I called the " hands " to do it, and was amused
to see the look on their faces when they found the
ship had gone to sea without them. It was a good
lesson for all concerned, and I continued to carry out
this practice of making the cadets do the actual work
till the completion of the cruise, as I considered it an
essential part of an officer's training to have practical
knowledge of what takes place when he gives orders
to others. In addition to taking the ship to sea, I
made the cadets carry out target practice with the
twelve-pounder. Each cadet was allowed to fire
five rounds, but this was not quite so successful, as
the target got shot away a good many times, which
caused considerable delay. Other cadets were
observed to shut their eyes and trust to luck when
they fired.

We anchored at Campbelltown and Holyhead on our way south, and eventually fetched up at Plymouth on July 31st, twenty-four weeks after our departure.

The *Cornwall* arrived a few hours after us, having come straight from Newfoundland instead of visiting Scotland as we had done.

We at once went on to Portsmouth, and passed the narrow entrance at exactly eight o'clock, which enabled us to salute with seventeen guns the Flag of Admiral Sir Cecil Burney, which was flying on board the old *Victory;* a fitting finish to a successful cruise, which had been the twelfth the *Cumberland* had carried out as a cadets' training ship. We had steamed in all 13,819 miles.

The cadets still had their examinations to do, a method of testing a boy's ability with which I never have great sympathy. In the meantime we had received orders that the battleship *Temeraire* was to replace the *Cumberland* and *Cornwall*, but luckily we were to go on as a training ship for public school cadets, and so carry out the thirteenth and last sea-going voyage of the *Cumberland*, though, as I will explain in the next chapter, it was not to be a cruise such as we had just had. When the cadets finally left the ship they landed from the quarter-deck, and were fallen in for me to inspect them and wish them good-bye. As they marched past the forecastle, the ship's company, of their own free will, had mustered in force to give them a parting cheer. I think they had appreciated the cadets taking the ship to sea.

On paying off the ship into " nucleus " crew, I went to the Admiralty to report to the Second Sea Lord and to call on the Director of Staff and Training Duties. I was very tickled when he told me that I had overworked the cadets, that my " clock " system in the West Indies was absurd, and that he entirely disagreed with the cadets being made to do seamen's work. I can only conclude this part of my story by saying that, if I had the same job to do again to-morrow, I would not only do the same things, but would try to improve on them, and make the " young gentlemen " do still more of the seamen's work, in order better to fit themselves as officers.

XIII

Public School Cadets

AFTER the cadets had left the ship, we all went on what I considered a well-earned leave, during which I was elected a Younger Brother of Trinity House, one of the oldest corporations in the City. I was very proud of the distinction. I had to attend a court of Elder Brothers, and for the first time in my life took an oath of allegiance to the King, this being one of the rules of Trinity House. Every year on Trinity Monday a Special Court is held, and a Master (for many years H.R.H. the Duke of Connaught) is appointed, and also a Deputy-Master. Both Elder and Younger Brethren then proceed to church, and I think it is about the only time nowadays when they sing the three verses of the National Anthem. After church, a big luncheon takes place at Trinity House, presided over by the Master, and the loving-cup is passed. Nearly all the Brethren, except the honorary ones, such as Baldwin, Churchill, MacDonald, etc., are old sea-dogs, and it is one of the events of the year to which I always look forward.

On returning to the ship, I found the " axe " in full swing, and we had to part with nearly all our ship's company, only maintaining on board the bare necessities for steaming the ship and keeping her more or less clean. It was a great come-down after being such a smart ship. Luckily, I was able to keep my Commander, Goolden, and most of my officers, though some changes had to be made. Just as we were due to leave Portsmouth towards the end of September, the great railway strike took place, and we got immediate orders to sail for Plymouth, calling at Portland with various ratings and stores for the Reserve ships there. When we arrived at Plymouth we found the strike was in full swing, and we were berthed alongside the dockyard ready to take a regiment to Wales if required. In the meantime, the Admiralty had called for volunteers as motor-lorry drivers. The Commander passed the word round, and practically the whole crew volunteered. I thought this showed a good spirit, but I doubted their driving capabilities. On going further into the matter, I discovered that most of them had volunteered out of sheer loyalty and the idea of a stunt. One man, for instance, said he thought he could drive, as he had a brother who could. In the meantime the cadets began to roll up bit by bit ; some came by car, others had got on board a collier in Northumberland, and so on.

I had forty-six cadets in all, and they were known as the Public School, or special entry. Thirty-one of them had already had a short training at Keyham, and the remainder had come direct from public schools. A finer crowd of young fellows one could not wish to meet. Much has been written and many arguments have been stated for and against this form of entry into the Navy. Having had the experience of training both the Dartmouth entry and the Public School entry, I have no hesitation in advocating the latter, and I would extend it further and include the Secondary Schools. Of course, these boys are older, which gives them an advantage, because they know their own minds better and whether they really want to go into the Service or not, whereas a number of Dartmouth boys join because their fathers were in the Navy or because they have been attracted by the brass buttons.

I didn't find a single point on which the Dartmouth production showed any superiority over the Public School, in fact the reverse, and I should like to see Dartmouth closed down or turned into a Public School—as there are many disadvantages to any Government establishment, and the more or less dual control which used to exist at Dartmouth cannot lead to efficiency. It is frequently argued that a boy must be taken young to the Navy, so as to learn its traditions and the power of command, etc. On the former point, I found the Dartmouth boy took all the customs for granted, whereas the Public School boy was for ever asking or delving into the reasons why one saluted the quarter-deck, and so on. As regards power of command, most of the new cadets had either been prefects at school or in the O.T.C., or both, and had great self-confidence. As regards their education, my instructor informed me that the

Public School boy was the better of the two, as he had been less crammed and better educated, and he was readily able to apply his knowledge of mathematics, etc., to any navigational, gunnery, or torpedo problem.

One small point that often comes to my mind is the matter of reading the Lesson on Sunday. Instead of my always reading it, I arranged that each officer should read it in turn, I taking the first turn. Now, I told the Padre to let the cadets take a hand at it, and found they were far less nervous and read far better than the officers. Incidentally, church on board ship used to be compulsory, but in the ships I commanded I made it voluntary for men over twenty-one. Under twenty-one I said it was part of their education. The Padres objected, and said they wouldn't get a congregation, to which I replied that if they had hymns and a sermon that sailors enjoyed, they would get a full house.

When the strike was over, we sailed for Queenstown, where Admiral Sir Reginald Tupper was then Commander-in-Chief. This was the thirteenth time that the ship had sailed as a cadets' training ship from Plymouth, but this time it was not for a cruise, as we proceeded to Queenstown and moored at Number Thirteen buoy, which we swung round for six months —and I am telling the yarn in my thirteenth chapter !

I think these six months were the happiest I spent in the Service. Except for breakfast, I messed in the Wardroom with the other officers ; the cadets were a pleasure to train, the ship's company gave no trouble, and I had practically no defaulters. I had my wife and son in a delightful little house ashore, and many of the officers and men were similarly placed ; yet the *Cumberland* was our home, and I have seldom, if ever, seen so fine a spirit as prevailed from bow to stern. We played games, we danced, we golfed, and we worked in as even proportion as could be arranged. All round us lay Rotten Row, with famous monitors and old cruisers who had done their bit during the War, and were now awaiting the fall of the auctioneer's hammer.

A " Duty Sub " of cadets, who had to remain on board when the others went ashore, was no new idea to the training service—but in our case, owing to having such a small ship's company, they had to do a good deal of ordinary sailors' work. They were entirely responsible for the cleanliness of the quarter-deck, one of the batteries, and two of the cutters, and the work was done both cheerfully and well. I was always proud to have people come on board.

One of the jokes of the ship was my motor-boat, which was always breaking down. I would send for my coxswain and tell him to " call away " my motor-boat. The Commander would hear it, and have his little joke and " call away " the picket-boat ready to tow the Captain.

Queenstown at this time was rather a dangerous place to live in. On one occasion a party of six soldiers were walking down the streets when they were held up by a batch of Sinn Feiners, who dis-

armed them, and shot one dead ; although the
incident took place at midday and was witnessed by
dozens of people, not a soul would give evidence. I
had very little anxiety as to the safety of the cadets,
as they always behaved themselves and were always
very popular, but I was anxious about my little boy
for fear he should be kidnapped. My wife and I in
our small house had two Sinn Fein maids and an
English nurse. The maids were the best I have ever
run across, but we found out, on our return to
England, that they had searched all our gear for
fire-arms, and that the English nurse had been
threatened with punishment should she inform us of
what they had done. Luckily, I never kept any
fire-arms in the house—well, hardly ever, and to
be exact, only once : when having heard that the
Commander-in-Chief was going down to the Naval
Base to witness the embarkation of prisoners, and
having some anxiety about his safety, I took a
revolver ashore with me. I did not tell my wife, but
just laid it under a dirty shirt in the linen basket.
Just as I was getting into bed I heard shots. I at
once jumped up, and much to my wife's surprise
seized the revolver, and rushed out. There was
nothing doing on the naval pier, so I proceeded to
Admiralty House, where I found that a Marine
sentry had let off his rifle by accident. Many
figures were at once seen in the dark, and a regular
round of shots took place.

The old cook in particular was a delightful old
soul, and when I used to put " Rule Britannia" on

the gramophone in the drawing-room, she would put on the kitchen gramophone, " Wrap the green flag round me, boys." I tried to persuade these two maids to come on board the *Cumberland*. One of them eventually did so to help at a dance, but the old cook, in spite of my promise to give her dinner in my cabin, refused to do so unless I hauled down the White Ensign. The Irish are a fine race, and have a great sense of humour. Happening to go into the house one day with my sword on, I asked the cook if she thought the Sinn Feiners would try and take it away, to which she replied : " No, begorra, it isn't sharp enough for our purpose."

Another time, a lot of recruiting posters had been put up in the railway station, " Join the Army and see the world." The following morning they had put up a new set of posters, " Join the R.I.C. and see the next world."

When the time came for us to leave Queenstown, both maids gave us a tremendous send-off, and both asked if they could come to England with us.

One of our frequent visitors at Queenstown was Miss Fitzgerald, who was a great character and, I believe, a Sinn Feiner. She had a way all her own, and generally dressed rather shabbily. She would come into the drawing-room and promptly take off her shoes and sit beside the fire. She promised to give my boy a Sinn Fein flag to hoist in the garden. So I sent him round with a message the next day to ask for the flag and to say, " Father is waiting for something to light the fire with."

In the unfortunate state of Ireland at that time, the Navy as a whole was looked on as a friendly neutral, while the Military, and R.I.C., not to mention the Black and Tans, were regarded as fair sport. I naturally did everything I could to ensure that the ship was kept outside of any of the unrest ashore, and when the Commander-in-Chief suggested that I should take a large party of prisoners to Milford Haven, I was obliged to protest strongly, as I would no longer have been in a position to hold myself responsible for the safety of the cadets. He agreed with my point of view, and other arrangements were made.

Football at Queenstown was rather a difficulty, as the number of schools we could play at Cork was very limited, and other teams used to go in for a good deal of " fouling." I generally used to get a priest or Padre to referee. I remember on one occasion attending a match at Cork where the " fouling " was really dreadful ; as was to be expected, the cadets behaved like gentlemen and didn't retaliate. Many of the opposing team were ordered off the field. After the match the Captain of our opponents came up to me and asked if he might be allowed to congratulate the cadets on their clean play. He said, " We fouled as much as we could and tried to make them lose their tempers, but there was nothing doing." Eventually Rugby became impossible, since it got more or less banned, as being an English game. We had a good many Soccer matches on our own ground, playing eight-aside for fifteen minutes each way. I had never played Soccer before in my life, but I was made to turn out and enjoyed many a good game—after my first experience, which was not much of a success. I had had a luncheon-party before the match, and someone had suggested a glass of port to give me Dutch courage. I took it, and about half an hour later, when I came to take my first " header," I thought all the stars in heaven had fallen on me !

We also had friendly matches between the cadets and ship's company, officers and ship's company, and so on. The ship's company also went in for and won the League Football Competition with the other ships in harbour.

We had, to a great extent, to make our own amusements. We invested in a cinema, and with the aid of the local people, we got films twice a week, Friday for the ship's company and Saturday for the cadets. We had a real thriller in the form of a serial. The cadets at one time thought they were treated too much like children, as I only gave them leave till 10 p.m. once a week to dine with friends, but when the serial started it was the other way round, and the cadet Lieutenants, Spreckley, de Pass, and Alcock, would come to inform me that Cadet So-and-so wanted to know if it would be all right for him to get out of dining with some big bug.

I was very keen for the cadets to attend lectures and debates, and to read and write essays, so as to broaden their minds as far as possible. The lectures, a good many given by people outside the ship, covered a wide range of subjects, and we had no less than sixty-eight of them. I could never get official recognition from the Admiralty for this form of education, but as they were all done out of working hours, it didn't particularly matter. I used occasionally to get the cadets to lecture if they had studied some special subject at school. I remember the first one who attempted it gave a lecture on the Peloponnesian War. As I had spent so short a time at school, I had never even heard of such a war. The cadet, Hilken, gave an excellent lecture, with maps to illustrate the battles and so on, but every now and then he would say, " Now that happened in the year 440. Two years later, in 438, so and so happened." After the lecture I sent for him in my cabin and congratulated him on his success and added :

" I am afraid you got a bit nervous and mixed up in your dates."

He said : " No, sir, it all happened before Christ."

Paper chases were other forms of recreation we used to go in for, and on one occasion I arranged for the chase to end at our house, where tea was waiting. My wife had laid out a huge spread, starting off with two sausage rolls each, but by the time they had finished there was one sandwich left on the table for politeness.

When the cadets went on Christmas leave, the ship was placed out of the way in the Basin, with only the Chief Gunner and four men on board. The Gunner felt his responsibility very heavy, as he was

frightened lest the ship might be captured by Sinn
Feiners. The Gunner's nickname was Von Tirpitz,
as he had side whiskers and looked rather like him.
One afternoon I met the Gunner ashore with his
wife, who had just arrived, so my wife and I crossed
the road to introduce ourselves, and I attempted to
make pleasant conversation, without much success.
On leaving them, I remarked to my wife :

" What a shy woman."

My wife replied : " I am not surprised, seeing
that you said, ' How do you do, Mrs. Von Tirpitz.' "

It was about this time that I was invited to dis-
tribute prizes at a school in Cork. I was advised
by the police not to go for fear of Sinn Feiners. I
insisted not only on going but on going in uniform,
and got what might be called a " popular reception."
The subject of my speech was " Loyalty to King and
Country," etc. etc. It not only went down very
well, but the following day the whole proceedings
and my speech were reported verbatim in even the
extremist papers—in fact, they had a leading article
about me, in which they accused me of being a
gentleman, and referred to my visit to France during
the War and the remark I had made about the V.C.

During the Christmas leave, I went to dine one
night with Colonel Hart in the Sherwood Foresters'
Mess, which was situated on the top of the hill, and
to get to it, I had to walk through a bit of a wood.
It was very dark, and as I was going through I suddenly heard a " Halt, who goes there ? " Luckily
I stopped at once and replied, " Friend," and found

myself surrounded by bayonets all about an inch off my tummy. At first I thought I had fallen into the hands of the Sinn Feiners till I heard some laughter, and then I realised it was a put-up job by Hart and his officers, who wanted to see what a so-called gallant naval officer would do under the circumstances.

When the cadets returned from leave, they paid myself and the officers the biggest compliment I have ever had by saying the leave had been too long, and they were aching to get back. Half our term had already passed, and the examinations were looming ahead, but they didn't worry much, except that the " axe " was already at work, and there were rumours that some of the cadets would have to leave the Service.

Persistent rumours of this sort have adversely affected all ranks of the Service ever since the War. Why not have a policy and stick to it ? As far as the examinations were concerned, I had arranged, in order to reduce cramming to a minimum, that throughout the term spasmodic examinations would take place, for which marks were awarded which counted in the finals. A Lieutenant would walk into the classroom and write a few questions on the board, the answers to which would be marked. This method had also the effect of enabling us to watch the progress of each cadet. Amongst other things, it was in my hands to award up to (I think) a hundred marks for officer-like qualities. Instead of doing it entirely on my own judgment, I got each

officer in the ship, including the Paymaster, Chaplain, and so on, to give me their confidential marks,
as we had all worked so much together that I thought
that each officer might have seen a cadet in a different
light.   It was extraordinary how in some cases the
marks would vary as much as 50 per cent.

Towards the end of our time, we had to put the
old ship into dock and prepare her for the sale list.
About this time, Easter Sunday came along with
rumours of another rebellion, and we had to arrange
to embark loyal subjects, if necessary, but the only
event that occurred was the appearance of a Sinn
Fein flag flying at the top of the flagstaff on Admiralty
Pier.   After some discussion it was decided that a
party of sailors should haul it down, but when they
got there they found that the flagstaff had been
greased and the flag had been nailed to the masthead,
so it remained flying for some time.

We had a good finish up to what had been a splendid time.   The climax came when the Wardroom
Officers gave a big farewell dinner to my wife and
myself, the Warrant Officers, and cadets.   We sat
down a big family party of sixty-six.   The speeches
were brief ; all I had to say was how intensely proud
I was of my ship, officers, cadets and men ; that
nothing was so good that it could not be improved ;
that our success during the term was not one man's
work but the splendid co-operation of every man and
lad who had put the Service before all else.   After
dinner a special movie show had been arranged,
with topical advertisements, etc. ; this was followed

by dancing to the jazz band, of which my great friend, Lieutenant Eric Brand, was the leading spirit. Unfortunately, one of the tunes played was the Marseillaise, the strains of which were wafted across the water to Admiralty House, so that the Commander-in-Chief thought a rebellion had broken out, till he was reassured that it was only the *Cumberland's* last night. What pleased me particularly that night was to see the Cadet Gunner, Mr. F. L. Maunder, enter most thoroughly into the show and, as is sometimes said, " let himself go." He was a Warrant Officer who had served with me twice before in destroyers, and I had selected him for the *Cumberland*. He had served through both commissions in the most difficult job of the whole lot, in charge of what one might call the domestic life of the cadets, a job requiring much patience and tact, and he had carried it through not only with efficiency, but in a way that made him loved by all the cadets.

At midnight we came to the end of not only a perfect day, but also of a perfect commission. Officers of all ranks held hands round the quarter-deck for " Auld Lang Syne," and then the National Anthem.

XIV

H.M.S. *Impregnable*

AFTER leaving the *Cumberland*, I was appointed to the War Course at Greenwich, and whilst there, much to my surprise, I was offered the command of H.M.S. *Impregnable*, the Boys' Training Establishment at Plymouth. It had always been one of my ambitions to command her, but I didn't think I was in the running.

On joining, I relieved Rear-Admiral Laurence Oliphant, who had been my Captain in the ship when I was there as Lieutenant. My Commander (Captain G. W. Taylor) had also served with me in training ships before. When Taylor was promoted, I was intensely flattered on receiving a letter from Commander R. N. Suter, asking if he could come as my Commander. I thought it exceedingly nice of him, as in the old *Impregnable* I had served under his orders, and I was very glad that I was able to get him.

The *Impregnable* training establishment, although still bearing the same name, had changed since I was there before. It was now composed of the old cruisers *Andromeda* and *Powerful* (of Ladysmith fame), joined together in line ahead, and joined alongside the *Powerful* was the *Black Prince*, which I have referred to in a previous chapter. We had about 1,600 boys, and with the staff and ship's company, we mustered over 3,000. A big command, but one of intense interest.

Previous to joining the *Impregnable* as Captain, with the knowledge that I was going to serve under my old friend Admiral Sir Montague Browning, and also knowing him to be a great authority on regulations, I took the trouble to get a copy of the Training Services Regulations and read them up beforehand. I found in them, in the chapter headed " Seamanship," the fact that the Captain was expected to live on board with his family, subject to the approval of the Commander-in-Chief. So on reporting myself after taking over command, I asked permission to allow my wife to live on board, as she had already joined the ship with me the night before when we stayed with the Oliphants. The Commander-in-Chief was somewhat taken aback, as he was not aware of the regulation, and told me I must put my request in writing. I informed him that my wife was already on board, so he said that she could continue on board provisionally. A few days later, however, he returned my call, and I introduced him to my wife. That night I got approval to have my family on board. I believe he wrote to the Admiralty, and said that he had given me permission to use the married quarters on board, but could not understand what relation there was between the Captain having his wife on board and " seamanship."

Our married quarters were very spacious, and

were situated in the stern of the *Andromeda*. I was
about the seventh Captain to live on board, and each
one had done something to improve the accommodation, with the result that, in addition to the whole
of the Captain's quarters and the Warrant Officers'
mess, we had two bathrooms and eight cabins. My
steward, Barnes, came with me from the *Cumberland*, and he ran the whole show in tip-top fashion.
The only difficulty we had was with the nurse. She
used to go ashore once a week and come off on the
late boat. She was allowed, by the courtesy of the
officers, to sit on the stern-sheets ; but my coxswain, who acted as a chaperon, thought he could
do the same thing, to which the officers naturally
objected, and this was privately conveyed to me by
the Commander, so it had to be stopped.

My daughter was born on board during the time I
commanded the ship. She selected 9 a.m. on a
Sunday morning for her debut, which was a very
awkward hour. The nurse who attended the
" launch " rather alarmed me on the same afternoon, when she came to me and said that, according
to the rules of her Association, she must go ashore for
two hours. I strongly protested, as I did not relish
the idea of being left alone with my wife and a baby
a few hours old, but the nurse insisted, so I told her
she could go if she swam ashore, in the meantime
giving strict orders that she was not to have a boat,
which gave me the winning card. My daughter,
Flora, was duly christened on board in the presence
of the boys and with the band playing.

On my taking over command of the *Impregnable*, the Commander-in-Chief complained that boys frequently passed him in the streets without saluting. I pointed out that boys often did not salute either the Commander or myself, because they generally saw us in uniform in an official capacity, and were so glad to get out of our presence, that they did not recognise us in plain clothes. Anyhow, I took the precaution of telling the Commander to warn all the boys that, if they saw a very handsome and distinguished-looking man with one arm walking in the Cornish lanes, they were to salute him ! In the meantime the Commander-in-Chief said he would come on board and make all the boys march past him. I was, of course, very honoured, but I pointed out that they wouldn't recognise him any better, as, if he came on board at 9.30, I would warn the Commander to have everything ready at 9.25 ; he would tell the Lieutenants to be ready at 9.15 ; they would tell the Instructors to be ready at 9 ; and for half an hour, these young boys would be practising " on " and " off " caps, and having it thoroughly rubbed into them that the Commander-in-Chief ranked next to God Almighty, so that by the time they got past him without being smitten dead or some such fate, they would be thankful the show was over, and simply have in their minds a lot of brass hats and gold lace. However, the march past turned out a great success for all that, and the Commander-in-Chief not only expressed his approval, but said he would stay to Church. I did what was a risky thing, as I tried to pull the Commander-in-Chief's leg. I suggested he should read the Lesson " in order to give the boys time to have a good look at him." He turned round at me, gave me one hard stare and said :

" The proper person to read the Lesson on board is the Captain."

David, my son, thoroughly enjoyed living on board. He was then about seven or eight years old, and was dressed up in uniform, the same as the other boys. I used to make him march past me every Sunday morning and salute, just like the remainder. On one occasion he remarked to his mother that he thought it was time the Captain got a new frock coat, as it was looking more shabby than any of the other officers' coats. After he had been on board for three months, I had him brought up with a party of other boys to my office to be awarded a Good Conduct Badge. He was, of course, kept waiting outside my office about half an hour, and when he eventually came in, he was very scared, as I treated him exactly like an ordinary boy and not as my son.

I said : " Have you been a good boy ? "

He said : " Yes, sir."

I said : " Can you swim ? "

And he said : " Not quite, sir."

So I said : " Here is a Good Conduct Badge for you, and take care you are a good boy, otherwise you will lose it, and when you can swim, you can come and ask the Captain for another badge."

That day at lunch, he was wearing his gold Good Conduct Badge and was obviously very proud of it.

I think he found it rather a nuisance on the whole, as every time he did anything wrong, his mother would say, " If you aren't careful, you will be sent up to the Captain, and you will lose your Good Conduct Badge."

It was very extraordinary the way he would know when to call me " Captain " and when to call me " Father." Sometimes I would say to him :

" Telephone through to the Officer of the Watch and tell him I am going ashore at such and such a time."

He would telephone through and say : " The Captain wants his boat at such and such a time."

On another occasion my wife would suggest asking one of the officers in for bridge or something of that sort, and David would telephone and say :

" Father wants to know if you will come along and join him and Mother at a game of bridge."

In due course he came up for his second Good Conduct Badge in a proper service manner, and having satisfied myself that he could swim the width of the bath, I awarded it to him. At lunch time he was wearing both his badges, and I remarked :

" I see the Captain has given you another Good Conduct Badge."

And he said : " Yes, Father."

I said : " Well, what sort of a mood was the Captain in to-day ? "

And he said : " Not very good, but not half so bad as he was the last time."

The education of the boys was one of the first

things I looked into, and was astounded to find the advance which had been made in what might be called the *x* side of the education. It is all very well for a number of boys to be specially selected to go on for higher technical education, but there will always be required the man behind the gun who does not need to know the fourth dimension or things of that sort. I was continually protesting against some of the examination papers set, including the General Knowledge papers, as they were far stiffer than anything I had ever had to pass myself, and I very much doubt if half the masters could have answered some of the conundrums themselves. I considered that the boys who had moved into what was called the Advance Class, i.e. higher education, should have been removed to a separate establishment, similar to Greenwich College, because, human nature being what it is, they didn't like staying behind in the training ship with all its training-ship regulations and limited freedom, when they saw other boys, who had joined at the same time as they had, swanking about with *H.M.S. Nelson* on their cap ribbons and more attractive to the girls than the boys who still had on theirs, *H.M.S. Impregnable*, well known as a training ship.

The Director of Naval Education, Mr. McMullen, came down, and we discussed the whole field of training. I found we had a good deal of agreement, but I am afraid his authority was rather too limited. I should have liked to have seen a body of Public and Secondary Headmasters set up thoroughly to overhaul the educational system. Naturally they would have taken the advice of naval officers as to special requirements.

The next thing I turned my attention to was punishments. When I saw my first defaulters, I rather shocked the Commander when I did not stop any of the boys' pocket-money, which was one of the routine punishments allowed by the Admiralty—but my experience as a Lieutenant in the *Impregnable* had taught me that this was a very poor form of punishment, because, in the first place, the pocket-money paid to boys was deducted out of their Service pay, and the balance was refunded when they were drafted to sea. In consequence, the boy who had had a lot of pocket-money stopped went to sea with a far bigger balance than the boy who had drawn his pocket-money regularly. In addition to this, I discovered that when a boy got his pocket-money stopped, it frequently happened that his mess-mates, out of sympathy for him, each subscribed 1*d.*, so that he might very well get more than his 6*d*. It was very rarely, therefore, that I stopped a boy's pocket-money, unless the regulations made it absolutely obligatory.

The best, and to my mind the most suitable, punishment for a boy is to cane him. It is quickly over, it does not stop his recreation, and if it hurts him sufficiently at the time, he does not want to have it again. I always had boys examined medically before being caned, and the caning was done in the presence of a medical officer and in private, as I do not believe in public caning. The rules about caning boys were very ridiculous. One was only officially allowed to cane them for certain offences, such as wilful disobedience of orders. It has always been a custom to cane boys who have been bowled out smoking, but when I sent in my first punishment return to the Admiralty, containing several charges against boys for smoking, I got it back to say that caning was not allowed for this offence; and thereafter, when I found it necessary to cane a boy, I had to word the offence so as to cover the regulations.

On one occasion a boy was had up for calling his instructor an insulting name, for which I gave him twelve cuts. The charge against him was for using insulting language against a superior officer. It came back from the Admiralty, " Caning not allowed for this offence." On the same day Admiral the Hon. Sir Victor Stanley came down for one of his routine inspections, and I asked him what he would do to a boy who called his instructor " a silly old fool." He replied, " I would give him twelve of the best." I said, " That's exactly what I did, and here is your reply." Apparently the matter had been dealt with by some civilian.

On another occasion when Admiral Stanley (commanding the training service) was inspecting the ship, I, in accordance with naval custom, " piped " for any boy wishing to see the Admiral to fall in outside the Captain's office. It was very unusual for anybody to make use of this privilege, and I was rather taken aback when it was reported that a boy wished to see the Admiral. I wondered what on earth his grievance could be—anyhow, he had the right to see the Admiral over my head and was brought in. The Admiral said, " Well, what is it, my boy ? " to which the reply was, " Please, sir, may I have your autograph ? "

In addition to smoking offences, the most frequent cause of canings I had to give was breaking into orchards and stealing apples on a Saturday or Sunday afternoon. Generally on a Monday morning I would have complaints from the local farmers ; my reply to which was to suggest that a shot-gun was a very good preventive for having apples stolen. And to the boy I awarded six cuts with the cane, not for pinching the apples, which I had frequently done myself as a boy, but, as I used to tell them, for being such silly young fellows as to be bowled out.

But smoking was the most frequent offence, and naturally so. The regulations stated that boys were not allowed to smoke till they reached the age of eighteen. The boys used to join at the age of sixteen, and I asked each one whether he was in the habit of smoking. About 90 per cent. replied " Yes," and of these about 40 per cent. said they did it with their parents' consent. By law (civilian), a boy is allowed to buy cigarettes and therefore smoke at the age of sixteen. I am not suggesting that we probably wouldn't all be better if none of us smoked till we were twenty-one ; but I did object to giving an order which I couldn't enforce, and which led to a lot of other misdeeds, such as smuggling and bribery. There was no limit to the methods the boys would employ to smuggle cigarettes on board ; sometimes they would arrive in dummy books or even bananas. They would, of course, conceal them if they could on their persons, even inside their socks.

I remember one little boy, about five feet in height, asking to see the Captain about two days after he had joined because, as he said, " he was fed up with the Navy and missed his —— smoke." I did my utmost to get the regulation altered, so as to allow of smoking at the age of sixteen at certain regular hours. This would have controlled the situation ; but the proposal met with a blank refusal.

The nearest I came to stopping smoking was by stopping a day's privilege leave for the whole division to which an offender belonged, so that he got not only a caning from me, but a rough time from his messmates ; but apart from that, most of the boys had a sense of playing the game, and didn't want to let their division down. It was often very difficult to catch the boys actually smoking, even if you saw a cloud of smoke, as they had a very good spy system, and if anyone approached used to shout out " Lobbo "—a contraction, apparently, for " Look out, boys, blooming officer." Another trick they had was to share one cigarette between six of them, passing it round from mouth to mouth for a puff, so that if bowled out, only one boy would be caught in possession.

The whole of the 1,600 boys were divided into divisions called after the names of great sailors, Nelson, Drake, etc. Each division had its own tune, which was played when they marched round me on Sunday or when they won some competition.

The divisional system led to good esprit de corps, and a divisional competition was held in nearly everything we could think of. In addition to cricket and football and such-like games, cleanliness of mess-decks and kits was included. Two friends of mine, Mr. Page and his brother, presented a beautiful challenge shield. The great event in the divisional sports was the tug-of-war, with a hundred boys a side, and the Commander-in-Chief kindly presented a very handsome challenge cup for this event.

We had an unhappy tragedy over the swimming test. One afternoon a boy suddenly went under, and in spite of the fact that several people dived in after him, he was not saved, and we had to send a diver down to recover his body. As a result of the Enquiry which was held, orders were given that in future boys were to pass the test with a life-line round their bodies.

We had the usual number of epidemics, the worst one being that of diphtheria, when we lost a number of boys. For a long time the medical authorities couldn't locate the source of infection, until one day I happened to be walking along the main deck of the *Black Prince* and noticed a very unpleasant smell. Some dockyard workmen were repairing the deck, and had one of the planks up, and the smell was coming from underneath ; apparently the many tons of water which must have been poured on the decks during her long life had worked under the wood and caused rot.   A sample was at once sent to the expert and declared to contain diphtheria germs. The Commander-in-Chief sent for me and ordered me to arrange for the 600 boys who were accommodated in the *Black Prince* to be housed elsewhere within twenty-four hours.   This was a big undertaking.   I thought of all the buildings in Devonport, but could not think of a suitable place.   As the weather was fine and summer was at hand, I decided to establish a camp ashore close to the ship, and, thanks to the help of the Army Service Corps and my own Marines, we had the camp rigged and occupied in the specified time.   I had commandeered some of the gunnery school buildings for cooking purposes, etc.   We were very proud of this evolution, and when the Commander-in-Chief came to inspect the camp we were hoping for a pat on the back, but all we got was that " some of the boys looked untidy."

The Commander-in-Chief took a great interest in the ship in many ways, and we always looked forward to seeing him in the field either officially or unofficially.   One day he came to inspect the battalion under arms, for a march past, etc.   It was a terribly hot day and, of course, the boys had to be landed about an hour before the Commander-in-Chief arrived. Admiral Browning expressed his great pleasure at the inspection, and commented on his surprise that no boys had fallen out in spite of the overpowering heat. I was also surprised at this, and when I returned on board, I sent for my Gunnery Lieutenant Denton, to pass on the Commander-in-Chief's congratulations, especially the part about nobody falling out. I then discovered the truth, namely, that about fifty boys *had* fallen out, but Denton, with good foresight, had taken fifty spare boys ashore for such an eventuality, and as each boy fell down with the heat, he was replaced by one of the spare boys.

The camp was a great success, and luckily we were favoured with a good summer, so the boys rapidly improved in health. I was able to obtain an extra week's holiday in the summer in order thoroughly to fumigate the *Andromeda* and *Powerful*, so as to ensure no recurrence of diphtheria. I hope it (the extra leave) has become a permanency, as the leave in the *Impregnable* used to be very meagre, namely, ten days at Christmas and Easter, and three weeks in the summer. Although with the unsatisfactory system of recruiting, it is quite possible that the boys might not have got stale or deserved long leave, yet the officers and instructors were, in my opinion, entitled to as long a leave as is given at Dartmouth or in the Public Schools, because nothing is more wearying than continually instructing boys, especially in a training ship like the *Impregnable*, where not only do the normal instruction hours have to be worked, but there is a lot to be done in the evening in superintending, even the boys turning into their hammocks. This is especially applicable to the Petty Officers compared with those in barracks. One day, no doubt, the training of the Navy will be put on a more satisfactory basis, and be more in keeping with modern requirements and times.

The boys used to join haphazard ; one day perhaps three would join, and another day twenty, according to how the Admiralty wanted recruits. During the many years I served in the Training Service, I never discovered what the Admiralty's policy as regards recruiting was, as it appeared to change from day to day—which not only was detrimental to the boys' training, but added to the difficulties of running a training ship. The proper system would appear to be to have entries similar to schools, i.e. three times a year.

During the great coal strike of 1921, I used to get quite a number of recruits from the coal-mines. They apparently joined for much the same reason as other boys, though I saw a special danger, not only from the fact that some of them had been earning considerably more than 1s. a day, but also because, as I grasped at my first interview, some of them had Communistic tendencies. Although they showed the same pride in their uniform and discipline as the other boys, I scented a certain amount of danger for the future, and pointed it out to higher authority.

The day after each boy joined, he was brought up before me to sign his agreement to serve for twelve years after the age of eighteen. The Admiralty, having spent a certain amount of money in the expense of recruiting and getting the boys on board, fed, and kitted up, did not like it if a boy changed his mind.

I remember one boy in particular being brought up before me at nine o'clock in the morning to sign his agreement, and all he could do was to howl and say he wished to go back to his mother. I pointed out all the benefits of the Service, but this was of no avail. I asked him if he had had a good supper and breakfast, whether he had slept well, and sounded him as to whether, by any chance, he had been bullied, but he had no complaints on any of those scores, so forming a conclusion that he was home-sick, I told him I would leave him till the following day. In the meantime I sent for the Padre and the Lieutenant in charge of new entries, and told them to take a particular interest in the boy, and to make sure he was well looked after, and made as happy as possible. I saw him the following day with the same result, that he could do nothing but cry and say he wanted to go home to his mother. I then adopted the other tack, and proceeded to let fly at him myself, telling him that at his age he ought to be ashamed of himself, crying like a child, and that he was of no use to anybody and so on and so forth. On the third day I again saw him, still in tears, and still wanting to go home to his mother.

I said : " All right, the Navy has no use for you, and you can go home to your mother, but you will regret it one day, because, in a few years' time, the boys of your age will be swanking down the streets of Tokio with a Japanese girl on each arm and not wanting to change places with the King of England."

This did the trick, and he at once said : " All right, sir, I will sign on."

Early in June I kept on pointing out that it would be inadvisable to continue the camp after the summer as the young boys would suffer in health during the winter months. I had already pointed out from the start that the camp could only be looked upon as a temporary arrangement. The *Black Prince*, much to my regret, was definitely condemned. I had suggested re-decking her, as otherwise she was an ideal training ship. The summer came to an end, and still the Admiralty had reached no decision as to what ship should take the place of the *Black Prince*. Being a matter of training of personnel, I suppose it was side-tracked for gunnery or some other matériel. The net result was that a large number of boys never completed their proper training, and were sent to a reserve ship, in my opinion a most unsatisfactory arrangement.

I was ordered down to Chatham in order to look over the famous battle cruiser *Inflexible*. I took my medical officer with me, and we both agreed that she was totally unsuited for a training ship, unless a very large sum of money were expended. Her decks were low, giving very little head room, and the ventilation was bad—not necessarily for able-bodied men, but certainly for young boys. But the Admiralty thought otherwise, and so the ship was taken out of the scrap-heap at Chatham, manned with a crew, and steamed round to Devonport to be fitted out. I entered a final and rather strong protest and the Commander-in-Chief came on board to inspect the ship, with the result that, within an hour, all work was stopped, and the vessel was paid off and returned to the scrap-heap. What this little adventure had cost the Admiralty, or I should say the country, I don't know. Eventually the *Colossus* and *Collingwood* were fitted out as training ships, and they lay for a short period at Portland as an independent command, under Admiral Collard. I had the pleasure of assisting him to some slight extent in fitting out the ships, and giving him the routine. I found him a most genial man to work with, and formed a great admiration for him.

During my command, I received many visits from distinguished people, who gave up their time to entertain the boys. Amongst the many I remember was Sir Harry Lauder, whom I had invited to tea with me, but who told me that he would be unable to give the boys any songs. It leaked out to the boys that he was visiting the ship, and I knew their disappointment would be terrible if they did not see the famous man. After tea, I arranged for all the boys to be assembled in the recreation room while Harry Lauder was yarning with me on my stern walk. He was telling me how the rhythm of all his songs came to him when he was a boy in sailing-vessels off Glasgow, and that even now the rolling of a ship gave him inspiration, and he started humming

15

to me several of his tunes. I asked him if he realised that there were 1,600 boys on deck who would simply love to hear him doing what he was doing for me, so he agreed to come up. The band, by pre-arrangement, was playing Harry Lauder's tunes, which I think pleased him very much, and he eventually got up and entertained the boys for half an hour, and he finished up by telling them that he hoped that, when they got into their hammocks between their white sheets and put their heads on their little white pillows, they would feel they had come to the end of a perfect day. On walking back with him, I told him the boys had been very tickled at his last yarn, as they neither slept between sheets nor had white pillows. He said :

" I know they don't, and that is why I always tell that yarn when I go aboard a ship."

Another well-known star to visit us was Arthur Prince, who had been in the R.N.V.R. during the Great War, and he brought his dummy, Jim, with him, wearing his medals as they had apparently performed in France.

Another kindness that I shall never forget was the visit of the late Sir Ernest Shackleton. He came into Plymouth for a few hours on his last voyage, and though very rushed for time, he came at my invitation to address the boys for twenty minutes, and made one of the most brilliant speeches on discipline and unselfishness that I have ever heard. As he left in the steamboat, in addition to the three usual cheers, I told the boys they could give as many as they liked, and they cheered him till he was out of sight.

That night my wife and I were invited to a farewell party to Shackleton and the officers of the *Quest*. He looked tired and ill, and when I wished him good-bye, I said :

" I wish, sir, I had half the guts that you have," and on going home with my wife, I said to her, " I feel that brave fellow will never return."

I frequently used to call on General Sir Reginald Pole-Carew and Lady Beatrice and her daughters. On one occasion, I gave a tea-party in her honour, and we had shrimps and spring onions for tea. I had these because somebody bet that I would not, but the tea-party went off very successfully, as I took the precaution of supplying finger bowls.

On another occasion Lady Beatrice honoured us by coming to a concert party with her daughters. They were all very young, and we had some artists from the local Hippodrome. One of them started by singing a rather shady song, which tickled us no end, and was encored over and over again. It got worse and worse, until eventually I had to stop it. In the meantime, I had apologised to Lady Pole-Carew for what had happened, but she said the only part that worried her was to see her daughters laughing so much.

In another concert party, we had on board a fair but rather stout damsel dressed up in sailor rig. The boys took a dislike to her, and I must admit her voice was not very attractive. Each time she started

to open her mouth, the boys fairly howled her down
—" gave her the bird " is, I believe, the correct expression. But she stuck to it and continued her
song throughout the uproar. After the concert
party had left the gymnasium (where our concerts
were held), I addressed the boys and reprimanded
them for their disgraceful behaviour, and I told them
that if they did such a thing again, I wouldn't get
any more concert parties for them. Having finished
my harangue, I went to join the concert party, who
were having supper, with the intention of offering
my apologies to the good lady concerned. Before I
could begin, she turned on me with : " What
delightful boys you have ! I have never had such a
wonderful reception and so much applause in all my
life ; I could have gone on amusing them for
hours ! ! "

In addition to our concert parties, I continued my
Cumberland scheme of having a series of short
lectures. The one that I think impressed the boys
most was given by Dr. Burnett Rae, of Harley Street,
on " Auto-suggestion."

One of the great days of the year for the boys was
the King's Birthday, as they used to have a whole
holiday, and were either taken up the river for a
picnic, or, if the weather was wet, they went to some
cinema show. I often used to feel that they should
be kept on board to celebrate the King's Birthday in
appropriate ceremonial fashion ; but, on the other
hand, I wanted it to be a day they would remember,
and a day away from the ship, when I rather think

the officers and instructors had blind eyes as far as smoking was concerned, left the greatest impression on their minds.

And as far as ceremony was concerned, I used to carry out a good deal of it. They had an especially good opportunity of letting their cheers be heard when the *Renown*, with H.R.H. the Prince of Wales on board, passed close to the ship on completion of his world tour. The guard and band were paraded, and the boys gave such cheers as I had never heard ; and we had to do things properly, as we flew the flag of the Commander-in-Chief and had to fire all the salutes on his behalf.

About the time of our regatta and that of the local one as well, the old *Impregnable*, one of the last of the old three-deckers, was to be towed out of harbour to the ship-breakers. I had a lucky idea for celebrating the departure of an old ship that had been as well known in Plymouth as the *Victory* at Portsmouth. I sent for the boatswain, and told him I wanted one of our " pinnaces " fitted out as an exact model of the old *Impregnable*, and to have her ready in ten days. He said it was impossible, but I reminded him of all the old pensioners we had on board who had not only served in the old ship, but also in sail. A beautiful model was soon rigged up, all done to scale. We borrowed two guns from the Yacht Club, and as the old *Impregnable* left the harbour, our model was towed towards her with a farewell signal flying, and with David at the helm. A salute of twenty-one guns was fired, whilst the boys on board the *Powerful* cheered ship and the band played " Auld Lang Syne." After this ceremony, I sent the model into the local regatta at Torpoint and " bombarded " the town. It created a great amount of enthusiasm amongst the older folk especially. I got permission from the Commander-in-Chief to keep the model rigged as a permanent model for the boys, to show what the old ships of the line looked like ; I had a certain amount of difficulty in getting this approval, as only just previously I had written saying how short I was of pinnaces, and here I was asking for a pinnace to be permanently demobilised from active service.

Owing to the haste with which the model had been fitted out, we had only been able to fit dummy sails on board. This was remedied by my successor, who had proper sails fitted, and at a later date, I had the pleasure of a sail in her with the then Captain, T. J. Lyne—and not only did I have a sail, but I was received on board with a boatswain's pipe, and the Captain ordered the main brace to be spliced.

Ever since the War I had continued to suffer from insomnia, which became worse and worse, and during the summer of 1921 I was suffering very badly and my nerves were on edge—no one can understand the complaint unless they have experienced it. Finally I had more or less to give in and get medical assistance, and arrangements were made for me to have six weeks' leave. Nobody could have been kinder and more sympathetic to me than the Commander-in-Chief in whom I was able to confide completely : I was indeed fortunate in serving under such a sympathetic and understanding man.

The way in which I was eventually placed on the sick list was rather curious. I had had a particularly restless night, being unable to place my head on the pillow without thoughts of getting torpedoed. My wife sent for the doctor about 6 a.m., and he injected some stuff which sent me off to sleep. I awoke about 10 a.m., very annoyed at not having been called and having missed prayers, which I regularly attended, but I found, on sending for the signal book, that the Commander had made a signal to say that I had been placed on the sick list suffering from insomnia. As I was fast asleep when the signal was made, my sense of humour took the place of my annoyance.

On returning from leave, I wasn't a great deal better, and offered to give up my command, but I was persuaded to stay on and leave more of the work to the Commander—very sound and correct advice, but very hard to follow, as I found myself sitting up halfway through the night thinking out all kinds of rubbishy details which were really the job of other people than the Captain. It is a form of illness in which you get very little sympathy, as you may look reasonably well ; you become a nuisance to yourself and to everybody else, you become intensely shy and self-conscious ; but in spite of all that, I am glad I went through it, as it has made me understand, from first-hand experience, some of the terrors that ex-Service men, who had shell shock or were torpedoed during the War, are going through at the present time without being " understood " and without the advantage that I had of the best medical attention available in the country. I have more sympathy for the man who lost his nerves during the War than for the man who lost his leg.

I stuck it out as long as I could, much longer than I could have done but for my Commander-in-Chief and Surgeon-Rear-Admiral Sir Daniel McNabb of the hospital. But eventually, at the beginning of the summer leave, I asked to be relieved of my command, and applied for three months' sick leave.

It was a bitter disappointment to have to give up my command, especially as I had attained one of my ambitions, but I thought it the only fair thing to do.

The Commander-in-Chief gave me a most cordial good-bye, and commended me on the fine spirit of the ship. He said I had made a mistake in not joining the Royal Yacht Club of Plymouth, to which all the other Captains in the port belonged, but my reason for not having done so was a feeling that I was by age completely out of my seniority, and I did not wish to swank.

I eventually turned over my command to Rear-Admiral Berwick Curtis, C.B., C.M.G., D.S.O. I had, as was my custom, told the Commander I wished to leave the ship in silence, but when I left about 6 p.m., the ship was manned from masthead to the water-line and I was cheered all the way ashore.

XV
Odds and Ends

ONE of the most outstanding men in the Navy and one for whom I have a great admiration is Rear-Admiral T. J. Lyne, C.B., D.S.O., who started as a boy in the *Impregnable*, and ended his career as Captain of the same ship. He was specially promoted from Warrant Officer to Lieutenant's rank for his gallant services during the South African War. In 1899, when he was in command of a torpedo-boat which broke down, with great skill and ingenuity he made sails for it out of odd bits of canvas on board, and sailed it a hundred miles back to harbour. In the Yangtze he commanded several boats with great distinction, and later held several other commands. During the War, he earned the D.S.O. in charge of mine-sweepers at Harwich. He has unfortunately retired owing to the age limit of fifty-five, and was promoted to Rear-Admiral on the Retired List. If there had been a Department of Imagination at the Admiralty, they might have made a special exception and promoted him to Rear-Admiral on the Active List, even if only for a day, and allowed the Navy, as I am sure it would have liked to have done, to salute him with thirteen guns. He was Captain of the training ship *Indus* whilst I had the *Impregnable*, so we saw a lot of each other and stirred up a certain amount of friendly rivalry.

One of the crew of the *Dunraven* who came very much before the public was Petty Officer Pitcher, who received the Victoria Cross, the Distinguished Service Order, and the Médaille Militaire. He has a very striking appearance with an old-fashioned black beard which is rapidly disappearing from the naval service. During the War, he was specially selected to attend at the Naval Exhibition of pictures in London, and he had the great honour of being photographed with their Majesties the King and Queen, Queen Alexandra, and Sir Dighton Probyn.

Whilst Captain of the *Impregnable*, I was invited by H.R.H. the Duke of York to attend his first camp at Hythe, and on their first night to address the members, who consisted of industrial and Public School boys. I think the boys will for ever be grateful to the Duke of York for initiating these camps, which have done so much towards improving the good feeling of the various communities which make up the country.

One has often heard of hero worship, which doesn't mean that the object of it is heroic, but simply that he has some quality which arouses an almost dog-like devotion in one particular person. During the War, I used to be a frequent visitor to a sloop, whose Captain was a great friend of mine. He had on board a very efficient young " sub," but beyond the fact that he generally received me at the gangway, and I casually yarned with him in the Wardroom,

I never got really to know him. At a later date, I
was fitting out one of our mystery ships, when I
heard in a private letter that this " sub " was ill and
had left the sloop. I didn't take much notice of it,
but the day before I was due to sail, something, I can't
say what, prompted me to go to the Naval Hospital
and see if by any chance this young fellow was there.
I made enquiries of the Sister, who said, " Yes, he
is here, but I am afraid he cannot see anyone, as he is
dying." I gave my name, and asked her to convey
a message. As soon as she heard my name, she
said : " Oh yes, you may come in, as he has been
asking for you each day "—it appeared that his
mother hadn't liked to ask me to come, because I did
not know her, and she thought our difference in rank
might make it against etiquette for me to worry
about a " sub." I saw the young fellow, who was
obviously dying ; and he told me that his one
ambition was to serve under me—would I take him
when he was well ? The following day he died.

Two incidents which left a great impression on me
after the War were the Burial of the Unknown
Warrior in Westminster Abbey, and the V.C. Dinner-
Party given by the Prince of Wales.

At the Burial, I had the great honour of being
placed in command of what was called the V.C.
Guard of Honour, consisting of one hundred of all
ranks and ratings, drawn from the Navy, Army, and
Air Force. Lieut.-Colonel Freyberg was Second-
in-Command. We assembled at Chelsea Barracks.
All rank was ignored, and the V.C.s fell in according

to height. We then marched to the Abbey and
formed a guard around the Unknown Warrior's
grave. I cannot conceive a finer service than was
held, among a congregation which seemed to consist
entirely of women in black. All seats had been allotted
by ballot, and Duchesses and cooks sat next to each
other. In spite of the solemnity of the occasion there
were no hysterical breakdowns. The choir, without musical accompaniment, sang " The Supreme
Sacrifice," bringing tears to many eyes, and then in
the distance we could hear approaching the procession
from the Cenotaph, and slowly the Unknown
Warrior was carried up the aisle. The pall bearers
were Field-Marshals and Admirals-of-the-Fleet,
followed by H.M. the King, the Royal Family, and
Ministers of State. The coffin was draped with a
Union Jack, and lying on top were a shell helmet
and bayonet. At the head of the grave was H.M. the
Queen, accompanied by three other Queens. After
the coffin had been lowered into the grave, the King
threw earth on it. When all the Royal Family and
high officials had left the Abbey, the V.C.s filed past
the grave on either side, and had a last look at the
Unknown Warrior. We then marched to Wellington
Barracks, headed by the band of the Irish Guards.

After changing into plain clothes, I walked along the
Embankment to witness the mourning men, women,
and children, some carrying large wreaths above their
heads, others with just a bunch of violets.

The V.C. Dinner-Party given by the Prince of
Wales was held in the Royal Gallery at the House

100 V.C. GUARD OF HONOUR AT UNKNOWN WARRIOR'S FUNERAL. SELF IN COMMAND.

of Lords, and it was one of the finest sights I have ever seen in my life. Some three hundred V.C.s had been in London all day, yet with everybody wanting to entertain them, they all turned up at the dinner-party stone-cold sober. The Prince of Wales had a word for each one of us as we filed past and shook hands, and a more admirable dinner-party has never been held. All the seats were arranged by ballot. H.R.H. sat with Viscount Gort on one side of him and a chauffeur on the other. Champagne was served, and a teetotaller from Lancashire told the waiter after his third glass of it, that he would not have any more, as the lemonade was nothing like he got in Lancashire!

I was very much touched when the four officers and men who had been awarded V.C.s under my command asked me to lead them past H.R.H., so that we all went together like old times.

The following day (Sunday) a special performance of *Journey's End* was given for all the V.C.s, and on the Monday—Armistice Day—we again mustered and marched with the ex-Servicemen past the Cenotaph, led by Admiral-of-the-Fleet Lord Jellicoe, who gave us a brief address in Wellington Barracks afterwards.

Later my wife and I gave a supper party to the V.C.s who had served under me, and their wives, and at the conclusion of the evening I suggested that it was an occasion on which their old skipper might be allowed to kiss the wives, which I proceeded to do amidst much merriment.

XVI

South Africa

On completion of my sick leave, I was appointed as Captain-in-Charge, Simonstown, South Africa. I took with me my Secretary from the *Impregnable*, and we went out in one of the Intermediate Union Castle ships. I had asked for a cabin to my-self, but was told that in the interests of economy this could not be permitted, so I had to pay the extra fare. The one stipulation the Admiralty made about Captains' passages was, that they could not have cabins to themselves, but they were not to share them with officers of junior rank, as being against good discipline—what absurd red tape ! As I wanted to be as quiet as possible on the way out, I got permission to dine at the officers' table instead of at the captain's table, to which I had been invited. I felt sure I had seen one of the officers before. We went through all the various ships we had been in, and he assured me he had never met me. But on the day of our arrival at Cape Town, he came up to me and said, " You are quite right, sir, I know you perfectly well, as I was a boy in the *Impregnable* when you were Lieutenant, and I deserted."

On arrival, I reported myself to the Commander-in-Chief, Admiral Sir Rudolf Bentinck, who had a beautiful house at Simonstown, where I received much hospitality from the Admiral, Lady Bentinck, and their daughter. I went to take over my command from Rear-Admiral Arnold-Forster, who showed me over the dockyard and house. I think he was a little taken aback when the first question I asked was : " Where is the nearest fire hydrant ? " but in one of my horoscopes many years previously I had been told that I would live in a Government House that would be razed to the ground by fire, and as this was my first Government House, I thought I would be ready for it. But it didn't happen there, so I shall now have to wait till I go to another one !

I lived in Muizenberg, about ten miles from Simonstown, for some time, whilst the house was being repainted. I had gone out to Simonstown as a bachelor, as my medical advisers had advised me to live for six months free of the worry of children, but on landing on January 1st, 1923, I wired to my wife to bring the family out at once, as it was too good a spot for them to miss, with its beautiful climate and ideal surroundings. They arrived a few weeks later, and much to their surprise I met them at Cape Town (about twenty-five miles distant) in a car I had bought. I had never had one before, nor even driven one, but in spite of occasionally accelerating instead of putting the brake on, I got them down safely.

Our house at Simonstown, which had been built by the Civil Engineer of Jacksons, Ltd., at the same time as the dockyard, was charming. It was on the side of the hill, but unfortunately it did not have much of a garden. The only thing it really needed was a garage. In forwarding my yearly proposals for new works, I placed last on the list the necessity of a garage at the Captain's house, as being of least importance, but it turned out it was the only item the Admiralty approved of. They were apparently taken aback at somebody being more or less honest.

Our staff consisted of four black servants, all of whom were splendid, except the cook, who, having been converted to Christianity, used to get horribly drunk on dinner-party nights, so I had to get rid of him. I have no doubt missionaries do a lot of good, but, on these occasions at least, I had no use for them. Had the cook remained a Mohammedan, he would have been just as happy and far more sober.

After getting rid of him, we imported a coloured gentleman of the name of Charlie Abrahams, who was one of the leading Mohammedans, and at night he would frequently call his fellows to prayer, which was rather disturbing. One evening, when the Commander-in-Chief was coming to dine with us, the boiler suddenly burst, which, to say the least of it, was disturbing, but Abrahams, being sober and faithful, assisted by my coxswain Cooper, managed to get the dinner cooked next door, and it was actually brought in without having become cold.

My two stewards were named Abou and Hamesi.

On arrival I found that Abou was only a second-class steward, and in order to get the best work out of him, I decided to make him a first-class steward with greater authority. I therefore sent for Abou to come to my office, and said, " King tell me make you first-class steward if you serve Captain and Missy well. If you no good, King tell me to chop your head off." He went back to my wife very excited, and told her the whole conversation, and had his extra badge on before the day was out.

Abou and Hamesi served us well, and the only trouble we had was when Hamesi came to me during a children's party and said that Abou was going to murder him. They had apparently had some row about their wives. I left the children's party for a few minutes and saw them both, and told them that if they wanted to murder each other, they must wait until 6.30, when the children would be gone. I also sent for Cooper, and told him to see that my orders were carried out. I was delighted to find after the party that they had adjusted their grievance.

Our English lady nurse was rather frightened of staying in the house when my wife and I were out, as there were only black servants there. I asked her if she would be happier with a revolver in her bed-room. She was delighted with the idea, so I gave her a revolver and a box of ammunition, but took the precaution of taking all the powder out of the ammunition, so that if she had ever tried to fire the revolver nothing would have happened. Needless to say, I never told her ; but the thought of having

16

a revolver by her side kept her from having sleepless nights.

On being appointed to the South African station, I made enquiries as to whether I could take my coxswain, Cooper, with me, but I was told that I was not allowed a coxswain. On making enquiries as to, if I got him out there, how long it would be before it would be bowled out, I was told it would be about six months. Anyhow, he came out in the same steamer with me—he had already served with me since 1915.

We had on the staff of the ·dockyard a famous character, an old Krooman called Tom Peter, who had been pensioned off several years before, but who, being the best cook in Simonstown, had been kept on in the Commander's house. It so happened that one day, when the Commander-in-Chief was away, and I was acting as Senior Naval Officer, I received a letter from the Admiralty enquiring as to why—

(1) Petty Officer Cooper was on the station ; and

(2) Tom Peter was still employed.

I was able to keep the correspondence in South Africa for some three months before sending back the reply, together with a private note suggesting it might be pigeon-holed. In the meantime, Tom Peter had been told that the Admiralty were going to pension him off altogether, and his reply was, " I don't care what Admiralty think, I want to know what King thinks," and of course when he found that he could remain in his job without being relieved, he went round telling everybody that Admiralty had

South Africa

said Tom Peter should be relieved, but " King say Tom Peter stay cook to Commander ! "

The South Africa Squadron consisted of two old light cruisers and two sloops stationed at Simonstown, and two more on the West Coast. A surveying vessel and a couple of trawlers comprised the South African Navy, under Commander Rankin, who in his turn came under General Brink, who in his turn came under the Minister of Defence. Although the Squadron proper only consisted of four ships, it took as large a staff and as much paper work as in pre-War days were required for a Fleet. For instance, there were two gunnery officers in the Squadron, one of whom was the Fleet Gunnery Officer. The impression on my mind all the time was that it was a case of the staff craze overdone. Luckily, being Superintendent of the Dockyard as well as Captain-in-Charge, I was allowed to communicate with the Admiralty direct, and so avoided having my papers sent round to a large number of staff officers to initial. I imagine that in war-time the ships would be used for protection of commerce duties, and what all the staff would do then, I cannot think.

As far as I was concerned, my duties for the ships were merely to berth them and refit them and look after the shore establishments, hospital, recreation rooms, etc. The Commander-in-Chief used frequently to go away for several months in his flagship and generally left his Secretary behind, so I again found myself in the dual capacity of Captain-in-

Charge and Senior Naval Officer, and had to carry on a correspondence with myself. On one occasion my Commander, W. C. Tancred, came to me with some new suggestion which I thought excellent, so I told him to put it in writing, and I would forward it to the Commander-in-Chief with my support, which I proceeded to do. The following day, when I was dealing with the Commander-in-Chief's correspondence, this letter was before me, and the Secretary pointed out that it couldn't be done, as it was contrary to one of the King's Regulations ; so I, as Senior Naval Officer, sent it back to myself, drawing my attention to the Regulations and telling myself to be more careful to observe them in future.

I had a very happy dockyard, and soon got into the new routine. Most of my officers were civilians, and they were a splendid crowd, and always gave me the greatest assistance when I found myself dealing with new subjects, such as building houses, etc. I left them to look after their own departments without interference, except when necessary, and found things went very smoothly.

A lot of my preconceived ideas regarding the administration of dockyards disappeared when I came to investigate matters. I spent a good deal of time interesting myself in the social and welfare side of the dockyard. I had a big Sale Room cleared of stores and turned into a recreation room, where dances, concerts, etc., were held pretty regularly. My only fear was that as it was immediately over the rope store there was a danger of fire, and as I had made the dance hall without the permission of the Admiralty, I should not have had a leg to stand on ; but the old boatswain I had, Mr. Rendle, kept a pretty sharp eye lifting for anybody smoking. I used to allow smoking in the dockyard after working hours, as I couldn't see any objection to it. The dockyard really consisted of two dockyards, a new one and an old one about half a mile apart. Each had its own flagstaff, and I found on arrival that the Union Jack was only hoisted in the dockyards and hospitals on a Sunday, so I at once had this remedied, and ordered it to be hoisted every day. The boatswain did not much like the idea, as so many flags got torn when a south-easter, the prevailing wind, was blowing.

The boatswain was a fine old character—one of the last of the real boatswains ; as he used to put it, he was a boatswain because he was a seaman, his father having been one before him, and not because he had failed to pass for gunner. Twice a year he would go to the Commander and ask for a day's leave—for the day after his birthday and the day after the dockyard regatta. I met him some years after his retirement, and asked him how he was getting on, and he told me a yarn about a row he had had with his landlord, in the course of which the landlord had said to him, " Well, who the 'ell are you, anyhow ? " " I replied," said the bo'sun, " looking him straight in the face, ' Who the 'ell am I ? I am an officer in His Majesty's Navy by Royal Warrant, and a gentleman by the Act of Parliament.' "

I was Chairman of both the Whitley Council and the Workmen's Industrial Welfare Committee. They were entitled to meet every quarter, but I pointed out that if they would trust me, I would deal with any grievances that might arise at the time, without waiting for the quarterly meeting, and I felt highly flattered when they didn't call another meeting till a few days before I left. I asked them what the agenda was, and they said, " None, except a vote of thanks to you—and also we want to confirm our right to hold a quarterly meeting when your successor arrives, if necessary."

When the King's birthday was approaching, I decided to do what is not the custom in H.M. Dockyards, and that was to muster all the employees, Englishmen, Dutchmen, black workmen, etc., and give three cheers for the King. I was warned that the scheme might fall flat, but far from it ; they not only responded, but they also sang the National Anthem of their own free will, and boasted about it a good deal, as the ships had got rather lax in the matter of the King's birthday since the War.

When I first took over the command of the dock-yard, I nominally belonged to a ship called *Afrikander*. She really consisted of a coal lugger. At that time the South African Naval Service came under my orders for discipline, but later on the South African Naval Service was placed entirely under Captain Rankin, a most suitable officer for the job. This change necessitated a new " ship " for our Navy. The cooking vessel was selected, and rechristened *Flora*, after a guardship which had been at Simonstown many years ago, a figurehead of which had been placed in the Admiralty grounds. As my daughter's name is Flora, everybody thought that was the reason for the name being selected, although, as a matter of fact, I had not been in any way consulted about the name. My Commander, one of the most splendid I have ever had with me, had a keen sense of humour. He was dining one night with the Governor-General, H.R.H. Prince Arthur of Connaught, who remarked to him, " I suppose you will be going to sea again very soon ? " and Tancred replied, " No, sir, I am too busy in the dockyard, cooking."

Among my other duties in South Africa was that of Steward of the Kenilworth Turf Club ; not that I knew anything about horses—but I found myself of some use in enquiries into bumping, etc., where it was simply a matter of judging which jockey was the biggest liar.

I drove in my car, with my wife, Tancred and his wife, to nearly every race meeting. We made rather an exhibition of ourselves one day when the hooter started hooting and nobody could stop it. Neither Tancred nor I knew anything about the innards of a car, and we stood with a crowd around us, each holding up one side of the bonnet and trying to look intelligent, until somebody came along and easily stopped the hoot.

The drive from Simonstown to Cape Town is a particularly pretty one, and I frequently had to do it twice a day, about twenty-five miles each way. On one occasion, coming back from a dance, we had the Padre of the Flagship as a passenger. A gale had been blowing, and the road was partially blocked by sand ; eventually we ran into the sand and were unable to move. While Cooper and I were trying to get some planks to wedge the car out, I heard the Padre say to my wife, " I think I had better put on my trousers now." One might have been suspicious, but I soon tumbled to the fact that he only had his full-dress knee breeches on, and was putting on his trousers to keep out the cold.

I found that in the dockyard the routine was to have " fire stations " at 7 a.m. the first Tuesday in every month. This struck me as a very inefficient arrangement, as everybody knew exactly when they were going to be, but it was obvious that any other arrangement would to some extent dislocate the work of the dockyard, so I compromised to the extent of having it alternatively at a fixed time and at any time I wished. One evening I thought I would have a proper surprise, and on strolling into the dockyard about 7 p.m., I ordered the policeman to ring the fire bell : at the same time I informed the Commander-in-Chief what I had done, and he ordered ships to land their fire parties. Much to my surprise, all the dockyard workers came tumbling in, full speed, and the hoses were soon squirting water on an imaginary fire. I was frightfully pleased with the way they had turned up, and mentioned the fact to the cashier, who was standing close to me. He asked me if I knew what it was going to cost, and then for the first time I realised that all the men who had come in had to be paid overtime. This was a complete surprise to me after being used to naval discipline. However, the accounts had to be squared up without the Admiralty knowing.

Amongst the many things that came under my jurisdiction was the famous South African Observatory. I was responsible for the safety of the wires for hoisting the telescopes, the fire stations, the pay of the staff, etc., and I used to visit them about once a quarter. I was faced with a difficult position when H.M. Astronomer at the Cape of Good Hope, Mr. F. S. Hough, M.A., died. It was an appointment that had to be filled at once. I therefore appointed the Senior Assistant temporarily without additional pay. I do not suppose it often falls to the lot of a naval officer to have to make such an appointment. Eventually Mr. Spencer Jones, F.R.S., was sent out as H.M. Astronomer, and we had very pleasant meetings together. I frequently used to go up at night when there was anything special to see.

Overlooking Simonstown, on the top of a hill was what was known as Klaver Valley, part of which was used as a rifle range. The whole of the valley was very thick brush and, except where the water-supply was, contained a lot of snakes. Our chief trouble in the Klaver Valley was the continual outbreak of fires. One in particular burnt the whole valley out and continued for several miles, and there was no way of stopping it—though on these occasions Tancred and I would go up with a party of sailors, and when necessary clear an area round important posts, such as the Sanatorium, Naval Hospital, etc.   On one occasion a sailor cutting down a tree cut a snake in half, and it so scared the remainder that we had the greatest difficulty in getting them to work again—they were all black sailors.

The greatest shock I ever had in my life was when, walking across the hills in the Klaver Valley, which was one of my favourite pastimes, I lost my way one evening and got into the long grass. For many months I had carried a snake-bite outfit about in my pocket, but having come to the conclusion that the presence of snakes was chiefly a legend, I had given up this habit.   But I had a rude awakening when I suddenly felt a snake inside my trousers. Luckily there was no one in sight, or I should probably have screamed. I could feel the slimy thing against my knee, and the thought quickly flashed through my mind as to whether I should take my trousers down or pull them up.   In the meantime I had seized the snake (which turned out to be a small puff adder) by the head, and wriggling up my trousers, shoved it out ; and it slithered away through the brush as hard as it could.   I was too terrified to know whether it had bitten me or not, and dashed down the hill to the nearest doctor's, where I arrived about thirty minutes later.   He told me that if I had been bitten I should probably have been dead by that time, and advised me to go to the Club and have a good drink, which I proceeded to do.   On telling the yarn there, I was referred to Mr. Fitzwilliam's Snake Book, in which it says that the safest place to have a snake is up your trousers, as it cannot throw its head back to strike. But in spite of this consolation, I never went over the hills again without having my trousers tucked into my socks.

Shortly after this we had a visit from a great expert on snakes, who brought a lot down with him and gave a lecture in the Sale Room. He claimed that both he and his father were immune from poisoning by snakes and allowed a snake to bite him without any ill effects ; but shortly after this he went to Australia, was bitten by a snake, and died.

One of my greatest troubles at Simonstown was the bathing-pool, which was allocated to officers of various ranks at different times of the day, and also to ladies of various grades at other parts of the day. It led to no end of complications, and the only time I ever had any peace about it was when a sea-cow got in and came on the beach, thus choking everybody off bathing. The bathing-pool was surrounded by an old torpedo-net to keep sharks out, as they frequently came to Simons Bay.

We had several visits from American men-of-war, and one I specially enjoyed was that of U.S.S. *Trenton*, Captain Kalbaus, U.S.N., who gave a delightful luncheon-party on board, to which my wife and I were invited. He was an excellent host and a very good speech-maker. I remember him telling a yarn about an American ship leaving Boston after the Captain and the Chief Engineer had had a row, accusing each other of not knowing their jobs. They agreed on leaving Boston that the Chief Engineer should take the bridge and the Captain have charge of the engine-room. After about half an hour, the Captain went to the bridge to find the Chief Engineer sitting in an arm-chair and smoking a big cigar. He said :

" Say, Chief, I give in. I cannot make these blasted engines go round."

The Chief replied : " I am not surprised, as we have been grounded for the last twenty minutes."

We had in the dockyard a party of black sailors, about a hundred in all; some were Kroomen from the West Coast of Africa and the others Seedie boys from Zanzibar. The former were chiefly Christians and the latter Mohammedans. They were in charge of the boatswain, who had great difficulty at times to prevent them fighting; in fact, at night we used to leave the light on in their quarters to make sure they didn't kill each other in the dark. They were stout fellows and good workers. They had a tremendous respect for the King, and didn't think a great deal of anybody below him, so when punishing them or awarding them good-conduct badges, I used to tell them that the King had given me instructions to do it.

On one occasion, when my Commander was away on a few days' leave, one of the Kroomen died, and being in the habit of attending all the funerals of any of my sailors, I attended his funeral. When the Commander returned from his leave I asked him if everything was all right.

He said, " No."

I said, " What's the matter ? "

He said, " All the Kroomen want to die."

I could not understand what he meant, till he told me that the Kroomen had said :

" Captain attend Krooman's funeral ; we all want to die before Captain go home."

XVII

South Africa *(continued)*

STATIONED at Simonstown was a South African training ship for boys, called the *General Botha* (previously H.M.S. *Thames*), which had been presented to South Africa by Mr. Davis, the great shipping man and owner of the yacht *Westward*. She was for a considerable time a source of great trouble to the dockyard, as she was run by a Committee of Management, and the control of her was somewhat confused ; moreover, she owed the British Government a large sum of money, and was yet demanding more stores. As, after investigation, I could not get any definite guarantee of payment, I gave orders that no more stores were to be issued. In the meantime I had learnt that the Chairman of the Committee had written direct to the First Lord of the Admiralty, behind both my back and the Commander-in-Chief's ; so when he came to see me and begged me to give him more stores, I replied : " You have appealed to Cæsar and you can wait for Cæsar's answer." Things, in due course, got cleared up as far as the dockyard was concerned, the Captain resigning and his successor also resigning a short time later.

A lot of people think that South Africa is a good place for people with a tendency to consumption. I believe this is correct, provided they go to the high altitudes of South Africa, but Simonstown itself was not very suitable for consumptive patients, and I had a lot of difficulty over this matter, as men would apply for the South African Station, thinking that the climate would put their consumptive troubles right, and then, when they were getting near death, they would apply to be allowed to return to England in order to die at home. One particularly sad case I had was that of an officer who suffered from consumption to such an extent that he was unable to walk to my office. He had a particularly affectionate wife, who nursed him through thick and thin, and who told me that if I relieved him of his work and sent him home it would kill him. I therefore allowed him to carry on to the bitter end, when he died.

I found the attendance in the Dockyard Church very poor, which I attributed to several reasons : firstly, because the service was very uninteresting ; secondly, because all the pews were arranged according to seniority ; and thirdly, because in these modern days people like to spend part of Sunday, their only day off, in going for picnics. I suggested to the Padre that the service should be shortened in order to enable people to go for their picnics, and also to enable those women who had to look after their husbands' Sunday dinners to get home in time for that purpose. We could not come to any agreement on the subject, so eventually I took a vote for a short or long service, the result of which was fifty-fifty. So we arranged for a long service one Sunday and a short service the next. Needless to say, the short services had the bigger attendance.

I had difficulties at a later date when a new rector arrived and at once got the backs up of all the naval people as he refused to recognise the Dockyard Church. I tried to smooth matters over, and eventually had a private meeting at my house, consisting of the magistrate, the rector, my own Padre, and myself. Previous to the meeting, Abou had put the whisky and soda, etc., on the table, and we were all smoking our pipes when the rector arrived and at once started to recite the Lord's Prayer. I did not dare look at the magistrate, or I should have burst out laughing, because I was trying to hide my pipe in my dinner-jacket pocket, and my eye was fixed on the whisky and soda, of which I felt sure the rector disapproved. He was one of those narrow-minded men who, in my opinion, render very little service either to the Church or to the State.

We had some small detention quarters in the dock-yard, which I occasionally had to inspect. On my first visit, I found that we were still carrying out a very old custom of making prisoners fill bags with stones, and then tip the stones out again and refill them. This struck me as a most degrading form of punishment for even the worst criminal, and as the detention quarters had been instituted with a view to educating men during their time of detention, I at once had this practice stopped, with a reservation that it could still be employed in a case such as mutiny or violence. On several occasions I found that men who had deserted from the Navy, and who wished to get a free passage home, would come down to Simonstown and give themselves up as deserters, for which I awarded them the maximum punishment I could give, namely, ninety days' detention, and then they got their free passage back to England. Sometimes they were men who had deserted over twenty years previously. I saw no reason why these men should get free passages home, so on one occasion, when a man gave himself up, I refused to recognise him as a deserter ; but this procedure was not approved of by higher authorities, and I was told that, in future, I must deal with all deserters who had surrendered themselves.

The new buildings which were being put up in the new dockyard were being erected at the expense of the Union Government as their contribution to the British Navy. It so happened that the Minister of Defence, Colonel Creswell, was also Minister of Labour. Owing to delay in contracts, we were unable to complete certain buildings for which money had been allowed, but I proposed to transfer the money to other buildings with which we could go ahead. This was not approved of by the Minister of Defence. I invited Colonel Creswell to visit the dockyard, and again asked him verbally if I could transfer the money, but he said : " No, it cannot be

17

done." I said : " Very good, sir, but I am afraid you will have another hundred men added to your unemployed to-morrow." At this, he pricked up his ears, and within twenty-four hours I got approval to transfer the money.

One of my pleasantest days at Simonstown was when the Governor-General, the Earl of Athlone (who had succeeded H.R.H. Prince Arthur of Connaught), accompanied by H.R.H. Princess Alice, honoured the dockyard by a visit. As was my custom when distinguished visitors came to the dockyard, I took the Governor-General into the victualling store to have a drop of Nelson's Blood (rum). He inspected the black sailors, and in honour of his visit they were given a "make and mend." Whilst the Governor-General was going round the dockyard, my wife took the Princess up the mountain to see the wonderful wild flowers. We had a picnic party at the top of Simonsberg, which we reached by an aerial railway. It swayed about so much that the Governor-General preferred to walk down.

Picnics were the great order of the day on the Station. We spent one of the jolliest Christmas Days I remember in some pine-woods at a place called Tokai. After a big picnic lunch, the children were all sent to sleep, and whilst they were slumbering, we decorated a growing Christmas tree in proper Christmas fashion as a surprise for them.

Climbing Table Mountain, some four thousand

feet, was another amusement—or shall I say amusing after it was all over, and one had got back to one's car at the bottom of the mountain and found tankards of beer waiting?

One New Year's Eve, my wife and I gave a party to the whole of the Shore Staff and their wives. Just before they arrived, I asked my wife how she thought we had better start things going, because some of the wives did not get on with each other—a very common occurrence. Observing a bit of mistletoe hanging at the front door, I decided to receive the guests there, and kissed all the ladies as they arrived. I rather expected a severe snub from one or two of the wives, but was intensely amused when they were the ones who turned out to enjoy it the most.

One of the great events of the season was a big ball, organised by Princess Alice, in aid of the hospitals. It was called a " Black and White Ball," as they were the only colours that were allowed. Different parties were asked to get up set lancers, so we organised a set at Simonstown, consisting of naval officers and their wives. The men were dressed in old-fashioned seamen's rigs, and the ladies in crinolines. Although the outfit only cost 5s. a head, we were adjudged the best set.

I occasionally used to play cricket at the Cape, and was once fielding at point in the annual match, the Navy versus the Law, when one of the strongest batsmen came in. The bowler moved all the fielders farther out, but unfortunately missed me.

The batsman gave a mighty swipe, the ball hit me in the heart and I fell down, but luckily had the sense to hold the ball in the air as I fell, so that they could see that I had caught it.   Everyone rushed up thinking I was dead, and someone told me afterwards the first thing they thought of was : " Thank God, he held the ball ! "   The doctor informed me afterwards that had the ball been half an inch lower it would have killed me.   I never before knew you could be killed at cricket.

The South African Government had generously given me a free pass over all their railways, but unfortunately it didn't include my wife ; and I didn't use it a great deal, except for a special trip to Rhodesia, of which I shall write later.   I had to go to Pretoria and Johannesburg on duty on several occasions : the former is a wonderfully laid-out city, and the Government buildings are, I think, the finest I have seen, having been designed by Baker. On one occasion in the Club at Johannesburg I was a bit taken aback when General Smuts walked up to me and said :

" You are the sea brigand I met in France during the War."

The ordinary amusements at Simonstown were very limited, except for those which we made for ourselves.   On one occasion we were visited by a circus of many wild animals ; in fact, too wild for my liking, as I felt sure the lions would break through their cages.   The night before the circus arrived, while it was on trek towards the town, the

Navigator of the Flagship, a very righteous, godly, and sober fellow—with incidentally a beautiful voice which he sometimes lent to the Dutch Church—was motoring back from Cape Town late at night. He ran into the tail end of the circus and bumped into and slightly damaged a baby elephant, which had no red light astern of it ; he then had a barging match with a rather bigger elephant. Needless to say, a few words ensued with the keeper, who spoke about prosecuting him for damages. The Navigator, on arrival at the dockyard, thought he had better put himself on the right side, and reported the whole matter to the police. The sergeant on duty knew, of course, that there were a lot of elephants in South Africa, but had not heard of the circus, and tried to pacify the Navigator by saying : " There, there, now, you lie down in the corner and have a good sleep. You'll be better to-morrow."

We had at Simonstown a small Naval Club, of which the Commander-in-Chief was President, and I was the Vice-President and Chairman of the Committee, which consisted, naturally, chiefly of officers of the shore establishments, as we were the ones who had to do the donkey work and keep the Club going when the ships were away. Sometimes there would be no ships in harbour at all. I took the opportunity when all the ships were present except one, of calling a general meeting and putting forward a proposition that up till noon each day our sitting-room should be put at the disposal of ladies, to give them a chance of getting together and seeing the English papers ; the motion was duly passed, and ladies were admitted to the Club. In due course, the missing ship, which had some form of Bachelors' Club on board, asked for a general meeting to be held. They packed the meeting, did a lot of propaganda, and some of the officers joined the Club the day before the meeting, in order to vote. The result was that ladies were turned out of the Club—which in my opinion was a very discreditable affair. I at once resigned, together with the chief members of the Committee. The Commander-in-Chief sent for me, and asked me to reconsider the matter, as he told me the Club couldn't be carried on if we shore members resigned *en bloc*. I said I quite agreed, but unfortunately the fellows in the ships didn't appreciate what we were doing for them, and that I thought it was an insult to the ladies to have admitted them at a general meeting, held well within the rules of the Club, and then to turn them out. After a long discussion I agreed that I and the other members of the Committee would withdraw our resignations, provided it was very clearly stated that we had done so at the personal request of the Commander-in-Chief and for no other reason. This was agreed to and carried out. The question of ladies was allowed to lapse, as so many of them said that even if a new rule were passed, they wouldn't avail themselves of it, as they weren't going to be allowed in one day and turned out the next. Anyhow, before leaving the Station, I again brought the matter up, because I wanted it

put on record in the minutes of the Club that I was
no party to what I considered a most uncalled-for
and ungallant insult to the ladies of Simonstown.
The motion was defeated by a smaller majority
than I expected. Anyhow, there the matter ended.
The members of the Club sent me a letter of thanks
for my services, etc., on leaving the Station.

XVIII

South Africa *(continued)*

IT was very enjoyable to meet men who had served both against us in the South African War and for us in the Great War. I was especially struck with the personality of General Brink, who was head of the Defence Department under the Ministry, and a typical Dutchman of the finest type. My wife was always of the greatest help to me when we entertained Dutch people, as her mother is Dutch, and she was able to talk the language. At the various official functions we attended at Government House and the City Hall, the person who always attracted me most was General Smuts, then in opposition. General Hertzog was a genial man to talk to, but I felt he had rather roaming eyes. Colonel Creswell was perhaps the easiest to get on with ; he belonged to the Labour Party, and appeared to have a certain amount of bitterness about him—but I liked him all the same. The Officer Commanding at Cape Town was General Tanner, and we saw much of him and his wife : he was a typical soldier. But outstanding above them all was General Lukin, an oldish man, who had fought in German West Africa, and then led the South African troops with much gallantry in

France. He was loved by everyone and supported by his wife, and they were regular attendants at the Race Meetings. He lived quite close to the course, and the Prince of Wales, when he came to South Africa, broke away from the race meeting to go and visit him, as he was too ill to attend.

One of the events of the year was the opening of Parliament, which was carried out with great ceremony by the Governor-General. I used to have to attend officially, and was always greatly impressed with the respect shown to the King's representatives here as in various parts of the Empire. In opening Parliament in Cape Town, the official language being bilingual, the Governor-General would read his speech in English, and it would then be read in Afrikaans.

When the Earl of Athlone came out as Governor-General, he became intensely popular, not only for his personality, but through taking the trouble to learn Afrikaans and so be able to talk to his Ministers in their own language. During my stay in South Africa the Right Hon. J. H. Thomas came to Cape Town as head of the British Delegation. As representative of the Commander-in-Chief, I attended at Cape Town for his welcome and at the City Hall, where he made a brilliant speech. I was in white naval uniform. After the reception, Mr. Thomas came into the ante-room, lit his pipe, and said : " Thank God that's over," and catching me by the arm said, " Look 'ere, you are just the fellow I want. I 'ave been looking for a railway official about my journey to Pretoria." He was somewhat taken aback when I informed him I was representing the Commander-in-Chief.

On the way out to South Africa, I had made great friends with a Dr. McKenzie and his wife, who lived at a place called Gatooma in Southern Rhodesia, not far from Salisbury. He was frequently inviting me up to go big-game shooting, but I could not afford the expense. But some kind friend had heard of my wishes, and the Union Government gave free passes to myself and my wife, and the Rhodesian Railways, which were not Government, gave assisted passages, which greatly reduced our expenses. Sir William Hoy kindly placed a reserved carriage at our disposal, and we started off on our long journey, which proved one of the most enjoyable and exciting holidays I have ever spent.

The actual journey through the veld is monotonous, and the red sand penetrates everywhere. We had glimpses of some of the old-time battlefields and war graves, and stopped several hours at Kimberley to get a glimpse of one of the famous diamond mines. We then continued our journey to Bulawayo. The Governor of Rhodesia, Sir John Chancellor, whom I had known previously at Trinidad, had kindly sent a car to meet us, and several of the members of the Club had come down to give us a welcome. My first impression of Rhodesia was that it breathed the spirit of that great man Cecil Rhodes. Most of the people we met had been out there since the early days, and had fought in the Matabele and Mashonaland Wars, and knew Rhodes intimately. We never got tired of hearing tales about him, and he seems to have been worshipped by the natives.

I had the pleasure of meeting, on several occasions, Sir Van Ryneveld, the first man who flew from Cairo to the Cape. He was a typical airman, and very quiet, with a strong, powerful face. During his flight he had been obliged to make a forced landing near Bulawayo. A native in the field, who had never seen an aeroplane before, fell down on his hands and knees when he saw Van Ryneveld step out of the machine in his air kit with goggles on, and then went up to him and in native language said, " How do, God."

We of course visited the Matoppos, where Rhodes is buried. It is known as the view of the world, and certainly no words of mine could describe the magnificent panorama one gets from the top, where one large stone with the simple inscription, " Cecil Rhodes," lies over the tomb of that great Empire-builder. We were accompanied on our trip by an old veteran, Major Gordon. His chief hobby, after his fighting days were done, was to catch snakes, and he had a reputation for being able to pick them up by their tails, and then with a swift click, break their heads. As we were driving along, we narrowly missed running over a green momba, a particularly dangerous snake. Gordon stopped the car and said, " Come on," and followed the snake into the long grass. I went timidly behind him, and was rather thankful that we didn't see any more of our friend.

From Bulawayo we travelled to Salisbury, to
spend a week at Government House with Sir John
and Lady Chancellor and their daughter. The
house was a little outside the town and in most
delightfully peaceful surroundings. The A.D.C.
and Private Secretary was the Hon. A. Lowther, son
of the late Speaker of the House of Commons. He
had a cottage near the house, and as the Governor
was in the habit of going to bed early, I spent many
an enjoyable evening with him, and sometimes sat
up till the early hours of the morning. The only
trouble was that on my going back to the house the
Governor's dog would start barking, which rather
gave me away.

One day the Governor's daughter suggested I
should go riding with her. I told her I knew nothing
about it, and the only time I had been on a horse was
in China, when it bolted. She assured me that
" Father's horse " was very quiet ; so next morning
I started off about 7 a.m., and luckily there were two
niggers to help me on. We got away all right, and
I was rather patting myself on the back for making
agreeable before-breakfast conversation, when suddenly we got to a railway crossing, and the horse
turned round and bolted at full speed. I put on all
the brakes I could think of, but without any effect ;
I then lost my stirrup, and was just wondering
whether or not, if I got thrown off, it would be best
to hang on to the reins, when suddenly I fell with a
heavy thump on the road—the horse continuing its
journey back to the stables. It was lucky it threw

me where it did, as a short way farther on, it would probably have landed me on some barbed wire. In the meantime I had got up, lit my pipe, and tried to look calm, though I was covered with red sand and terribly sore. Miss Chancellor, who was naturally rather upset at the so-called " distinguished visitor " having a toss, was soon on the scene, and I assured her I was all right and started to walk back with her. To my horror one of the servants had brought the horse out again, and as I didn't like to say I was frightened I mounted again. It turned out that the horse hadn't been exercised for some time. Lowther was very perturbed at the incident, and I was stiff for about a week.

Whilst at Government House a big garden-party was given, at which I met Mrs. X. I was introduced as Captain Campbell. Some months later I again met her in South Africa, and she would insist on addressing me as Major Campbell. After some time I asked her why she called me " Major," and she said she knew I was only a Captain really, but she had been brought up always to address officers with a rank higher than the one they held.

After leaving Government House, my wife went camping with Mrs. McKenzie and I went to Gatooma to shoot.

The area we were going to shoot in was known as the Sehunge Territory, where the tsetse (sleeping sickness) fly exists, Dr. McKenzie being on a Government Expedition to investigate the effect of the fly on the savages who lived in the territory.

There were three white men in the party, the doctor,
a friend called Woodforde, and myself. We had two
native policemen and about seventy natives in our
party to carry our guns, rig camp, etc., etc. A
fellow called Wheildon motored us out to the
territory, passing Golden Valley and several disused
mines, where many of the original explorers of
Rhodesia had lost their money.

We arrived at our destination, a place called Goma,
about four in the afternoon, and camped near the
Zambezi.   Much game was in sight, and we had
one or two shots without success. The following
morning Wheildon left with the car. How he had
ever got us there it is hard to believe, since there
were no roads. We were off early in the morning on
foot, as owing to the fly, no domestic animals such as
horses or dogs can live in the area.

Owing to the danger of getting sleeping sickness,
we had to smother our faces, hands, and all exposed
parts, in the most evil-smelling kind of oil I have
ever met.   The flies in places were thick, and would
settle on our backs, when the natives would beat them
off.   I was only bitten four times—it was just a sting
like a needle being put into you, but I quickly sucked
the spot and I suffered no ill-effects.   Yet it served
to remind me of the warning given me before the
start—that I went at my own risk.

Our daily routine was much the same as far as our
hours went. We would turn out at 4 a.m., have a
cup of coffee and a jam sandwich, and then set off
after the game, which included nearly every known

wild animal. We stopped for breakfast at any time
between noon and 3 p.m., according to whether or
not we were on a hot scent. The natives would rig
temporary covers for us from the sun, the temperature
being about 147°. About 5 p.m. we would move
out again till about 7 p.m., when we would camp for
the night. If we were near water the natives would
dig a big hole in the ground and put a tarpaulin over
it so that we could have a hot bath ; a double ration
of gin and quinine followed, then supper, consisting of what we had shot—including buffalo—some
tinned fruit and a double whisky ; and so to bed at
9 p.m., thoroughly tired but thoroughly fit. We
were the only three white men within 200 miles, we
had no wireless, and we cared about nothing. Each
night we could hear the lions roaring, sometimes quite
close to the camp. At first I felt a bit nervous when
it came to going out into the bush for the " laws of
nature," with lions roaring, but one soon got used to
it. I had a great ambition to get a lion, and so we
spent a whole day following their spoor without
success. The doctor, who had spent over twenty
years at this game, told me that lions were extraordinarily hard to find, as, like other animals, they
concealed themselves during the day in grass which
matched their coats, but he had often come upon
them unexpectedly.

On our very first day out we sighted several hundred
head of game, including zebra, roan, impalla, sable,
baboons, etc. The wind was wrong for us, and
beyond Woodforde wounding a roan we had no luck.

The doctor had to visit a certain village, and as it was over a hundred miles distant, and our time was limited, it more or less meant marching straight there and back ; and if the wind held in the same direction, there appeared to be little chance of getting any sport. Of course the doctor and Woodforde were old hands at the game, but for me it was the chance of a lifetime, so I suggested to the doctor, that instead of our going to the village he should send a message to tell the village to come to us, to which he agreed ; and he sent one of the police with two or three boys and guns to fetch the village and arrange for them to meet at a set rendezvous. This saved us a lot of trouble, and we were able to get on with the sport.

Our most exciting day was when we got on the spoor of some buffalo, which we followed for over three hours. Eventually we heard a tremendous crash and about fifty buffalo charged through the Sanonga a little way ahead of us. Woodforde and the doctor fired and both got hits. I fired, but could not claim a hit, as I was so surprised at the sight I didn't have time for steady enough aim. One buffalo was killed and the other wounded. We followed the blood spoor for several miles, and then, much to my annoyance, the doctor called a halt and refused to let us go on. He explained that a wounded buffalo is the most dangerous animal to follow, as it doubles back and gets you from behind before you know where you are. I was very disappointed, but the doctor was in command and was very firm. One

SHOOTING IN SOUTHERN RHODESIA.

SHOOTING IN SOUTHERN RHODESIA WITH DR. MACKENZIE.

of the natives followed the trail, and eventually brought in the tail of the buffalo, as he was unable to carry the whole lot.

It was this night that the " village " arrived—men, women, and children—and the doctor spent several hours taking samples of their blood from their ears, and then they enjoyed a meal of buffalo and danced round the camp fire till the early hours of the morning to the music of a drum and sticks. Real jazz music. They got more savage as the night wore on, but the rhythm of their music was the same as is danced in the high circles in London at the present time.

The best day I had was when I got a small rhinoceros. We were going through some thick stuff, and I saw what I thought was a large ant-heap, but the doctor whispered " Rhino," and suddenly I saw this brute get up and make for us. I loosed off a ·45 which did the trick.

We saw a lot of wild boar, or, as they were more commonly called, pigs. They took a lot of killing, and when wounded would utter the most awful scream and try and get under earth. I got several, but I remember one fellow that took three ·45's before I got him. The boar being part of the coat-of-arms of the Campbell Clan, I presented the head to my eldest brother.

We had a most marvellous time, but a trip of this sort isn't all plain sailing, and we struck one bad day when we ran out of water. The doctor had warned me that it was better either to drink no water at all

18

or else have a drink of water every hour. We all selected the latter course, the natives carrying water for us in skins. We generally fetched up for breakfast or evening camp near a river or tributary and got a fresh supply. All went well till the day when, expecting a new supply at a small river about noon, we drank all the water we had—and then found the river dry. It was terribly hot, but one of the guides said he knew of a spring not far distant, so we tramped on for another two hours. When we eventually found the spring the water smelt like nothing on earth and was full of ants. However, the doctor said it was " fit," and we drank it. I never thought I should live to drink such putrid stuff, but thirst in a hot climate is a terrible thing.

All good things come to an end, and after a fortnight of absolute happiness with two of the best companions one could wish to have, we found ourselves back at Goma—alongside the Zambezi with the crocodiles and hippopotami. Our bag had been 1 rhino, 2 buffaloes, 2 roan, 5 koodoo, 1 sinabie, 2 water buck, 2 sable, 1 eland, 2 impalla, 5 bush buck, 1 Sharpe steer buck, and 14 wild boar.

Wheildon met us with his car, and as our ration of gin had been worked out to the day, we were glad to find that he had brought something with him, which enabled us to " splice the main brace." We motored back to Gatooma and found our wives waiting for us—a few celebrations, a visit to Woodforde's farm, and we set off for the Victoria Falls.

There are still " white men " in the world, and

McKenzie is one of them, nobly supported by his charming wife and family.

On our return journey, we stopped at what one would call a " one-eyed " place called Wanki, where there are some coal-mines. A fellow called Ferrari, who had served under me at Holyhead in airships, and was now an official on the Rhodesian railways, met us with a car, and suggested driving us round the town. I pointed out that, according to the Railway Schedule, we only had a few minutes, but he said that the train couldn't start without him, so off we went for our very interesting drive, and I am afraid we delayed all the passengers on the train.

On our way up to the Victoria Falls, I noticed in the train a remarkably nice-looking fellow, who appeared to be doing himself well and enjoying life. We arrived at the Victoria Falls Station about 8 a.m., and on going to the hotel, I was surprised to find our friend there in the capacity of clerk. He had just returned from his yearly fortnight's holiday. He was a most delightful fellow, who had been at Oxford, served all through the War and under General Ironside up in Archangel, and then, unable to settle down, had started to roam, like many another fellow I met in South Africa, and had fetched up in the hotel.

The heat at the Falls was terrific, and rather upset my wife, but we went down to see the Falls both by day and by night. They have often been described before, and I can only add my testimony to the fact that they are a wonderful sight and well worth a visit.

We crossed over to Livingstone, the capital of Northern Rhodesia, and had lunch with Sir Herbert James Stanley (the Governor of Northern Rhodesia) and Lady Stanley. I had met him before when he was Imperial Secretary.

Whilst at Livingstone we saw a rehearsal of the Armistice Day celebrations by the Northern Rhodesian (black) Regiment—now disbanded. They left a marked impression on me, as their marching and drill were as precise as that of any Guards regiment in London.

Coming back through Bechuanaland, we picked up a lot of toys made by the natives out of wood, which were sold at the various stations at which we stopped. I remember in particular a wooden monkey, with a tail curled like a " C." On my return to Simonstown, I kept it in my office, and Tancred, with his sense of humour, would put " tails up " or " tails down " according to whether or not he thought it was a suitable day for people to come and ask me for a day's leave !

On our return from the Victoria Falls, we arrived at Bulawayo about eight o'clock in the morning. I was dressed in my oldest clothes, as the train journey was very hot and the carriages full of red sand. It happened to be Armistice Day, and I was asked to take the salute at the War Memorial for the march past. I had no better suit with me to put on, but luckily I had my miniature medals with me, so with them pinned on one side and a poppy on the other, I took the salute after the Two Minutes' Silence.

Colonel Towse, the blind V.C., had performed a similar function the previous year, when he had gone out to " see " the Victoria Falls. He has told me since that he could picture the whole thing and feel the spray.

We stayed at both Pretoria and Johannesburg on our way south, and at the latter place received much hospitality from Mr. Izod, of the Navy League, who got me to inspect the Sea Cadets, a very smart set of lads, in the heart of South Africa. We also met Bishop Nash, a fine parson, who knew how to preach a good sermon, which is all too rare, and of whom we saw much later on at Cape Town. He was the number two Bishop to the Archbishop of Cape Town, Carter, a very old and dignified man who had a most charming residence just outside Cape Town.

Whilst at Johannesburg, we went down the Village Deep Gold Mine, one of the deepest—if not actually the deepest—in the world, about eight thousand feet. At that time the talk at the famous Rand Club was rather mournful, as some people thought that the days of the gold-mines were coming to a close, and as platinum had been found in the locality, there was a great boom in that. But I imagine that the gold will last many years yet.

We eventually returned to Simonstown, after one of the most interesting and wonderful trips I have ever had. It was difficult to settle down to dockyard routine again.

When staying at Johannesburg on our way back from the Victoria Falls, I received a telegram from

the Admiralty asking me to remain on the Station for
six months after my time expired. I demurred
until I had got into communication with the Commander-in-Chief to make sure that if I accepted it
would not adversely affect my employment as a Flag
Officer, by its being said that I had spent too much
time in shore appointments ; but a reply was
received from the Admiralty saying that it would in
no way affect my future employment. I therefore
accepted and remained on the Station six months
over my normal time. I thought, anyhow, that it
would help to qualify me for an Admiral Superintendent's job later on.

The routine of the dockyard went on much the same
except for a surprise visit from the Special Service
Squadron consisting of the *Hood*, flying the flag of
Admiral Field, the *Repulse*, and four light cruisers.
The first intimation we had of their visit came from
the Admiralty, in rather a curious way. As Captain-
in-Charge, the Canteen came under my jurisdiction,
and I received a cypher message asking me if I had
plenty of supplies for the Special Service Squadron.
I passed on the information to the Commander-in-
Chief, who had heard nothing about it. The next
cable I had was one ordering me to arrange for
special Christmas fare, so many turkeys for the *Hood*,
so many ducks for the *Repulse*, and so on, so I went
to the Commander-in-Chief and told him I thought
the Squadron would be at Cape Town about Christmas time. In due course he got a message from
the Admiralty to that effect, and also to the effect

that Admiral Field had been given acting rank over his head. It showed good organisation on the part of the Canteen Department, but I cannot believe that it was the correct way to treat a Commander-in-Chief.

However, they duly arrived, and received a great welcome. The chief impression left on the town was when a large party of men were landed and marched through under arms. A round of festivities of course took place. My chief duty lay in looking after the more uninteresting part. H.M.S. *Dragon* had a collision in the docks, and damaged her stern—which necessitated her being dry docked at Simonstown. It so happened that a big dinner-party was taking place at Admiralty House that night, and after dinner I was called into consultation with the Commander-in-Chief, Admiral Field, Brand, etc., and asked if I could dock the *Dragon* at 9 a.m. the following day. I said I would let him know in the course of an hour. I well remember one of the Staff turning to me, and although my junior officer, saying :

" You are Superintendent, aren't you ? Can't you give an answer without consulting other people ? "

I said, " No, I am not such a fool as to waste my time in carrying the tide tables in my head or the exact position of the blocks in the dock when I have a highly efficient Harbour Master and Constructor to do it for me."

Typical Naval War Staff ! !

I went straight to my house, and after consulting

the officers concerned, arranged to dock the *Dragon* the following day. We worked day and night on her right through the Christmas holidays, so as not to keep her away from her important cruise a day longer than was necessary. Her Captain, Fairbairn, was a first-rate fellow, and with his co-operation we got through the work very smoothly.

In the meantime a certain amount of entertaining went on, and my wife and I attended a delightful dance on board.

In due course the Admiralty sent a letter to me expressing their Lordships' appreciation, etc.

Our time at Simonstown came to an end in due course, and, although I had overstayed my time, I was very sorry to leave, as I had got to like the people, and I had a most loyal and cheerful lot of officers and their wives to support me.

Our last few days were very much occupied, as in addition to packing up, selling the car, etc., H.R.H. the Prince of Wales started his tour of South Africa, and I had to be present at a good many functions. He came down to Simonstown one day and was received by the Mayor and Naval Authorities. He then proceeded on board the training ship *General Botha*, after which he visited Admiralty House, and then went on to the Racecourse. I had to make a good many of the arrangements for his reception, in conjunction with the Deputy Mayor, who as it happened was also under my orders in the dockyard, which saved a lot of trouble in arranging who was to be present on the platform, etc. My chief difficulty was in arranging for H.R.H.'s Standard to be transported from one place to another, and to be hoisted at the correct moment. There were only two Standards available. As Steward of the Turf Club, I had to receive him when he arrived there after luncheon. I hired two cars, and got a permit from the magistrate to exceed the speed limit. One car went on ahead with the Standard, and the other conveyed me, after shifting from uniform into plain clothes, so as to arrive at the Turf Club before the Prince. We rushed there at about sixty miles an hour, and the police tried to stop us, as we were travelling too fast, but I got to my second place of duty in time. We received a good many cheers *en route*, as some of the crowd thought it must be the royal car. The following day two summonses were issued against me for exceeding the speed limit, so it was lucky I had taken the precaution of getting the magistrate's permit.

We had a lot of Moslems in the dockyard, and I received a deputation one day from their leader and representatives to ask whether the Admiralty would give them a grant towards rebuilding their place of worship, which I am glad to say the Admiralty did. They took it as a personal act of kindness from me (which of course it was not), and when we were leaving Simonstown they did a most unusual thing, as they invited both my wife and myself inside their place of worship in order to hear an address of regret on our departure and their hope of our return to Admiralty House (we received many of the same sort from other quarters), and also to make some presentations to my wife.

Our last week at Simonstown was a continual succession of farewells. The Commander-in-Chief (the late Admiral Fitzmaurice) gave a dinner in our honour, also the officers of my command, not to mention deputations and presentations from all sections of the community.

At the farewell dinner, when my health was proposed, the proposer remarked there was one thing he liked about me, and that was that I was accessible at any hour of the day or night, though he understood I was unapproachable when I was having my breakfast. On the morning of leaving, I gave a large breakfast-party, and tried to carry out my reputation of being unapproachable at breakfast. I therefore appeared at the breakfast table, said " Good morning," and sat down and proceeded to ring my bell for the steward, then for the coxswain (both of whom had been primed up for the job), proceeding to curse them roundly—my guests naturally thinking all that they heard was seriously meant. It was not until I had disrobed myself from my dressing-gown and appeared in my uniform that they discovered I was pulling their legs.

Our journey to the station was like a triumphal procession. Two cars fetched us, and we drove through crowded streets which were lined with black children waving Union Jacks. The station itself was packed with our friends, from the Mayor downwards, and with the seediboys and Kroomen forming a Guard of Honour. I was intensely nervous, as I always am on these occasions, and the only thing I could think of doing was to kiss everybody, after my success on New Year's Eve. We arrived at Cape Town, and I met the Commander-in-Chief, who had already heard the news about the kissing. I went into the Civil Service Club to say good-bye to the Secretary. I had only a few minutes to spare, and had a hurried cocktail with him. The Derby Sweepstake book happened to be lying on the table, so I wrote my name in it without even troubling to look at the number, paid my 10s. and asked the Secretary in a joking way to send me a wire when I won—on my arrival in England I got the telegram, and later a cheque for £100.

Amongst the many honours paid us before leaving South Africa, there was none I appreciated more than a private luncheon given by the Governor-General and Princess Alice to my wife and myself. Then we sailed in the *Garth Castle*, and so ended two and a half years in the Land of the Sun.

On my arrival back in England from South Africa, my faithful friend Truscott, who had served throughout " Q " ships with me, came out in a tender to meet me at Plymouth, a thing he invariably did whenever I arrived there. How on earth he found out by what ship I was returning, or when, I never discovered, but he used to watch my movements like a cat watches a mouse, and it was a sad day for me when he died in 1931.

XIX

H.M.S. *Tiger*

AFTER my foreign service leave I was ordered to a war course at Portsmouth. The day before I had to set off, I was suddenly seized with a terrible pain in my side. The doctor was called in about six in the morning, and a second one was sent for about seven. I could just hear them discussing at the end of my bed as to whether it was appendicitis or gall-stones, when the pain passed away as quickly as it had come. They advised me to stay in bed about ten days in case I got a recurrence of it, but in spite of their orders, I proceeded to Portsmouth the following day, and—touch wood—have not had the pain since.

On completion of my course I was offered and accepted the command of H.M.S. *Tiger*, a fine battle cruiser with a good war record and scars on her sides and turrets which she had received at the Dogger Bank and in the Battle of Jutland. On her quarter-deck was a memorial plate to those who had lost their lives in her. The *Tiger* did not belong to any particular squadron, being employed on special duties, such as gunnery firings and all kinds of experiments, most of which were of a highly con-

fidential nature, though we did have one fairly
public one, namely, testing a new electric bakery.
We made the trials last as long as possible, as we
found the bakery a great convenience to us. On
one occasion some distinguished visitors came
aboard, and I personally escorted them round the
ship, going out of my way to let them see all the
wonders inside the turrets, the torpedoes, etc., etc.,
and telling them that the *Tiger* was the best ship
in the Navy after the *Hood*. I thought and hoped
I had made a great impression, but when I got down
to my cabin and said, " What do you think of the
ship ? " the reply I got was, " Isn't it wonderful to
think you have an electric bakery on board and can
make your own bread ! "

We frequently had on board the Rear-Admiral of
Submarines, Admiral Haggard, and carried out
submarine exercises. The submarines would be
in any position between Portsmouth and Lamlash,
and we would proceed, escorted by destroyers,
whilst the submarines made an attack on us, if they
could. It was a job I never particularly liked, as
I was always frightened of ramming, though most
of the responsibility rests on the submarine, whose
business it is to keep out of the way of a big ship.
On one occasion, a submarine fired a torpedo
that hit our propeller and burst the air vessel,
which went off with a tremendous bang and shook
the whole ship. All the ship's company was
quickly on deck, and I turned to the Admiral and
remarked : " By Jove, sir, they have put a war

head on by mistake." I really thought we had been torpedoed.

We were stationed chiefly at Portland, but our home port was Portsmouth, where we served first under Admiral Sir S. R. Fremantle and then under Admiral O. de B. Brock. It so happened that at this period my elder brother Jim, who had been four years senior to me, was Captain of the Dockyard and King's Harbour Master. He was now four years junior to me, as during the War I had been specially promoted to the rank of Captain at the age of thirty-one ; and some curious situations used sometimes to arise. On one occasion I left the jetty when it was blowing pretty strong ; one of Jim's pilots was on board, but this did not relieve me of my responsibility for the safety of the ship. In turning round in rather a narrow space, we missed hitting the Royal Yacht by a few inches—had we done so, we would of course have sunk her. My brother was watching from the signal tower, and remarked to the signal-man, " I believe my brother is going to get the Royal Yacht." The Yeoman, who was looking through a big telescope, replied, " No, he isn't, sir ; he still has his pipe in his mouth and is smiling."

On another occasion we were due to sail at two o'clock in the afternoon, and it was blowing a whole gale of wind. My brother came on board at 11 a.m. to discuss with me as to whether we should sail or not. We discussed the matter over cocktails, and he eventually made a signal to the Commander-in-Chief to say he considered the weather too bad for the ship to be moved, so we had to remain in harbour overnight and wait for the next tide. As I had a dinner-party on board that night, I think most of the sailors imagined the thing was a put-up job between the brothers, but, needless to say, it wasn't.

One night we were dining together, and were both in uniform and having a heated argument. When it came to the point of saying " Good night," he saluted and said, " As your Junior Officer I say Aye, aye, sir," and then gave me an uncivil salute (a long nose), and said, " As your elder brother I think you are a silly ass."

The Admiral Superintendent of the Dockyard was Admiral Thesiger, a rather small but very important person and a rather strict disciplinarian. I had arranged one day to send all the sailors ashore for a route march at 9 a.m. Just at the last moment my Gunnery Officer came to me and reported that he had discovered that men weren't allowed to be marched under arms through the dockyard without the permission of the Admiral Superintendent, so I rushed up to Admiral Thesiger's house, and asked him if he would do me the honour of taking the salute if I marched my men past him—so all was peace.

I received orders whilst in the *Tiger* to give every facility to two film companies to produce naval films. One was " The Flag-Lieutenant," by Mr. Elvey, and the other was a play called " Second to None," by Miss Shurrey. I protested against the order, as I didn't think it becoming for the Service,

but got a written order, which of course I had to
obey. At first the sailors were rather amused at
taking part in the film, but they soon got fed up with
the whole show when they found boats had to be
lowered and hoisted two or three times to please
the cinema people.

We had one amusing scene over " The Flag-
Lieutenant." The Flag-Lieutenant himself was
Henry Edwards, a charming man with a delightful
wife. At first he wore his uniform wrong, but he
soon tumbled to the right way of doing things, and
always saluted his " Senior Officers." Part of the
show was to dress ship overall, with an Admiral's
flag at the masthead, and carry out the proper
ceremony for the King's Birthday. We originally
did it out of sight of land, but this not being successful, we had to do it again when lying alongside the
dockyard at Portsmouth. It was on October 3rd,
and I had to get permission from the Admiral to
hoist his flag (he wasn't a bit pleased ; but I pointed
out that it was his own order, " to give every
facility "), and to dress the ship overall at 11 o'clock
in the forenoon. We then manned ship, and the
officers, except myself, appeared in full dress. The
guard and band were paraded, and when the Marines
presented arms, the band went through the motions
of playing the National Anthem without actually
making any sound. I heard two stokers near me
say, " Do you 'ear that band ? it must be miles and
miles away ! " On the Commander blowing a
whistle, the crew waved their hands as if cheering,

but did not actually cheer. A dockyard matey, who happened to be watching the performance, went straight to the surgery and said that he had been suddenly stricken deaf, as he had been watching the *Tiger's* band playing, but could not hear it. A full account of this extraordinary proceeding appeared in the evening papers.

On another occasion, part of the Falkland Islands film was done on board, and the actor representing Sir Doveton Sturdee strutted about in naval uniform with all his medal ribbons on. About five o'clock in the evening the Commander came into my cabin and told me that Admiral Sturdee was going ashore in a felt hat, monkey jacket with medal ribbons, and plain-clothes trousers, so I had to order Admiral Sturdee either to put on uniform, or to go in plain clothes. There may have been some idea that, if naval films were to be made, they should have the proper surroundings, etc., so as to bring credit to the Navy, but the chief actors were non-servicemen who did not know how to wear their uniform properly and were more likely to discredit it. Another case was when a young " Actor-Commander " went ashore with his face smothered in grease paint, and was saluted by all the bluejackets he passed.

One evening at Portsmouth my wife and I were attending a very big dinner-party at Admiralty House, and Jim and his wife were also present. We were in mess dress with medals on, and after dinner I was told off to sit alongside the charming wife of a Commander to make conversation, but not being

19

very good at that sort of job, I did not get on very well until we discovered some mutual friends who had been married from our house in Simonstown. She asked me what job I had had out in Simonstown and I said " Captain-in-charge," and she said, " Did you by any chance relieve that fellow Gordon Campbell ? " Without thinking, I said, " Thank goodness I did not relieve that silly ass," and she said, " Yes, I hear he is a bit of an ass." Before I could stop her, she went on to say, " I am sick and tired of the name of Gordon Campbell, but his brother, who is sitting over there, is a charming man." She went on to say, " I should like to meet Gordon Campbell, though I hear he is a bit queer." Eventually, when she stopped, I said, " I hope when you meet him you won't find him so bad as you have heard—and, as a matter of fact, you are talking to him now."

The poor woman nearly fell through the sofa, and spent the rest of the evening trying to explain that she had not said what she had said. She went up to my brother afterwards and told him the dreadful thing she had done, but he assured her that I had a sense of humour, and would probably add the yarn to my repertoire.

When I first took over the command of the *Tiger* she was not a very happy ship, chiefly because the Admiralty was continually changing the officers, and the Drafting Office at Portsmouth was continually changing the men, a most hopeless way to attempt to run a ship smartly and efficiently. On one occasion when we were in dry dock at Portsmouth, it was reported to me that some dockyard workmen were singing the " Red Flag " under the ship's bottom, whilst the National Anthem was being played on the quarter-deck. Amongst other steps I took, I arranged for one or two of my officers to be walking under the ship's bottom next morning in case of a similar occurrence, but I gather it had already become known that I would not tolerate that sort of thing.

On another occasion I happened to notice two " dockyard mateys " on the quarter-deck with their caps on whilst the colours were being hoisted and the band was playing the National Anthem. I approached them and asked them what they meant by not taking their hats off, to which they replied that I had no authority to make them, which was perfectly correct. They were decent fellows, and I invited them down to my cabin (they took their hats off there) and showed them a picture of the King. I said, " Aren't you proud of that man, and can't you show you are ? " They said, " Yes, sir, but our Union won't let us." I had to be content with a compromise ; they managed to be ashore instead of on board whilst the Anthem was being played.

I was rather glad when the *Tiger* was recommissioned and I was able to start with practically a new crew, and I also met with some slight assistance from the Admiralty in not changing the officers so often. I carried out my old custom of paying particular attention to the welfare and recreational side, and even started Lectures and Debates for the men.

One amusing debate was on the question of " Prohibition," and I remember a Leading Seaman, who was well known in the boxing world, telling us that when he was in training, his trainer advised him to have a pint of beer every day, and if he felt over-strained, to make it two. I found that dancing was the thing that appealed to the modern sailors most, and they had frequent dances at Weymouth, which I used generally to attend. We had a ship's dog on board, by the name of " Tiger "—a white bulldog— who caused great excitement, because he couldn't stand the sight of a Marine, and when the Marines " doubled off " the quarter-deck, " Tiger " followed at full speed, and bit the trousers of the first man he could catch. He generally lived in my cabin, as on the whole he was not popular, and not having " joined " the Navy till the age of six, did not take too kindly to ship life, and eventually, after I left the ship, he was " discharged, services no longer required."

When I went to the *Tiger* I was getting near the top of the Captain's list and, knowing it would probably be my last command, was particularly anxious to have a happy ship ; and it was a very unfortunate thing that it was the only time during my career that I had to try two officers by court-martial ; but as the Admiralty sent me at one time no less than six officers who were in the " special report " category, it was not surprising. It was also in the *Tiger* that I received my only admonition from the Admiralty during the time I was in the Navy, but this one did not disturb my sleep, as it was a case of a man being wrongly advanced, and as the case had nothing to do with me, I kept it as a curio.

The last steam trial I did in the *Tiger* was supposed to be one of an hour's duration on passage from Southend to Portland, after carrying out bombardment practice there. The thrill of steaming at 26 knots with the stern nearly awash was too much for me, and when the Engineer-Commander reported that the steam trial was complete, and that he proposed to reduce to the economical speed of 13 knots, I told him that I would not reduce to anything less than 21 knots. He asked me what about the explanation of expenditure on fuel, and I told him to wait and see. Anyhow, we dashed down-Channel at 21 knots, and instead of arriving at Portland at 8 a.m. as I had signalled, we arrived there about 2 a.m., and I went to bed thoroughly contented with life. On waking up in the morning, I began to think what explanation was going to be made. The Chief very kindly offered to help me, and we discovered an old regulation which said that Captains were to take every opportunity of training any new batch of stokers at cruising at high speed. I therefore, on my official report, simply stated that I had maintained high speed in accordance with the regulations, a new batch of stokers having recently joined the ship. I heard no more about it, but the regulation was in due course altered.

In the summer of 1927 I received information from the Admiralty that I would be relieved at the end of July. The then Naval Secretary, Admiral Sir F. Larken, K.C.B., was extraordinarily nice about it, as he had already extended my time over my original appointment, and he allowed me to select a date for being relieved convenient to me. Realising that this would be the last ship I would be likely to command, anyhow as a Captain, I decided to make the best of my remaining time. In May I sent in an application to go for a cruise to the south-western ports—Falmouth, Torquay, Plymouth, etc.—in order to train the cadets, together with Marine Officers, whom I had on board, as we had spent so much time in harbour.

In spite of frequent applications, I could not get any answer out of the Admiralty one way or the other as to whether my programme was approved or not, so when the day of sailing came, I sailed without their approval. The Commander asked if he should take the drifter with us (each big ship has a drifter attached for taking men ashore), and I said, " Of course," as I thought that if I was taking a battle cruiser on a cruise, I might just as well include the drifter. We had a thoroughly enjoyable time. I had assembled the crew to tell them that it was my last cruise, and asked them to let me leave with a good impression and have no leave-breakers. They played the game 100 per cent. Our first call was Torquay, and unfortunately the drifter had a collision, but in order to avoid having to report it I paid for the necessary damage myself. Whilst on this cruise at Torquay we celebrated the King's Birthday. I have always had a fancy for ceremonial, provided I do not have to take a prominent part. On this occasion I surprised everyone by arranging for the quarter-deck to be manned by sailors in white uniform ; in the centre were the remainder of the seamen and stokers in blue, and on top was a guard of Royal Marines—red, white, and blue. I had the Mayor of Torquay on board for the ceremony, and in the evening entertained all the Warrant Officers to a big dinner-party.

We next proceeded to Dartmouth, in order that I might pay my respects to Admiral Bayly and his niece. I dined with Admiral Nasmith, V.C., who was Captain of the College there, and joined in one of the Cadets' Dances. I remember dancing with one very small Cadet, and half-way through the dance I suggested I was not much good at dancing. His reply was, " You are getting on very nicely, sir."

I next went to Plymouth in order to salute my old Commander-in-Chief, Admiral Sir Rudolf Bentinck. Our last port of call was the Scilly Islands, where I had one of my brain-waves. On leaving Plymouth I handed the Gunnery-Lieutenant secret orders for landing a battalion of sailors, together with field guns, etc., and had an imaginary scheme worked out for him. On arrival at the Scilly Islands, as the anchor was let go, the landing party left the ship, amidst the cheers of the Marines, who thought at last they were left out of a landing party. I shifted into plain clothes and took the Captain of the Marines, also in plain clothes, ashore with me to act as umpire together with myself. As I was leaving the ship, I handed a letter to the Lieutenant of the Marines, a fine old Marine called Petley, which contained instructions for the Marines to land immediately to rout the sailors! So we finished up with a pitched battle ashore, which I think amused nearly everybody.

On returning from the Scilly Islands to Portland on the completion of our cruise, I received a wireless message informing me that the Admiralty had approved of the cruise!

Amongst the many pleasant evenings which took place before I left the *Tiger* was one occasion when I was entertained by the Wardroom officers, and another when I was entertained by the Gunroom officers, about eighteen midshipmen and cadets with a very fine Sub-Lieutenant. I spent one of the most enjoyable evenings I had had in the ship, watching these young fellows acting exactly as I had done when I was a midshipman, doing their best to try and make the skipper have " one over the eight," whilst they themselves pretended they were teetotallers. Grace was said before dinner, and an obviously pre-arranged " Amen " was forthcoming. After dinner, they sat me down in the arm-chair in the mess, and gathered round me like a lot of children, trying to get me to spin them some snappy stories.

I left the *Tiger* on July 31st, and the day before leaving I had another sham fight ashore with practically the whole of the ship's company, as I greatly believed in these sham fights : although they are not perhaps extremely instructive, they are a relief from the monotony of ship routine, and they combine with exercise a certain amount of instruction and fun. Just before I left the ship, the officers gave a dance, followed by an enormous one given by the ship's company. The total number present must have been about 2,000. They had asked permission to give me a present on leaving, which I had to decline, but during the dance, much to my astonishment and gratitude, they got my wife into a prominent place, and made her a beautiful presentation of a silver inkstand, whilst the officers presented her with a silver tray. My wife and children have many souvenirs given them by officers and men of the ships in which I have served.

I was given a great send-off on leaving the ship. I intended sailing ashore, as was my custom, and the officer of the watch had my galley all ready, with the mast up. Unfortunately it was blowing a gale, and as soon as I got clear of the ship, I lowered the sails and pulled ashore.

After going through a war course at Portsmouth, I settled down at Plymouth, waiting to hear whether or not I would be placed on the retired list on promotion to Flag rank. I thought that my chances of being kept on were only twenty-five out of a hundred. I knew the Admiralty had great difficulty in deciding who could stay, and having had a nervous break-down, coupled with the fact that my age was com-pletely out of my seniority, I thought I should probably have to go, especially as I came in a batch of Captains who had all been specially promoted for War service. I had also only been a " salt horse," and specialists appeared to have priority. My chief hope was that my experience as Superintendent of the Dockyard in Simonstown might be made use of for one of the home dockyards. One morning, early in November, I was lying in bed when I received two letters from the Admiralty. The first one I opened was from the Naval Secretary saying it was proposed to put my name forward to take command of two of the brand-new 10,000-ton cruisers during their trials. I turned to my wife and said, " By Jove, they are not going to axe me after all ! "

The second letter was one to inform me that on my promotion to Rear-Admiral I should be placed on the Retired List. The Admiralty have a sense of humour entirely their own ! The letter informing me I had to retire was a regular stereotyped letter, probably written by someone who had no sea sense, and rather less gracious than one would send to a cook who had served you for two years. I had heard many other Captains who had received similar letters complain about the tone of them, and when I saw the letter, I was not surprised ; but since the

War more attention has been paid to matériel than to personnel. I suppose such trivial matters as retiring Captains were simply part of the routine. I was given the opportunity of retiring at my own request, but I declined to do so.

I was rather surprised that, two days after my receiving the letter, the information was made public in a newspaper, although I had had no correspondence directly or indirectly with any paper, a fact which the then Naval Secretary, Vice-Admiral Eric Fullerton, C.B., did not appear to believe. I was also rather surprised to find that I was being retired without the First Lord having been informed, but this was to some extent made good by my receiving a very charming three-page letter from Lord Bridgeman, in his own handwriting, which gave me an opportunity of replying and putting forward certain points. I then had a very pleasant interview with the then First Sea Lord, and I pointed out to him that I had no grievance about being retired, and quite expected to take my turn with my brother officers, but I did object to the manner in which it was done. I then went so far as to tell him that had I been one of the Sea Lords, I should probably have retired myself !—only in a different manner. I also put on record at this time that I considered there was a growing want of confidence in the Board of Admiralty, a fact which I had noticed in the various commands I had held since the War.

I declined the command of the cruisers, as, apart from my own feelings, it struck me as absurd, when it was already so difficult for officers to get as much sea experience as they needed and used to have in pre-War days, to employ a person who was about to be retired.

I had the honour of being made an A.D.C. to the King for a short period, and also got a Good Service Pension, but as these are awarded by seniority and not by merit, a certain amount of the honour disappears.

Naturally I was very upset at my naval career coming to a close at the age of forty-two, and the first thing I did was to take a trip to the Sahara Desert, where I sat by myself for two days and said good-bye to the Navy. On my return I sat down and set about writing my first book, which has since been published in England, the U.S.A., France, Italy, Japan, Norway, and Czechoslovakia.

I eventually retired in April 1928, when I received another formal letter, rather more human, from the Admiralty, also an Order in Council awarding me a special pension of £100 a year.

" AT THE COURT AT BUCKINGHAM PALACE,
" *The 7th day of May*, 1928.

" *Present*,

" THE KING'S MOST EXCELLENT
MAJESTY IN COUNCIL

" Whereas there was this day read at the Board a Memorial from the Right Honourable the Lords Commissioners of the Admiralty, dated the 13th day

of April, 1928 (C.W. 11370/27), in the words following, viz. :

" ' Whereas by Section 5 of the Greenwich Hospital Act, 1865, it is enacted, inter alia, that Your
Majesty may, from time to time, by Your Order in
Council, appoint such pensions as seem fit to Officers
of the Royal Navy and Royal Marines and others for
the time being entitled to the benefits of Greenwich
Hospital :

" ' And whereas we are desirous of awarding a
Greenwich Hospital Pension of £100 a year to Rear-
Admiral Gordon Campbell, V.C., D.S.O., in recognition of his distinguished and exceptional services during the Great War, such pension to be in
addition to those authorised by Your Majesty's
Order in Council bearing date the 16th January,
1924 :

" ' We beg leave humbly to recommend that Your
Majesty may be graciously pleased, by Your Order
in Council, as an exceptional and isolated case and
not to be drawn into a precedent for the future, to
approve of the establishment of an additional
Greenwich Hospital Pension of £100 a year accordingly, and to sanction the award of this Pension to
Rear-Admiral Gordon Campbell, with effect from
the 6th April, 1928, until the date of the Officer's
death, when the pension is to be regarded as lapsing.'

" His Majesty, having taken the said Memorial
into consideration, was pleased, by and with the
advice of His Privy Council, to approve of what is
therein proposed.

" AND the Right Honourable the Lords Commissioners of the Admiralty are to give the necessary directions herein accordingly.

" M. P. A. HANKEY."

Even with this, which was an exceptional honour and one I much appreciated, my pension did not amount to the maximum retired pay of a Captain or the minimum retired pay of a Rear-Admiral. The moral is, do not play the fool in war and get promoted too young.

XX

Lecturing

AFTER completing my book, I looked round for something else to do, and once having opened my mouth, I thought I might try my hand at lecturing. By a fortunate coincidence, my literary agent, Leonard Moore, is partner to Gerald Christy, of the Lecture Agency, Ltd., in England, so I consulted Christy as to lecturing, and have worked with him ever since. A better combination than Christy and Moore for lectures and books would be hard to find.

Christy, the elder man of the two, has had a very wide experience in dealing with the very best lecturers in England and elsewhere, and I have always felt on safe ground in taking his advice. Moore had the misfortune to lose a leg through a disease contracted during the War, but so little does he complain or grumble about it, that it was not until I had known him several years that I discovered he had a false leg ; one day I noticed him walking lame, and asked him if he had rheumatism, and he said, " No, I put a new leg on this morning." To watch him playing tennis, it would be difficult for anybody to detect his suffering, and after the game, he goes off and changes his leg.

As a trial run, I gave my first lecture at Salcombe, Devon, where I happened to be staying for the summer. I took my son, David, then aged thirteen and a half, to listen to it, and on walking back I explained to him that my pension would not enable me to keep him at Winchester, so that his education would be dependent on my success as a lecturer. I asked him to think the matter over carefully and to give me some practical suggestions for improving my lecture. After a short pause, he said, " Well, to be quite honest, I think it was a very good lecture, but really, Father, you must try not to look quite such a silly fool when they clap you." I tried to overcome this disadvantage of mine, but was rather discouraged when, some months later, I was lecturing at a public school, and the Head Master and his wife were present. After the lecture, I was talking to Mrs. Head Master, and told her the yarn about David. She, without thinking, said, " Yes, isn't it extraordinary the way these boys come straight out with the truth ! "

The first big lecture I gave was in the Kingsway Hall for the Prudential Insurance Company. I got my wife, Gerald Christy, and Admiral E. R. G. R. Evans, the most experienced lecturer I know of, to come and hear it, and to give me some candid criticisms afterwards. The hall had three tiers, and when I arrived on the platform I was as nervous as a cat, and thought I had better picture myself shouting to sailors on the forecastle from the bridge of the *Tiger*. I therefore let fly with a full blast. Evans was sitting in front, my wife in the middle, and Christy at the back. They all had the same criticism to make, and that was, that I shouted too loudly. Incidentally, I had been warned when lecturing to try and pretend that I felt at ease (which I never do). So for a change I tried sitting down during the course of the lecture on a sort of raised part of the platform, with the intention of talking to the audience in a conversational manner. To my horror, I saw the slides going on one after the other before I was ready for them, and I discovered that I was sitting on the bell that did the trick !

I didn't realise when I started lecturing what a strenuous job it is, and what a lot one has at times to put up with. In my first season in England I got through over sixty lectures between October and the middle of December, which meant travelling nearly every day, lecturing in the evening, and very often staying at an indifferent hotel.

I think the two most difficult lectures I gave in England were, one to a Blind College, and the other to the inmates of a Lunatic Asylum. At the Blind College the audience consisted of people who had been born blind, and I wondered how they could possibly understand the first thing about a ship, let alone mystery ships. The Principal, Dr. Campbell, assured me they would. I felt terribly nervous, and each time when I said, " Now you see," I could feel the sweat trickling down my back. It turned out a great success, and they not only talked about it for a long time afterwards, but invited me to go down

20

again and give them a talk on how a battleship is run.

The Lunatic Asylum was what one might call a fashionable one, with people who paid big fees and lived in a lovely house, with gardens, tennis courts, dancing, etc. Some of the cases were most pathetic. A Varsity fellow was one : he had overworked himself, and could only talk Latin or Greek ; another had a great athletic record, but had lost his reason on the matter of heat and cold. The audience were nearly all in evening dress, ladies one side of the room, and gentlemen the other. Except for the presence of a number of nurses, one would hardly have realised one was talking to more or less lunatics, except for the fact that they never smiled or applauded till the end. The only interruption I had was when a man asked me, " If you get torpedoed and go to the bottom of the sea, do you come up again ? "

After the lecture, a fellow with a good war record came up to me and told me he had written some twelve books about war from the Crimea onwards—he gave me his card and the names of his publishers, and asked me to go and select any three books I liked as a small present from him. On making enquiries, I found he had never written a book, but always thought he was writing one. One thing that struck me about the place was that they all seemed happy.

The lectures that I enjoy most are those at Public or Preparatory Schools, though I have noticed that the boys and girls in the schools in the U.S.A. take a far greater interest (or should I say, show far more enthusiasm) than the young people in this country, who very likely are sick and tired of hearing their fathers talking about the War, little realising what a great anxiety they were to their parents when food was scarce and sorrow was hovering round many homes. At one Preparatory School to which I went, I had been spinning them a yarn about how the magazine caught on fire and eventually exploded, when a small boy said, " Please, sir, why did you keep a special room on board for magazines, and what magazines did you keep in it ? "

I have many times had most delightful chairmen at my lectures : the one that comes most readily to my mind is Lord Burnham ; yet I could almost write a book on " Chairmen I have suffered under." On one occasion I was giving a lecture in a city where the Mayor had done me the honour of presiding. He arrived twenty minutes late, and as we went on the platform together he turned round to me and said, " My dear old chap, I'm awfully sorry, but I've clean forgotten your name and what you are talking about." I whispered the correct answer, when he started off with a twenty-minute speech explaining why he was late and how many committee meetings he had attended during the day, and what improvements in the town would ensue, etc. By this time he had again forgotten my name. I tried to get it to him—and he finished up by saying, " I now have much pleasure in introducing to you—er—

er—Admiral Gordon, who will give you an interesting lecture on—er—er—well, I will leave him to
speak for himself."

One of the nicest lectures I had in England was at
a girls' school called " Calder Girls' School " at
Seascale, Cumberland. I had neither heard of the
school nor the place before—but on arrival there I
was greatly impressed. Seascale consists of a
station, " pub," church, golf-course, and about
four or five shops. I dined with the Misses Wilson,
the head mistresses, previous to the lecture, and was
greatly interested in hearing their views on education. Each girl is carefully watched on joining, and
a specialist in psychology tries to find out where
the girl's talent really lies. The girl is then particularly trained in whatever subject or art is suitable,
so that when she leaves school she is qualified for
some profession. The appearance of the girls also
greatly took my fancy, as they all looked so happy
and well. Without saying what my impressions
were, I got my wife to visit the school, which impressed her in the same way as it did me, with the
result that my daughter is there now.

In touring the schools I enjoyed meeting the
Head Masters and hearing their views on the modern
boy ; personally, I think he is just as good as—if not
a better fellow than—we were. I was particularly
anxious to find out what effect the War had had on
boys, mentally and physically. I found that mentally they were apt to be exceedingly sensitive, shy,
and somewhat nervous ; physically they are as

healthy as ever, except that they apparently get tired more easily than we used to do, and are not so energetic. This I think is not due to the War, but due to the change of transport and life generally. Whereas I used to walk to school, a boy now takes a bus or train, or even his father's motor-car—and why not ? In the long run they play more tennis and golf, and if England wants four hundred thousand men again to-morrow, as she did in 1914—she will get them, and they will be just as good. This was shown by the way they behaved at the General Strike. I am very much against the youth of this country being run down—if they follow the advice of the Prince of Wales and give some of their spare time to the service of their country in some small way, all will be well—and let them remember that democracy is going to win, and they can't afford to be snobs.

During the summer of 1928 one of the lecture managers of New York, Lee Keedick, was over in London. He happened to have read an advance copy of my book, and approached me as to lecturing in the States and Canada. His visit was a very rushed one, so I had to fix things up in a great hurry. I met him in his hotel, and after preliminary discussions, he telephoned to one of the well-known halls in London and hired it for ten minutes. I could not imagine what he was doing till we went along there together in a taxi, and on arrival, he asked me to get on to the platform in the empty hall and talk for five minutes on anything I liked, whilst

he sat at the back of the hall. After this performance, we got on with the contract, his idea being that
if I could talk in such unfavourable circumstances,
I ought to be all right for America, and also for
publicity purposes he would be able to say that he
had heard me talk in one of the most famous halls in
London.

I sailed in the *Berengaria* early in January 1929.
One of the most interesting men I spoke to was Mr.
Doran, of the American publishing firm of Double-
day, Doran & Co. I was particularly pleased to
meet him, as they were my American publishers, and
on receiving the manuscript of *My Mystery Ships*
had wired me asking permission to " glorify " it.
I had borrowed the saying of Joseph Chamberlain,
and replied, " What I have said, I have said, and
will alter nothing." I discussed the matter with
him, and asked exactly what they had meant by
" glorifying " it. One incident he referred to was
the sinking of my ship, the *Dunraven*, and he said
I hadn't mentioned that I was the last man to leave
the ship. I replied, " Surely to goodness you don't
expect any Captain of a ship of any nationality to say
he was the last person to leave his sinking ship ! "
to which he answered, " That is all right, but you
must remember that the U.S.A. is a vast country,
and people in the Middle West, unlike you in Great
Britain, have no ' sea sense,' and don't know either
the customs or traditions of the sea." He pointed
out that my refusal to alter the book would very
seriously affect the sale in America, and he was

perfectly correct, as it hardly "went" at all. I found later that what Mr. Doran had told me was more than correct, from many points of view. Just as we in England don't take a vast amount of interest in wars in the Middle East of Europe, so it was in the Middle States; they couldn't for a long time realise that the Great War, which we could see with our own eyes, had much interest for them.

On the voyage out, I read a book about New York, which fairly scared me, as everything seemed to be wrong about the place. It is extraordinary what false impressions the average Englishman has about the States till he gets there. I met with nothing but the greatest civility from the Customs and Immigration officials; in fact, it was the same with everyone I met in shops, railway stations, hotels, etc. The only possible exception one might make is when one runs across a disgruntled Irishman.

A lot of the New York porters had served in Europe during the Great War. On arriving at the Grand Central Station to catch my train, I handed my luggage to one who had been over in France. He read my rank on my luggage, and went ahead of me into the train. When I followed afterwards, he was very effusive in his salaams, and said, "I recognised at once by your walk that you were a military officer."

I was terrified at the thought of meeting the Press, but there again, I was agreeably surprised, as I found that, taken as a whole, they were perhaps persistent at times with their cameras, but always very pleasant to talk to, and I never saw anything reported that I took exception to. I took out with me, with malice aforethought, a walking-stick which had been made out of the wood of the *Victory*, and when the interviewers turned on to the subject of cruisers, I generally managed to switch them on to the stick.

Thanks to my many friends, I was made an honorary member of a lot of the New York Clubs, including the Union, Knickerbocker, and Century, and I joined the British Commonwealth as an ordinary member. Colonel Thatcher was the kindest friend I met in the States. He had a beautiful house in Park Avenue, where I enjoyed many a happy evening, but perhaps the times I enjoyed with him most were those I spent at his office, or various clubs. He had been adviser during the War to the Government on the burning question of " continuous voyage," which caused so much friction between the States and England. When the U.S.A. joined in the War, he came over to France and commanded an American regiment, receiving the Congress medal for distinguished service in the field. I can never convey, in words or otherwise, all the thanks I owe to Colonel Thatcher for his help in my lectures, for his hospitality, and for his great friendship.

Prohibition—what a word ! It is not for me to criticise the laws of a foreign country ; I can only relate some of my personal experiences. Besides attending several private champagne dinner-parties

during my first few days in New York, I got " put
wise " as to how to get my own personal supply in
my bedroom at the hotel, and an introduction to a
very respectable " speakeasy," where one could get
a good dinner and a good glass of wine. During the
War, I had serving with me an old sea-dog who, for
the four years he was with me, never smiled. I ran
across him in New York and invited him to my
room, and when I produced a bottle of whisky, I
saw him smile for the first time, so I won a second
smile by suggesting that he should take the whole
bottle with him.

I must admit that I never met an employer of
labour who didn't say that he had had better work
out of his employees since the days of prohibition,
but as I was generally told this over a highball
(whisky and soda), it appeared to me to be one law
for the rich and another for the poor, a thing which
rather surprised me in a country which prides itself
on being the most free and democratic in the world.
A result of prohibition which really disgusted me
was to see ladies in evening dress drunk—not just
tipsy—and the sad part of it was to think they had
probably only had a couple of cocktails. I found,
on going out to dinner-parties, that one never knew
in advance what to expect. Occasionally, but very
rarely, I would go to a house which was really
" dry "—the host would say, " I don't (or do) agree
with the law, but anyhow, it is the law, and I feel
it my duty as a citizen to obey it."

At another house, the host would say, " I am

afraid I can only offer you a whisky and soda, as I can't be bothered with getting good wines from the bootleggers." Yet another would give you a full champagne dinner. At one house the host said, " I am afraid I can only offer you a cocktail, and I wouldn't have even that in my house, except that my daughter makes me." Many a man told me he had never had a whisky and soda in his life till the Government said he wasn't to—and they might just as well tell him not to eat radishes, as they would give him indigestion.

One night I went to a dinner-party, and the hostess greeted me by saying, " I am awfully sorry, my bootlegger has failed me ; I have no sherry in the house, and I know you like it." I, of course, said I didn't mind, and anticipated a dry dinner ; but not a bit of it : there were cocktails, champagne, liqueurs, whisky and soda, etc., the bootlegger having only failed in the sherry. On another occasion I was one of the guests of honour at a big dinner for some six hundred people. We dined in public and I happened to sit between a leading legal authority in the State and a Judge. It came to my turn for my speech ; I remarked to my legal friend that I hated making speeches, and that it didn't help one much when one was full of iced water. He replied, " If you feel like that, Admiral, I have a flask in my pocket, and you can take it outside for a minute." The Judge, the legal authority, Mayor of the City, myself, and several others had some good " Scotch." I asked the legal authority if he minded me putting to him a candid question, to which he replied, " Go right ahead." I said, " We often talk in England of a man's house being his castle, where he can do what he likes, but I can't understand a legal authority who has to help administer the law, carrying about a flask of whisky on him." He replied, " Say, boy, the answer is simple ; I don't hold with the law."

I made two separate lecturing tours in the United States and Canada, both of which were full of interest, and I met a large number of nice people. During one of my stays at Montreal, I received a telegram from Sir Esme Howard, our Ambassador at Washington, saying that President Hoover wished to receive me the following day. I had a long journey to Washington, and got there about seven in the morning. My appointment was for twelve noon, which gave me very little time to have a look round. I first went to a hat shop to find out what was the proper headgear in which to go to White House, and found myself buying a Derby. Sir Esme Howard took me in to see the President, for whom I have always had a great respect, and I was very much surprised at the lack of ceremony attached to the office of President of the United States. I should have expected there to be more outward signs of the fact that the President is not only President of the United States, but also a great power in world affairs.

President Hoover received me most cordially, but I was a little bit disappointed in that his appear-

ance did not come up to the impressions I had
formed from his photographs. He appeared to be
a very quiet and level-headed man. My visit
happened to be at the time when the Naval Conference was taking place in London, and it was interesting to hear from him some contradictions of various
statements which were appearing in the morning
papers. He expressed a hope, with which I entirely
agreed, that there will be some more exchange of
visits between people from England and the U.S.A.
I was able to tell him how completely my opinion of
the States and its inhabitants had changed since I
had been over there, and what great hospitality
I had received on all sides.

On arriving at Toronto about seven o'clock one
morning, I went out of the station the shortest way,
straight to the hotel. I had no sooner got to my
room there than a fellow arrived in a great state of
excitement to tell me that a Civic Reception had been
arranged for me, and that the band and mounted
police were waiting at the station. I expressed my
regrets, but said that I had received no information
about it ; so I made enquiries as to when the next
train arrived, which happened to be about 11.30.
I suggested that he should go back and say that I had
missed my train and was not arriving until 11.30.
In the meantime I had a comfortable bath, shave,
and breakfast, and got hold of my old friend Hargraft
who had served under me at Holyhead, and together
we arrived at the station about 11.30, when I received
a great welcome. The traffic was held up, and I was

driven through the streets behind a band and mounted police, etc. On arrival at the Town Hall, I was received by the Mayor, Mr. McBride, a very famous and genial character. At the top of the Town Hall steps he read an official address of welcome, referring to me as Rear-Admiral, etc. He then turned round to me and said : " Come on, General, I would like to introduce you to some of the Aldermen." About half-way through the introductions he looked up at my face, and apparently thought that I looked too young to be a General, so he started to call me " Colonel." By the time I had laid my wreath at the foot of the Cenotaph, I was addressed as " Major." I found, throughout my tour in the States and Canada, that I was rarely called by my proper rank.

Whilst at Toronto I was labelled in the papers again as the " Mystery V.C."

About nine o'clock one morning I was just stepping out of my bathroom without a stitch of clothing on, when a newspaper correspondent, without even knocking at my door, burst into my room with his hat on, a large cigar in his mouth, and a camera in his hand and said : " Say, Admiral, I have come to take a snap." I replied : " Go right ahead now, and once and for all disclose the mystery."

Whilst at Ottawa I had the honour of lunching at Government House with the Governor-General and Lady Willingdon. I also went to Kingston to fit in a brief visit to the Canadian Legion, which is a branch of the British Empire Service League. In nearly every place I went to I paid similar visits, as they were not only intensely loyal, but also gave me a most hearty welcome as coming from the Old Country, and it was rather unusual for them to receive a naval officer. What always struck me most in Canada about the members of the B.E.S.L. was their friendly comradeship, which was perhaps more noticeable than in England, where we are more reserved.

In all my lectures I showed a picture of Admiral Jellicoe, which invariably brought down the house, as he was a man in whom all seemed to have implicit confidence and faith. Whilst at Kingston I also visited the Royal Military College, which used to be a naval station. I gave the cadets there a short address. Their turn-out was smart in the extreme, and their discipline was, I should say, second to none.

It was whilst in London that I met for the first time General Armstrong, C.B., whom I was to have the pleasure of meeting many times afterwards. He was smothered in medals, and I found him a most enjoyable man to yarn with, and very popular with all ranks and ratings. Nothing ever seemed to perturb him. He was a lifelong abstainer, as he did not like alcohol, but it didn't prevent him (as I have seen him do) sitting up till the early hours of the morning, joining wholeheartedly in the yarns and jokes of a sometimes rather rowdy and convivial crowd.

From London I went to Windsor, Ontario, where

I stayed with Colonel Prince and his wife. He has the reputation of being Prince by name and Prince by nature. Of the many houses in which I stayed, I have never stayed in one where I have been more at home. Prince is Colonel of the Essex-Scottish Regiment. He was one of the youngest Colonels in the Canadian Army during the Great War, and then took command of the Militia at Windsor. I, together with my son, spent a short time with them in camp, and the spirit of the regiment was typical of the spirit of Canada. Prince, although a strong disciplinarian, had but to express a wish and it was instantly carried out. I gave two lectures at Windsor, both run by the Essex-Scottish Regiment. The Armouries in which the lectures were held were decorated with the Union Jack and the flag of Canada. Pipers played at the ends of the room, and the Sea Cadet Corps was present in full force. The surroundings were ideal. It made one absolutely stir with patriotism.

The officers did me the honour of making me a Life Honorary Member of their mess, a thing I much appreciate. Their honorary members include many Americans from Detroit, a furlong away, who help to support the Regiment, which is chiefly run on a voluntary basis. They gave a rather unique dinner-party to myself and all the other honorary members. I say unique, because here we had British and Americans united to do honour to a Canadian Regiment. I paid several visits to Windsor ; in fact, I went there whenever I could.

It was whilst at Windsor, nearing the end of my second tour, that I had a bit of a breakdown, together with bronchitis, and was laid up in Prince's house for some time with an Army doctor to look after me. I was advised to cancel the remainder of my tour, which included a visit to Bermuda. This I declined to do, and though some kind anonymous friend generously sent a cheque to the bank to make good any loss I might incur through cancelling it, I went on with the tour, and only missed one lecture. At a later date another anonymous person sent me a cheque for $500, on condition that I spent it on myself, and saying he had long wished to pay a small tribute to someone connected with the British Navy. I have never to this day found out who it was, and if ever he reads this book, I hope he will accept my grateful thanks and my assurance that it was spent profitably.

At the end of one of my lectures, one of the ladies gushed to the extreme about it, saying how wonderful it was and so on. I was beginning to feel quite flattered till she said : " Now, do tell me exactly what it feels like to be *inside* those submarines "— I was somewhat taken aback till the fellow next door nudged me and said : " It's all right, sir, she's stone deaf—never heard a word of your lecture, and has only read the posters."

At Buffalo, New York, I met my old friend Robins, who had been Senior Officer of the U.S. Chasers at Holyhead, and was now a big man, and Vice-President of a big Company. One evening at Buffalo I

motored over the Peace Bridge, which had been
opened recently by the Prince of Wales, and gave
a lecture at the Lions Club. The following day I
had one of the most enjoyable half-hours I can remember in the States. I was invited to visit the
Bennett High School, the Principal of which is Dr.
Rhodes. It was my first visit to an American school.
I went at 9 a.m., in time for Prayers, which were held
in a big auditorium holding some 3,000 boys and
girls between twelve and twenty. The Principal
told me that he had the previous day circulated the
words of " God Save the King," and, much to my
astonishment, the whole audience got up and sang
" God Save the King." I never witnessed such a
thing before. One has often, out of politeness or for
ceremony, played the National Anthem of a foreign
country, but never before had I heard a vast audience
sing the words of a foreign national anthem. It was
just during the time of the King's illness, and was a
very first-hand example of the great respect and
affection in which H.M. is held throughout the world.
I pulled myself together, and after asking the children to sing " America," I made what I believe to be
the best speech I have ever made, as I was so thoroughly inspired by this wonderful scene.

I went all over the College. Although in the
States there appear to be varied opinions on the
advantages and disadvantages of a mixed school,
Dr. Rhodes assured me it was most advantageous.
I was much interested in all I saw, and the whole
building, especially the lighting and ventilation,

21

seemed much superior to anything I have ever seen in this country.

I paid an early call on the Mayor of Buffalo, who handed me the " Key of the City." The newspaper photographers wanted two photographs taken in different positions of the Mayor handing me the key, and as he remarked, " Now you have the key to the front door and the back door." My first lecture at Buffalo was not a great success, but on later visits I had better luck ; in any case, I enjoyed my visits, and made several good friends.

From Buffalo I continued my journey through New York State. I stopped at Albany in order to dine with the Governor, Franklin Roosevelt, to whom I have referred before, a man with iron pluck, as, although stricken with a serious illness in his middle age, he was carrying on his duties, practically a cripple and unable to walk unassisted, but with his brain as clear as ever. Then I went on to Hartford, where I had my first of many experiences of what may be called a " social lecture "—very common in the States and very pleasant to take part in. I was the guest of the Twentieth Century Club, and we had a sumptuous dinner, after which, while the company, about 200, were enjoying their cigars, coffee, and—I forgot, it is a prohibition country !—I got up and gave my lecture.

A man I met who left a great impression on me was the Hon. William Marshall Bullitt, who was in President's Taft's Government. He invited me to stay at his wonderful home at Louisville, in Kentucky, a very old estate which he had modernised, but it still contains slave quarters. He also had staying at the house a doctor, B. S. Hutcheson, V.C., M.C., M.D., of Cairo, Illinois, the only American citizen who holds the Victoria Cross. He had, on the outbreak of war, crossed the border and joined the regiment at Toronto as medical officer. He went to France, and not only won the Victoria Cross, but also the Military Cross. After the War, he had great difficulty in recovering his American citizenship, but eventually he did so, and has now a good practice of his own. Mr. Bullitt had one of the best libraries that I ever saw in the States, and is a great authority on the Victoria Cross and other medals. He took the trouble to come to Toronto, together with Dr. Hutcheson and his wife, for the Annual Dinner of the Navy League of Canada, after which I gave a lecture, followed by a small supper-party in my room, and we had a rather unique gathering of an American V.C., a Canadian V.C., and myself.

In addition to having some Scottish cousins in New York and Grand Rapids, I had some very great friends who lived out at Scarborough-on-Hudson with their family of five daughters. Whilst staying there on one occasion, I had a delightful motor drive, and paid a visit to the Military Camp at West Point. It did not come up to the expectations I had formed of it, although undoubtedly the Cadets were very smart on parade, though I did not think they compared favourably with the ones I had seen at Kingston, Canada.

On sailing from New York on the completion of my first tour, a fellow-passenger was Count von Luckner, who had commanded the German raider *Seadler* during the War. He was the first German naval officer I had met since the War, and I had a good yarn with him. He was very popular everywhere he went, as he had a great personality, and was an expert at conjuring and that sort of thing.

On one of my tours I dined at Hamilton with the Hamilton Regiment, under Colonel Baldwin, and after the lecture, which was arranged by the Canadian Legion, I visited the men of the 91st Argyll and Sutherland Highlanders under Colonel Fearman. I don't think many people in this country realise the fine spirit which pervades Canada, and enables these Militia regiments to carry on with very little financial support from the Government. The Essex-Scottish of Windsor was the only regiment I actually saw on parade, and there is nothing in the world that could touch them, but from what I saw of cinema records of the Trooping of the Colour of the Argyll and Sutherlands of Hamilton, they would take some beating.

Whilst at Hamilton an old sailor of seventy-two came to call on me, and we exchanged some yarns of his old days in sailing ships and my more modern days. During my tour I met many ex-Service officers and men from the Royal Navy, some of whom had retired with good records—others with bad ones, who had gone to the West and made good. They would frequently come and call on me privately at my hotel and say : " I knew you in such and such

a ship," or " Tell us how the old Navy is getting on."
I always had to be on my guard for men who claimed
to be ex-Servicemen, but who weren't really ; the
same thing of course happens in this country. On
one occasion I went to a place, and the secretary of
the lecture told me there was an officer there by
name X, who had served with me in " Q " ships. I
assured him that no such person as X had ever
served with me in " Q " ships, but he was quite persistent about it, so I asked to meet him. After the
lecture, X was produced, and pretended to remember
me well, so I asked him on what ship we had been
together, and he said H.M.S. *Stockforce*. I said
" Oh yes, of course. Where did we fit out ? " He
said, " Don't you remember, sir, all the trouble we
had fitting out at Chatham ? " I said, " Of course
now, I remember ; and where were we when the
Armistice was signed ? " He said, " Don't you
remember, sir, we were anchored off Gravesend ? "
and I said, " Of course, I remember well, but you
have only made three mistakes. I have never
served in a ship called *Stockforce*, I never fitted out
a ship at Chatham, and I have never been to Gravesend in my life." X departed hurriedly.

On another occasion I was having a shave when
the barber said to me : " Are you Admiral Campbell ? " and I said, " Yes, how did you know that ? "
He said, " I used to know you in the Service,
although I have never been shipmates with you."
I said, " How long did you do in the Service ? "
And he said, " Eight years." This struck me as

rather a funny period, and I suggested he might have been invalided out. He said, " Oh no, when I came home from the Straits in H.M.S. ——, we were given nineteen days' leave on arrival at Portsmouth, and instead of going back to the ship, I came out here." I said, " In other words, you are a deserter." He said, " Got it right first time, sir." This was only one of the many deserters and others who had been dismissed from the Navy whom I met in Canada ; most of them had served with the Canadian Forces during the War.

I ran across rather a strange case in the Far West, where a retired naval Captain was working alongside a deserter stoker, laying stones on a new Government road, the stones being carried there in a one-ton Ford lorry by an officer who had received the V.C. and D.S.O. I had a most enjoyable lunch with them.

Early in March I found myself in the comparatively small town of Sherbrooke, Quebec, and had the pleasure of meeting the fellow who was wounded in the hand in the bomb incident at Holyhead, and was glad to find he had a good job. I then went on to Halifax and Sydney, Nova Scotia, where I was kindly put up by Commander Oland, R.C.N., an old shipmate of the *Tiger*, and his wife. I saw as much as I could of the Canadian Navy, establishments and officers' mess, and, although small, I was very much struck by the fine spirit shown by the personnel, both officers and men, under the command of Commander Brodeur, R.C.N., and they certainly make the best of the small matériel with which the Canadian Government supply them. Anyhow, it is the personnel that matters, and I feel sure if war came again to-morrow, that Canada would provide a very fine body of trained seamen.

Whilst at Boston on one of my visits, I stayed with Professor Merriman, the Professor in History at Harvard University. I also made many friends and renewed many old acquaintances, especially with Admiral Sims, who was staying there for the winter with his charming wife, sons and daughter, a large, happy family party. It was chiefly through the recommendations of Admiral Sims and his sons that I was able to lecture at a number of boys' schools and colleges round Boston, such as St. Paul's School, Concord, Middlesex School, where there were two English boys doing a sort of " change over " for a year—a very excellent idea—St. George's School, Newport, Milton Academy, and Harvard University.

I gave several lectures at Detroit, including Cranbrook School, the Detroit Athletic Club, and the University Club, where I was very honoured that my lecture had, unknown to me, been attended by a German naval officer, who came up afterwards and congratulated me. I had the opportunity at Detroit of seeing over some of their great works, and was greatly impressed by the Calculator work, the President of which was Standish Bacchus. The work was almost entirely done by girls, and I was particularly fascinated by their quickness. The factory itself was a model of efficiency and, like so many United States factories, they had big parking spaces for the employees' cars. Bacchus frequently entertained me, and I especially remember one night when he gave a stag dinner-party in my honour. I had been used to seeing Americans smoking during their meals, but this night they didn't till Bacchus had stood up and proposed the health of the King, to which I at once replied with the health of the President. These small acts of extreme courtesy and thoughtfulness on the part of our American friends are too often overlooked in this country. Amongst many other American friends I made here were Mr. Joyce and Bill Lalley, who entertained me right royally during all my visits to Detroit. He had a very warm spot in his heart for this country, having worked over here.

From Detroit I went on to Cleveland, which I visited on several occasions, and stayed with Mrs. Baldwin, whose husband was a distinguished barrister, and had also taken an active part in the Great War. Mrs. Baldwin looked after me like a second mother.

After one of my lectures, I had to go to a large tea-party which consisted entirely of females. One lady came up to me and gushed in the extreme, telling me that my lecture was the most wonderful thing she had ever heard, and after remarking that she thought submarines must be very dangerous things, she added, " But what strikes me as the most marvellous thing about you and your crew, is the fact that you went through it all without being sea-sick. I can never put my foot on board the *Mauretania* without being ill."

Whilst at Cleveland I was entertained at the Tavern and University Club and also the English-Speaking Union. I had a delightful week-end at Mr. Baldwin's farm about forty miles outside the city. On the way there we stopped and had lunch with the Hon. James Garfield, the son of one of the Presidents of the United States—a most interesting man, and one who understood our problems in England as well as in his own country.

I had a wonderful example at Cleveland of the efficiency of the American telephone system. I had arrived about 7 a.m. by steamer from Detroit, and was met by Mr. Parker, who had taken me to the Club for a bath, etc. Whilst I was having my shave, a receiver was placed in my hands, and someone was talking to me over the 'phone. I used generally to get shaved by a barber in the States, as this was the easiest way to have one's boots cleaned, as one had a " shave and shoe shine " combined.

From Cleveland I went on to Chicago, another place to which I paid many visits. I arrived about 8 p.m. rather depressed, as I did not know a soul in Chicago, and felt very lonely. I heard a lot of what I thought were shots, and I said to myself, " Well, anyhow, I have arrived at the right place." On looking out of my window, I discovered it was a display of fireworks, being Easter Saturday. On the following morning, Sunday, not having anything to do, and as it was pouring with rain, I decided to remain in my room and read. I was rather surprised when, at eleven o'clock, Mr. —— sent his card up and then came up to see me. He said he had heard from Mrs. Baldwin of Cleveland that I was arriving, and he wished to offer me his hospitality ; and as he did not think it right for a Scotsman to arrive in Chicago without his native drink, he gave me a present of some Scotch whisky. Such is the hospitality of the American.

Whilst at Chicago I dined with Mr. ——, one of the big magnates of the city. His dinner was a beautiful show, and he supplied the best of wines, the extraordinary part being that his grandfather was one of the original advocates of teetotalism in England. His father was the same, and he himself drinks nothing alcoholic, nor does his son, a man of over thirty. Yet he is most particular in taking a personal interest in the wines served to his guests, and selects them according to the distinction of those he is entertaining. I, for instance, had brandy 1865 ; had I been more distinguished, it would probably have been 1815.

At one of the new industrial centres outside Chicago, where I was invited to go and talk after luncheon, they did me the honour of calling the new library the " Gordon Campbell Library."

Whilst at Chicago, one of my hosts was Mr. H. H. Porter, who asked me if I would mind giving a short lecture to a few of his friends after dinner. I was only too glad, as I thought, of returning some of the hospitality he had given me, and readily consented, and after an excellent dinner, I gave a short talk to about twenty people. I was rather astounded next day when he arrived with a cheque in payment for my lecture. I at once refused it, but he pointed out that I was a professional lecturer, and had he engaged anyone in any other profession he would have paid him, and he insisted on my taking it. To clear my conscience, I sent the cheque to my wife to buy herself a fur coat, but I grew rather hardened to this sort of thing on future occasions, and came to the conclusion that I was just as much entitled to a fee as a Harley Street doctor.

Previous to going to Canada I had been warned, from the experience of other British lecturers, that the fact that I had had a New York Bureau as a manager would be unpopular, and it certainly turned out to be the case, as I was frequently told that people could not understand why a British Admiral had a New York manager, as Keedick's name naturally appeared on the posters. At one place I went to the criticism was so strong that at a big luncheon that was given in my honour, I referred to the matter, and asked if anybody could give me the name of a Canadian Lecture Bureau, to which I received no reply. I then asked if anybody would care to join with me and form a Lecture Bureau in Canada, and there were great shouts of, " For God's sake, don't try such a thing." The fact is, that the population of Canada is so small compared with that of America that practically all the lecture tours are run from the States, just as most of the magazines you buy in Canada come from the States.

Victoria, British Columbia, which claims to be

super-British, was particularly annoyed at my having an American manager. I was therefore rather amazed when I went to the Lecture Hall to find that they had an American machine which would only take American slides, and not mine which were British, so that the machine had to be altered, and I also found that very national song of " Oh, Canada," was also on an American slide.

An interesting party I attended at Winnipeg was given by the Ladies' Press Club. I was the only man present, and happened to remark that I did not know so many ladies were connected with the Press, and I thought it would be a change for me to occasionally have a lady interviewer instead of a man when I visited various places. I think they must have taken me seriously, as the next three places I went to, I was called on by lady correspondents, all of whom were very charming. In one case, a lady visited my room at eight o'clock in the morning. She came in when I was just completing dressing. As bad luck would have it, my collar-stud broke, and so she heard me using a good deal of language, which formed the subject of her interview, saying that although I had retired from the Navy, I had not forgotten my nautical lingo. Another lady correspondent asked me when I had been most frightened in my life. I told her when I had a snake up my trousers in South Africa. She thought I was pulling her leg, so she did not put it in the Press.

Whilst at Winnipeg I was asked to inspect and address 250 sea cadets. I was astounded at finding such a large body in the centre part of Canada, over a thousand miles from the sea, though of course they had lakes on which to get some sea training during the summer months. But at Victoria, British Columbia, I found that, in spite of the fact that Victoria lies at the entrance to one of the greatest sea-ports of the Western Hemisphere, they were unable to muster more than twenty-five cadets.

It was very interesting to see the great changes which had taken place in Winnipeg since I was there as a midshipman, the town having grown out of all recognition, and containing a large quantity of foreign immigrants. I was told that the British immigrants were not a great success on the Prairie, as they were too much under the rules of trade unions, and would only work for eight hours a day, etc., not realising that in a wheat-growing country, it is a question of making hay while the sun shines.

From Winnipeg I made my way westward to the coast, stopping at many places *en route*. The first was Regina, where I had the privilege of being taken over the headquarters of the Royal Canadian Mounted Police, under the command of Colonel Worsley. A finer body of men it would be hard to equal. Their history and record of daring deeds and hard and continuous service are worth reading about. I also had the great privilege whilst there of being made a life member of the Regina Branch of the British Legion.

Soon afterwards I went to Edmonton. By this

time I was feeling very weary, but with the help of a friend of mine, Mr. Fowkes, from Toronto, who was travelling west, and who had volunteered to act as my secretary, I was able to arrive without being met, and enjoyed a quiet game of golf. When my arrival became known, I had to go through the usual procedure, but Fowkes helped me no end.

At Medicine Hat I was particularly touched at meeting an ex-Marine who had come thirty miles to see me and hear my lecture, and who asked me to get in touch with his mother at Portsmouth when I returned to England.

On the steamer that took me across the lake to Nelson, I found that the Captain, who had never been away from the lake until the Great War, had then crossed to England and served with our Naval forces. He was quite a middle-aged man, and his description of how some young Lieutenant at Whale Island had tried to teach him discipline was most amusing. He eventually fetched up in command of one of our naval vessels in the Persian Gulf.

I found a lot of retired naval officers living in the vicinity, chiefly on non-paying fruit-farms. I had a delightful drive through the country to Kamloops. My chauffeur was a University fellow, who found he was not making enough out of his farm, and so did a bit of " taxi " work during the winter. At Kamloops, in addition to my usual visit to the ex-Servicemen's Club, I visited the Old Men's Club, where I do not think anyone was younger than ninety, and I had the pleasure of shaking hands with a man of one hundred and nine. I travelled to Vancouver, and although I arrived at 7 a.m., I found a big number of friends to meet me ; in addition to the Mayor were several old shipmates. I was surprised to see how Vancouver had developed, and no doubt it will one day be one of the biggest shipping ports in the world. I had a rattling good time there, and this being practically the end of my tour, I could spend more time on golf, etc., but I didn't miss out my visits to the ex-Service Associations and Missions to Seamen. I was also invited to visit the Military Hospital, full of men who had been wounded during the War. I was asked to be there at 10 a.m. on a Sunday, and was rather surprised on arrival to find they were in the middle of Church. I sat down till the hymn they were singing was concluded, when the Padre announced my arrival, and said I would give them a talk instead of his sermon. This rather flattened me out, but I had to get on with it.

During my first lecture at Vancouver, a letter was brought on to the platform to me, and in a joking way I said to the audience, " Please excuse me a minute ; I expect this is from one of my old ' flames ' of over twenty years ago," and sure enough it was. After the lecture, the lady (who I am afraid I didn't recognise at first) came up and introduced herself and her husband, and started off with Admiral Campbell this and Admiral Campbell that. I said, " Look here, last time we met I called you N——, and you called me Gordon, and that is all I am now." She then told me, " Well, Gordon, I must admit you were the first man that ever kissed me," so I replied, " And I've been waiting twenty years for a second one," and gave her one there and then, much to the amazement of her husband.

After my lecture I was entertained to supper by a party of young people. It being a Saturday night, dancing ceased at twelve o'clock, and we adjourned to a bedroom to continue our yarns. I noticed a lot of whispering going on amongst the pretty young things, and thought it was an indication that it was time for me to go, and made a move to do so, but one of them said, " I expect you wonder what we have been whispering about, but we want to know whether it would be in order for us to ask an Admiral to come to a night club with us." I jumped at the idea, and we drove about twenty-five miles to a night club, outside Vancouver. Just as we were entering, a fellow met us and said, " For goodness' sake, don't go in, as there is a policeman inside—the place has been raided." It would have been a bad ending if I had been caught in a raided club. Anyhow, we went to another one, and had a jolly time.

From Vancouver I had a delightful crossing to Victoria. On arrival at Victoria, British Columbia, I stayed with Commander Murray, the Senior Naval Officer, and his wife. He had been my navigator in H.M.S. *Tiger*. I also had many other friends at Victoria, and thoroughly enjoyed my visit there. I went to Esquimalt from Victoria on the steam trials on one of the big C.P.R. liners. The Superintendent kindly offered to place a ship at my disposal to take me back to Vancouver, and to sail at any hour that suited me, so I crossed at one in the morning, the only other passenger being Captain MacMurray, who had served under me during the War, and we each had a spacious suite to ourselves.

During my various visits to Washington and Boston, I had the pleasure of meeting the two greatest American Admirals, Sims and Rodman. They were both men of great distinction, but of different types. Sims was a calm, collected, brainy man, with great enthusiasm for the Navy, and a great man for saying in public what he thought. But Admiral Rodman appeared to have more of the bull-dog and fighting spirit in him, and I was not surprised to know how well he had got on with Admiral Beatty in the Grand Fleet.

On both my visits to Washington the United States naval officers gave luncheon-parties for me, which enabled me to renew many friendships I had made during the War. I was particularly glad on one occasion to be able to sit next to Admiral McVae, who had commanded one of the battleships at Berehaven, and was now about to go as Commander-in-Chief to China with the rank of Admiral.

On one occasion in New York I attended a tea-party given to enable me to meet some distinguished Americans. It was an extraordinary coincidence that twice in the same afternoon I was taken for an American Admiral. The President of one of the railways said to me, " Where have you settled down,

Admiral, now you have retired ? " I replied, " In London," and he remarked that that was a funny place for me to settle down in. I said that it was not a bad place, and he replied, " I have never heard of one of our Admirals settling down in England before."

A few minutes later another American, much younger, said, " I guess you've retired from our Navy, Admiral ? " I said, " Retired from the British Navy," and he said, " Oh, I didn't realise you were a British Admiral," and after a bit he said, " You must have been mixed up in that War they had in Europe some years ago."

Towards the end of my second tour I crossed over to Bermuda and gave several lectures over there, but on my return to New York, to complete a couple of lectures at Bedford and Chester, I had a breakdown in health, which was not to be surprised at, seeing that I had spent pretty well two years in continual travelling and lecturing ; but as the saying is, " A friend in need is a friend in deed," and I was surprised at the number of friends both in Canada and the States, who invited me to go and stay with them to have a rest. It was very hard to make a choice, but Colonel Thatcher took the wind out of my sails by inviting me to dine quietly with him one night and then to meet one of the leading specialists in the States, and between them they arranged a rest. After I had rested in New York, my old friend, Colonel Prince, came down from Windsor, which enabled me to arrange a meeting between him and Colonel Thatcher, the two men I have more respect and affection for than any I met.

I was not too ill to give a farewell luncheon party in New York, and then I went to Windsor, Ontario, and spent a delightful three weeks with Colonel Prince and his wife, playing golf, etc., and I eventually sailed from Quebec.

I left the American Continent full of gratitude to my many friends, and with great admiration for the people of Canada and the United States.

On returning to England, I decided to give up lecturing for a time, and joined the Ford Motor Company of England, in which I remained ten months before resigning. My most interesting experience was when at Detroit on behalf of the company I went " on the line " as " Mr. Campbell " and assembled a motor, which, much to my astonishment, ran the test.

EPILOGUE

IN the summer of 1931, my wife and I decided, in view of the " depression " and the expense of living in London, to move into the country. Meanwhile, in August I was on a motor tour in Scotland with David when the crisis took place and a temporary National Government was formed.

At the time when I retired from the Service, three years previously, I had considered attempting a Parliamentary career, and had made approaches through the usual channels of the Conservative Party. But they did not eye me with much favour, as my views were rather too Socialistic to the extent that I said, even at that time, 1928, that I would like to serve under a Government composed of men like Mr. Baldwin and the leading men of the Labour Party, such as Mr. Ramsay MacDonald and Mr. Thomas. The Liberal Party appeared to me to be too split up amongst themselves, and the Socialist or Labour Party too much influenced by the extremists, so I decided at that time not to tackle politics.

But when the crisis arose, I at once communicated with my brother, the member for Bromley, and told him that I had definitely decided that I could not support the Socialists who had let the country down, but that, in the event of an election, I was willing to work, for preference, on behalf of a National Government, and failing that, a Conservative Government. I saw no other alternative. I was invited to stand for Parliament (this was the third invitation I had had since I retired), and I again declined, but was quite prepared to assist in the donkey work.

Early one morning, a few days before leaving our house, I received a telephone message from a friend of mine at the Bath Club, asking me if I would oppose Mr. Arthur Henderson at Burnley. This was followed by a similar request about half an hour later, and I was told (whether truly or not I do not know) that no candidate could be found to oppose him. The temptation of engaging the leading ship of the enemy line, backed by the soreness I was feeling over Invergordon, was too great for me, although I knew it meant a heavy financial sacrifice. I agreed to go to Burnley to stand as a National candidate in support of a National Government without any Party, as I had no political axe to grind.

Various parleys took place, and on October 12th I presented myself at a non-political public meeting at Burnley, and offered myself as a National candidate. My wife accompanied me, which I thought very plucky of her, as a rumour had got round that the meeting might be packed with Communists. On October 16th, when the nomination papers were handed in, I shook hands with Mr. Henderson, but the Communist candidate, Mr. Rushton, turned his back when I offered my hand. Both the Conserva-

tive and Liberal Associations placed the whole of
their organisations unreservedly at my disposal, thus
showing by their action the general feeling of the
country that it was the time to stand for a United
Government.

I feel I must mention the names of three people
who did more from my point of view than anybody
else to assure my success. The first was my wife
who, with her grace and tact, won the affection of
a good number of the women voters of the consti-
tuency ; the second was Lady Alice Reyntiens, J.P.,
who lives on the outskirts of Burnley, and who not
only received myself and my wife as her guests
throughout the election, but also entertained the
various distinguished speakers who came to Burnley
on my behalf, and the third was her daughter, Mrs.
Worsthorne, a Chairman of one of the Education
Sub-Committees of the London County Council,
who volunteered to act as my secretary. She was
not only an ideal secretary and friend, but had the
extraordinary tact of knowing exactly how to handle
me, and I am not an easy man to handle. As I had
not known her before, I thought she was extraordinarily brave to take on the job. I christened her
the Pilot, as she navigated me through very difficult
and dangerous waters, and when anybody con-
gratulates me on getting in for Burnley, I tell them
the " Pilot " did it.

At the first meeting I attended, somebody shouted
out : " What the 'ell do you know about politics ? "
I said, " Thank God, nothing ; I am only an honest

man." I was intensely struck with the spirit and friendship of the people of Burnley regardless of any political creeds that they might hold, and I very soon formed a great affection for them in the place which previously I had always looked upon as rather a washout. The police very kindly offered me protection during the election, but I declined, except on the night of the Declaration of the Poll, when they told me they could not be responsible for my wife's safety in the great crowd ; so on that occasion my wife, who had previously driven about with me in an open car, very kindly lent me by Mr. Brierley of Burnley, had to go in a separate car.

My last appeal speaks for itself (see page 344).

The result of the Poll was announced about 11 p.m. I did not go into the room until the count was almost completed. Mr. Arthur Henderson, who had fought a straight fight, was unfortunately ill, but his wife and son were present, and I had the pleasure of shaking hands with them.

By a curious mistake, when the Mayor arrived on the balcony of the Town Hall to announce the result of the Poll, Mr. Henderson's son was standing on his right, and I was standing on his left, so that for some time it was thought that Mr. Henderson had been returned, whereas I had been returned by a majority of 8,209. After the Declaration I was carried shoulder high through a cheering mob of supporters.

I cannot close this passage without expressing my

National Headquarters
Burnley
24th October 1931.

Fellow Countrymen

On Tuesday next the 27th inst, the fate of our great Nation will be in your hands.

So serious is the crisis that it is the duty of every citizen to register his or her vote, so that whatever the result of the election maybe, it will represent the opinion of the Nation as a whole.

I ask all men and women, whether of Labour, Liberal or Conservative principles to support a National Government.

The eyes of the world are on us and I appeal to you all to sink party prejudices, forget all personal feelings and think only of the welfare of your country, for which alone I stand

Yours very sincerely,

Gordon Campbell.

thanks to the various speakers who came from London and elsewhere to speak on my behalf. Once again it would be invidious to describe any of them or their speeches in detail, but I particularly appreciated the visit of Colonel Towse, V.C., who volunteered to come of his own free will ; Commodore Sir Bertram Hayes, K.C.M.G., who did the same thing ; and I also felt highly honoured that my supporters included Lord Bridgeman and the Right Hon. Winston Churchill, both of whom had been First Lords of the Admiralty, and the Right Hon. George Lambert, who, for many years, was Civil Lord.

Others who very kindly spoke for me include Lord Lloyd of Dolobran, Major Duff Cooper, Lord Meston, Viscount Erleigh, Lord Fitzalan, Sir Wyndham Portal, Lady Maureen Stanley, Mr. Derwent Hall Caine, Mr. J. Gibson Jarvie, Major Fletcher, and my brother, Mr. E. T. Campbell.

I was greatly disappointed that Lady Snowden, who had hoped to come, was debarred from doing so owing to her husband's ill-health.

And so on November 5th, 1931, I took my seat in the House of Commons, and swore for the second time my allegiance to H.M. the King.

INDEX

(Names of Ships are printed in Italics)